Living Treaties
Narrating Mi'kmaw Treaty Relations

Marie Battiste, Editor

CAPE BRETON UNIVERSITY PRESS
SYDNEY, NOVA SCOTIA

Copyright © 2016 Cape Breton University Press

All rights reserved. No part of this work may be reproduced or used in any form or by any means, electronic or mechanical, including photocopying, recording or any information storage or retrieval system, without the prior written permission of the publisher. Cape Breton University Press recognizes fair dealing uses under the *Copyright Act* (Canada). Responsibility for the research and permissions obtained for this publication rests with the authors.

The editor and contributors wish to thank the many contributions and funding provided to make this book possible, including the Social Sciences and Humanities Research Council of Canada through the Animating Mi'kmaw Humanities Project, Mi'kmaw Kina'matnewey and Unama'ki College of Cape Breton University.

Cover Image: *Empowerment* (detail), by David Brooks
Cover design: Cathy MacLean Design, Chéticamp, NS.
Layout: Mike Hunter, West Bay and Sydney, NS.

First printed in Canada.

Library and Archives Canada Cataloguing in Publication

Living treaties : narrating Mi'kmaw treaty relations / Marie Battiste, editor.

Includes bibliographical references and index.
Issued in print and electronic formats.
ISBN 978-1-77206-053-9 (paperback).--ISBN 978-1-77206-054-6 (pdf).
ISBN 978-1-77206-055-3 (epub).--ISBN 978-1-77206-056-0 (kindle)

1. Micmac Indians--Claims. 2. Micmac Indians--Land tenure. 3. Micmac Indians--Government relations. 4. Micmac Indians--History. I. Battiste, Marie, 1949-, editor

E99.M6L59 2016   971.5004'97343   C2016-902111-4
                                            C2016-902112-2

Cape Breton University Press   Distributed by
PO Box 5300   Nimbus Publishing
Sydney, Nova Scotia B1P 6L2   3731 MacKintosh St
Canada   Halifax, Nova Scotia B3K 5A5
                                      Canada

Narrating the Treaties

Contents

Introduction – Marie Battiste – 1
Narrating Mi'kmaw Treaties: Linking the Past to the Future

1. Stephen J. Augustine – 16
Negotiating for Life and Survival

2. Pamela Palmater – 24
My Tribe, My Heirs and Their Heirs Forever:
Living Mi'kmaw Treaties

3. Fred Metallic – 42
Treaty and Mi'gmewey

4. Patrick J. Augustine – 52
Mi'kmaw Relations

5. Jaime Battiste – 66
Treaty Denied: The 1928 Trial of Grand Chief Gabriel Sylliboy

6. Stuart Killen – 83
Memories of an ex-Indian Agent

7. James [Sa'kej] Youngblood Henderson – 95
Alexander Denny and the Treaty Imperative

8. Russel Barsh – 115
The Personality of a Nation

9. Jaime Battiste – 138
Treaty Advocacy and Treaty Imperative through Mi'kmaw Leadership: Remembering with Joe B. Marshall

10. Natasha Simon – 166
Beyond Cultural Differences: Interpreting a Treaty Between the Mi'kmaq and British at Belcher's Farm, 1761

11. Daniel N. Paul – 178
Racism and Treaty Denied

12. Douglas E. Brown – 196
Litigating Section 35 Aboriginal and Treaty Rights in Nova Scotia

13. Kerry Prosper – 222
Born to Fish

14. Victor Carter-Julian – 235
Tables, Talks and Treaties

15. Naiomi Metallic – 241
Becoming a Language Warrior

16. Eleanor Tu'ti Bernard – 253
Kina'matnewey Education:
How Our Ancestors Imagined Our Success

17. Marie Battiste – 259
Resilience and Resolution:
Mi'kmaw Education and the Treaty Implementation

Appendix 1 – 279
Declaration of Aboriginal Rights

Appendix 2 – 283
Archival Research, Treaties, and the Nova Scotia Mi'kmaq:
Aboriginal Rights Position Paper and Acknowledgements

Appendix 3 – 290
Communication to the United Nations Human Rights Committee
About Treaty Violations (1980)

About the Authors – 307
Index– 311

Marie Battiste

Narrating Mi'kmaw Treaties: Linking the Past to the Future

Educating Canadians to their treaties and their meanings is long overdue. Negotiated and signed by our Mi'kmaw traditional chiefs with the King of Great Britain and his representatives in the early 18th century, the Mi'kmaw treaties are a significant part of the history of Canada and of the United Kingdom, yet marginalized in the Canadian education curriculum and in the minds and hearts of Canadians. Treaties were central to the legalization of the settlements of early Europeans and later immigrants in Canada, and to the acquisition of land and resources that today are still being contested.

Most Canadians think the treaties are irrelevant and most politicians and resource-extracting corporations view them as inconvenient, but they *are* still relevant and will continue to be. The treaties have a textual message that is clear enough; they articulate a shared relationship of peace and friendship, as well as negotiated principles and outcomes, yet governments, lawyers and judges are constantly reinterpreting them for contemporary contexts from various perspectives, few of which are focused on the Mi'kmaq. Mi'kmaq are also contesting interpretations, urging the courts to hear and understand our ancestors' understandings and meanings of the treaties through our knowledge systems and oral traditions. It is significant that the Supreme Court of Canada has admitted oral testimonies affirming the knowledge systems are a key to understanding treaties; their negotiation and subsequent implementation continue to reside in memory and in stories that remain part of the Mi'kmaw knowledge system. Sometimes our stories and testimonies offer different words and meanings that contest what lay in written text and beyond court decisions.

Treaties between the king of Great Britain and the federated districts and tribes of the Mi'kmaq nation (1630-1794) impart relationships of sharing based on negotiated peaceful settlements and shared resources that enable Mi'kmaq and the settlers to live together peacefully as friends. Through treaties, settlers from foreign lands become beneficiaries of Canadian settlement though settlement did not give land to newcomers as is often thought. King George III in his Royal Proclamation of 1763 assured the Indians that all lands needed for settlement had to be purchased, and with their full consent (RSC 1985). The treaties, then, are a silent constitutional affidavit connecting us to the past, to agreements and to an oral and written history, one that is often forgotten among those who arrive on the shores of this country or across southern borders.

The imperial treaties are often also viewed by the Canadian public as irrelevant to contemporary relations, negotiated powers and resources, and that the source of power ended with Canada's independence from Great Britain. They fail to comprehend that the Mi'kmaw chiefs delegated authority to the King and Canada, accepting those treaties as the very foundation of Canada. That is why aboriginal and treaty rights are delegated to a separate section in the 1982 Constitution—section 35.

The administrative arm of the government, however, either ignores the Mi'kmaw treaties or constantly contests them, making Canadians believe over time that treaties are not an important issue for civil society, but only a political issue to be resolved by the government of Canada through their administrative methods or the courts. Superiority and indifference have flowed throughout colonial history through the relations of the government with the Mi'kmaq nation and—based on attitudes of entitlement, denial or bad faith—they have little to gain from the impoverished Mi'kmaq nation contesting the big powerful government. Regardless, the Mi'kmaq nation has continued to take their complaints and submissions to the federal government, sometimes to the Monarchy, sometimes to the Pope, leading to a long trail of correspondences that are often dismissed or ignored. The trail seems to end invariably with yet another long trail of court cases that are similarly lost or won—and those summarily dismissed and ignored still by Canada, the provinces and their citizenry.

To the Mi'kmaq nation, treaties are sacred pacts and legal covenants that are held as the fundamental source of their relations with successive waves of colonists and colonial governments. The treaties are the resource that they depend on for their present and future. Regardless of Canada's governmental attitude of entitlement, First

INTRODUCTION – LINKING THE PAST TO THE FUTURE

Nations, Métis and Inuit lands and resources are still tied to treaties and other documents negotiated in good faith with the King or Queen with an objective of shared benefits to both parties and members. So it is important to know about them, to read them, to hear them, and to comprehend their constitutional significance in contemporary life.

It is a duty and a requirement of Canadian citizens in Atlantic Canada to know their own constitution and history; most schools provide this foundation. It is their duty to include the perspectives of the Mi'kmaq nation on treaties as the courts have continuously affirmed. Mi'kmaq have always held the treaties to be an important part of our oral tradition and, while many of our traditions have been eroded by colonial education and residential schools, such traditions are still held in memory.

One such tradition, the taking out of the wampum belt or string, was firmly implanted in my parents' memory. They recalled with me how the wampum belt would be regularly and ceremonially recanted in oral stories of the event and the terms of the agreements by the *putu's*, or wampum keeper, of the Sante Mawio'mi, or Grand Council. I was raised under the understanding that the wampum belt symbolically represented our treaties with other indigenous nations and the kings of France and Great Britain. Over the last sixty or more years, most of these significant documentations have been lost, stolen or sold. For many Mi'kmaq today, the testimonies are still held in the memories and stories of our Elders. At the Nova Scotia Museum of Natural History are photographs of the late Grand Council Putu's Andrew Alex at Chapel Island Reserve holding wampum string and a wampum belt.

Andrew Alex with wampum string and belt, Chapel Island, 1930. William (Clara) Dennis collection. Courtesy Nova Scotia Museum, Ethnology Collection, 73.180.624; N-6107.

When I took my mother Annie Battiste there with Ruth Holmes Whitehead one day to show her these old pictures in a book, she

3

recalled the names of people in the pictures, by the landforms she recognized, where they were taken.

Written documents and oral testimony have shown to be not always the same. The treaties were written in the king's English, sent to England, returned to Nova Scotia and then stored. For more than two centuries, the written treaties negotiated in Nova Scotia area were not seen until recovered from the dusty dark public archives in the late 70s. Those shadowy documents, held for so long in their undignified quarters, concealed their importance and meaning from peoples they were meant to serve, both the Mi'kmaq and the settler society. However, the memory of the tradition, the power of the promises and their meaning could not remain hidden from the conscience and consciousness of settler society forever, as was probably hoped, judging by their humble storage.

When the Mi'kmaw treaties with the king were brought back to life by archival research by the first Mi'kmaw college students and the Union of Nova Scotia Indians in the 1970s, the treaties as written rejected the silent, racialized and colonial explanations for the losses Mi'kmaq had to endure for more than four centuries and the losses to their language, culture, land, resources and livelihood. In 1920, the Nova Scotia courts rejected Grand Chief Sylliboy's defense that the treaties protected his hunting rights, holding instead that, as uncivilized savages, the Mi'kmaq did not have treaty rights, they held no right of sovereignty. This kind of racism has been a major feature of Canadians relations with Mi'kmaq and other First Nations, Métis and Inuit men, women and children.

The treaties make sense of the idea, in the Mi'kmaw language, of *elikewake* (the king in our house), just what was aspired and committed to in living with the king as a friend and ally, not as oppressed subjects. The treaties affirm Mi'kmaw wisdom and tenacity in what they sought and provide the extra energy and commitment for the leadership of the Grand Council with Union of Nova Scotia Indians (UNSI) to reveal definitively how the colonists had failed to live up to the treaty vision and to urge final acceptance and implementation of the treaties. In particular, Grand Council Captain Alex Denny, who was then the president of UNSI, began the Mi'kmaw quest to resurrect the treaties and to mobilize a significant movement to ensure they were constitutionally protected in the patriation of Canada from Great Britain in 1982, and also in their future deliberations affecting access to resources among Mi'kmaq and other treaty nations. Many of the essays in this book touch on the influence of Alex Denny's treaty imperative and Aboriginal rights initiatives.

Treaty mobilization began an alternative narrative to the meaning of a Mi'kmaw perspective in Atlantic Canada. Their story of the battle to have the Mi'kmaw treaties recognized and their Aboriginal rights understood is a more accurate story than the existing colonial narratives of dispossessions of the Mi'kmaq based on racist discourses and presumed cultural inadequacy.

The treaties are, decidedly, documents with a written text, but, equally important, they have multiple layers of history and perspectives told in many narratives since that time. They include colourful animated stories of diverse people, places and events, along with the deceit, treachery and racism of pre- and post-treaty colonial era. Some of the history and the stories have been lost with the erosion and loss of the Mi'kmaw language and with the governments' complicity to deny Mi'kmaq anything, and to take everything from them.

Several historians have attempted to capture the archival history written in colonial languages and these are shared here in this book as well. They bear witness to colonial perspectives of deceit and overt racism, both used in pursuing the domestication and acculturation of Mi'kmaq. We recognize that they have been written in the context of the times and address specific events, times, places and interests of importance surrounding the treaty-making period of the relations between the Mi'kmaq and the king and, later, with the federal government. Many writers, including some in this book, have researched the background of treaties in the course of their work and university or legal research to reveal the various ways the governments and Mi'kmaq used treaties, understood them, ignored them or have responded to them. These documents have served as valuable resources to the courts and to the parties involved in the court cases surrounding treaties, although most of that written research material retains the dominant narratives of and repeated biases and perspectives of one party—the English or the French, the church and the governments.

This book aims to reveal another side of the histories of the treaties, focusing on the stories from perspectives of Mi'kmaq and their allies who worked among them during various times over the last fifty years. These authors, both Mi'kmaw and non-Mi'kmaw allies, have had experiences contesting the Crown's version of the treaty story, or have been rebuilding with the Mi'kmaq nation with the strength of their work from their understandings of Mi'kmaw history and the Elders' stories. They share how they came to know about treaties, about the key family members and events that shaped their thinking and their activism and life work. They elevate their Mi'kmaw leaders: people significant to them who taught them about their history and about their treaties' meaning from Mi'kmaw perspectives, about their ancestors and relatives who shared stories and memories of the meaning of the treaties, and of the backlash of racism that aimed to push Mi'kmaq back—into the forest, onto the reserves and into the black hole of history. That black hole of omission and marginalization of Mi'kmaw history has been constructed so as to erase the understandings among those who signed the treaties and the promises of the resources the British gave in return for Mi'kmaw favour and peace.

Racism and Eurocentric superiority and apathy have been effectively used as strategies for hiding the governments' and citizens' complicities in denying the treaties, to gain access to land and resources, thus reducing Mi'kmaq to poverty, marginalization and the fool's gold of welfare. Herein, the authors offer the stories of those who have lived under the colonial regime of a not-so-ancient time. Here are the passionate activists and allies who helped uncover the treaties and their contemporary meaning to both Mi'kmaq and settler society and speak to their future with them. Here also are the voices of a new generation of indigenous lawyers and academics who have made their life choices with credentials solidly in hand in order to pursue social and cognitive justice for their families and their people. Their mission to enliven the treaties out of the dark caverns of the public archives, to bring them back to life and to justice as part of the supreme law of Canada, and to use them to mobilize the Mi'kmaw restoration and renaissance that seeks to reaffirm, restore and rebuild Mi'kmaw identity, consciousness, knowledges and heritages, as well as our connections and rightful resources to our land and ecologies.

As a result of the stormy disputes in courts between settler interests and Mi'kmaw interests, it is significant that the Supreme Court of Canada has recognized the intended fundamental rule of construction of the treaties and how they are revealed. They have dismissed colonial interpretation of the Mi'kmaw treaties as dishonourable and lacking persuasion. The Court has been guided by the constitutional reforms of 1982 that affirm Aboriginal and treaty rights. It has been persuaded by the arguments for reading the Mi'kmaw treaties as they should be read—as the Mi'kmaq would have understood them. This method reflects the most faithful application of the original meaning of the treaty negotiations and text. Therefore, while our Elders and families continue to share their stories in their homes, over tea, at their camps, on the land and in their fishing boats, we feel that it is important that Canadians also read about those stories and hear what the original meanings are from the people themselves.

Mi'kmaw treaties with the King are now a significant part of the supreme law of Canada and of the United Nations. The future of the Atlantic Provinces depends on a fair and just constitutional reconciliation between the treaties and other constitutional powers. Such constitutional reconciliation has to replace the colonial traditions of being legal adversaries. The hardened responses of the provinces and the citizens to the constitutional affirmation of the Mi'kmaw treaties by the courts ought not to perpetuate the colonial adversarial attitude—as reflected in J. M. Coetzee insights in *Waiting for the Barbarians* (1980: 133)—that the colonial mind is preoccupied with one thought alone: "how not to end, how not to die, how to prolong its era."

In the process of constitutional reconciliation it will be crucial to have the treaties comprehended by every government, every institution and every person. Constitutional reconciliation has been a theme of annual October 1 Treaty Day observances in Halifax, and other places, over the last twenty years. It has to be a theme of Mi'kmaw month in Nova Scotia and beyond, as well as Aboriginal Peoples day (June 21). These treaties have to be explained; they have to be read according to the principles of the Supreme Court, and everyone has to hear and think about what they mean from the perspectives of many, not just the self-interested party that holds sway with the media, schools, universities, politicians and churches. These events should be held as equal in importance to Victoria Day and Canada Day. The people of Nova Scotia have only to look at the handshake on the original seal of Nova Scotia as part of the ancient reconciliation of friendship between the peoples. The Courthouse on Spring Garden Road must be remembered as the site of the 1761 treaties with the Mi'kmaq.

The ancient wampum belts and written Georgian treaties have to be moved from the Nova Scotia Museum and the dusty, nondescript boxes in the public archives of Nova Scotia to a new consciousness of constitutional reconciliation and belonging to the foundational vision of Canadian society.

Mi'kmaq know that constitutional reconciliation by implementation of the Mi'kmaw treaties leaves Atlantic Canadians in an uncomfortable situation. We have been uncomfortable for centuries when the settlers denied our treaties. To begin treaty implementation, Atlantic Canadians and provinces must reject the tired old paths of denial and repression. Few people believe they are guilty of generating the denial and repression of the past, or at least would like to think so; most would like to see themselves as innocent, though evasive, victims of the past while they benefitted from the land, the resources, and their self-government. But, as the commissioners of the Truth and Reconciliation Commission have offered to Canada, everyone is now responsible for forging a better relationship with Aboriginal people in the present and in the future. To do this, they must begin to understand the meaning, significance and the need for implementing the treaties of peace and friendship from the Mi'kmaw perspectives.

Courtesy Province of Nova Scotia.

Since the court decisions, the status quo in Atlantic Canada is no longer a neutral and morally defensible starting point. The status quo presumes that Mi'kmaq should accept what their existing reserves and welfare poverty provide under the *Indian Act* of Canada, but it is not clear why they should be content with that situation. Now is the time for Atlantic Canadians to live up to the high ideals they value, and to challenge the status quo as unacceptable. For many generations, most of the children in Atlantic Canada have learned historical and ideological misinformation and have not learned much about the Mi'kmaq nation and its treaties. While they are taught the relations between the federal government and the provinces, they are not taught about the idea of treaty commonwealth or federalism that continue, against all odds, to live as the supreme law of Atlantic Canada. They do not understand the ongoing constitutional relationship that needs to be reconciled and implemented. One old saying comes to mind and is useful here: while the truth, at first, may make one uncomfortable, it will eventually set one free. The treaties are about sharing what the Mi'kmaq had in abundance and the idea of equal opportunity through trade and respecting human rights. They are not about military conquest, "might makes right," or other theories leading to injustice. Mi'kmaq and Atlantic Canadian educators need to rewrite the curriculum so that all our children understand the importance of the treaty process and how it has created the baseline of democracy and respect for the land.

—

The chapters in this book are written from various perspectives of the authors—how they personally came to understand the importance of the treaties from Elders and teachers, their personal learning about the treaties and about the obstacles created to discredit the treaties both in and out of courts, as well as in schools and in the media. These stories are narratives of insight, integrity, dignity, hope and vision reflecting of Mi'kmaw consciousness and humanity at the beginning of the 21st century. In their stories are the justly emotive reactions to colonization, to maltreatment in society, to residential schools and their lament to the erosion or loss of their Mi'kmaw languages and cultures. These are stories that reveal the pain and passions of the past and feelings of hope of today's youth and their elders in the post-residential school and post-truth and reconciliation era. All of this is what we call treaty education and a beginning for all Canadians and their students to understand. Herewith we can expect a new society and new relationships built on respect, reciprocity, reverence and responsibility.

Note on Writing Systems

The authors come from various parts of Mi'kma'ki—the Mi'kmaw territory that reaches a land base covering five provinces, from Gaspé Peninsula of Quebec through New Brunswick, Nova Scotia, Prince Edward Island and Newfoundland. The Mi'kmaw language and its written form varies depending on districts from where the author comes, as their orthographies were created in other times and contexts and were never standardized. All diversities are accepted as norm for Mi'kmaq; therefore, three distinctive orthographies are evident in the writings in this book. No attempt is made to standardize the orthographies, as standardization does not exist in Mi'kma'ki. The editor is from Cape Breton, Nova Scotia, and uses the Smith-Francis orthography; those in New Brunswick use the Pacifique-Millea system while also adapting increasingly to the Cape Breton usage, and Quebec uses the Listuguj or Metallic system.

Chapter Overview

Stephen Augustine, former curator at the Museum of Civilization, is hereditary chief and *keptin* from Elsipuktuk, in the district of represent Sikniktok "district" on the Mi'kmaw Grand Council, and now dean at Cape Breton University. Beginning with his own family history, he positions his knowledge of Mi'kmaw oral traditions and ancient traditional teachings living on the land, as learned from his paternal grandmother, who learned from her father-in-law, who in turn learned from his great-grandfather. Stephen's story is a multilayered exposition of Mi'kmaw humanity, values, beliefs and livelihood that led to the historical relations of treaties with settlers and their continued importance to Mi'kmaq. Important to this story is that Mi'kmaw treaties, unlike the numbered treaties, are peace and friendship treaties that were not land transfers but promises of protection for settlement in exchange for promises of protection from conflict and guarantee of trade truckhouses, a term used in the 1752 treaty referring to government regulated trading posts, some types of staple foods and goods, blankets and ammunition.

Pam Palmater is a well-known Mi'kmaw activist, lawyer and professor at Ryerson University. Her essay relays her family upbringing with activist relatives passionate to keep her connected to their perspectives about their history and culture as learned from their ancestors. This strong familial socialization in Mi'kmaw perspectives, together with her strong educational foundation, supports an affirmative view of Mi'kmaw history of treaties and a strong voice for Mi'kmaw treaties and sovereignty. In her essay, she offers to Canadians why treaties should be important to them and how they might view them from a Mi'kmaw perspective.

Fred Metallic, a Mi'kmaw fisherman from Listuguj, shares family teachings living on the land and off the water. These Elder teachings, drawn from the covenant with the Creator, provide the rights and responsibilities to the water, to the land and to the generations. Shared in wampum are the protocols and teachings of sharing — not just stories, food and hospitality, but their time, resources and, when needed, activism by allied peoples in their nation and beyond. Fred shares the inside story of the dispute over the fishing guidelines at Burnt Church, a story of violence enacted against the Mi'kmaq on the water, that brought them together in solidarity, as well as their calling on allied nations such as the Mohawk to support them.

Patrick Augustine, a member of Elsipuktuk First Nation, sketches Mi'kmaw concepts of law in the form of several Mi'kmaw relationships, among them Mi'kmaw cosmology, or how we know who we are and where we come from. In part, these reveal our relationships with the land, the water, the animals and ecology, as well as the importance of our relationships with each other and the spirit realm. He offers explanations and connections to the ancient stories of the Six Worlds, to the concept of *netukulimk*/sustainable harvesting, to the traditional districts, the impacts on Mi'kmaq resulting from colonial relations in trade, treaties and Canadian legislation.

Jaime Battiste, law graduate from Dalhousie University, a resident of Eskasoni First Nation, and a member of Potlotek First Nation, recalls his coming to understand treaties, first at home at the table with his parents (J. Youngblood Henderson and Marie Battiste) in conversations with Kji-keptin Alex Denny and many well known Mi'kmaw leaders, among them his neighbour, Cape Breton University professor, Joe B. Marshall. His essay shares the history of a case he first heard about at CBU, involving Grand Chief Gabriel Sylliboy, that was based on Aboriginal people's right to hunt in their own land and the values that still hold to the land, the animals and their respect for their ecologies. He relays the resulting deteriorating authority of Mi'kmaq in their land to settlers' laws, once promised to be the way to settle conflicts in a good way, and how it has been used to erode Mi'kmaw rights to their land and resources, language, indigenous knowledge and their ability to sustain themselves on their land. The court overturned that early decision, and Jaime concludes with urging a posthumous pardon for Gabriel Sylliboy and his family.

Later in this collection, Jaime, in conversation with **Joe B. Marshall,** relays the wealth of knowledge an elder statesman such as Joe B. can impart when in conversation and story. Joe B shares how he came to be involved in and remains the elder statesman for the Union of Nova Scotia Indians and its allied leadership organizations such as Atlantic Policy Congress of Chiefs and Kwilmu'kw Maw-klusuaqn also known as Mi'kmaq Rights Initiative. With Joe B.'s permission for the use of his writings and ideas, and from their conversations, Jaime offers reflections on the history of Union of Nova Scotia Indians and other leadership organizations among Mi'kmaq and how they create a better understanding of Mi'kmaw advocacy for, and successes in, affirming treaty rights in Nova Scotia.

Stuart Killen is a former superintendent of the then federal department of Indian Affairs, assigned to Nova Scotia in the early 1960s. His story reveals that the object of Indian Affairs was made quite clear: assimilation and control of the Indians. Eventually he was sent to a position in La Pas, Manitoba, where he began a movement of supporting indigenous empowerment by his refusal to be the conventional controlling Indian agent boss on the reserve. His role on his return from Manitoba with his new training in popular education was finally used to help secure funds to fight the White Paper policy, which he secured for the Union of Nova Scotia Indians, thus leading to his many enriched years of service seeking to fight both the department's policies through researching treaties and generating the Nova Scotia Micmac Aboriginal Title Position Paper.

J. Youngblood (Sa'ke'j) Henderson, a law graduate of Harvard, a scholar of Aboriginal and treaty rights, and current Director of the Native Law Centre at the University of Saskatchewan, Sa'ke'j (a name given to him by Mi'kmaw Elder Annie Battiste) shares his early Eskasoni years and stories of finding a new mandate for justice emerging from his relationship with Grand Captain Alex Denny, stemming from his family relatives. Alex's vision in bringing him to Eskasoni with his wife Marie Battiste was to pursue the restoration of Mi'kmaq, Aboriginal and treaty rights and Mi'kmaw language education, both aspirations that were part of a well-articulated dream. Finding a fully inspired and capable team at UNSI—with energy, humour and tea in rich supply—he set out to carefully unlock the hidden treaty relationship between the Mi'kmaq and settlers. Insisting on organized, educated, strategic thinkers, like his ancestors, Alex advocated for the right research, mobilization of Mi'kmaw natural justice, and taking Mi'kmaw treaty infractions to the courts to inform Mi'kmaw people, the public and their politicians. The risks, plans, strategies and humour combine for an important story for the next generations.

Russel Barsh, a Harvard lawyer and geological scientist, a friend of the family of Alex Denny and Foreign Affairs Ambassador of the Mi'kmaw Grand Council, offers anecdotal scenarios of European-Mi'kmaw diplomacy in Europe during the 1980s and 1990s, leading to the final affirmative vote for the Declaration of the Rights of Indigenous peoples. He reminds us that residential schools, ignorant politicians, misguided bureaucrats, rising Canadian nationalism, neglectful scholarship, inadequate books and one-sided mass media have all eroded Mi'kmaw memory and self-confidence. Yet, in the hands of local leaders, and in particular guided by Alex Denny's profound and inspiring strategies, there came a change in climate at the end of the last century, ensuring that treaties are brought back to life and the path through the traumatic dark colonial history of misguidedness, racism and ignorance can be illuminated. His stories of Alex Denny and his work at the United Nations demonstrates a humanity in action, cultivating love with humour and connecting nations as friends and neighbours.

Natasha Simon, a Mi'kmaq from Elsiputuk, begins with many curious questions about treaties with her family setting her on a journey to find the answers. In so doing, she begins to read the text and consider the context to the 1761 treaty between the Mi'kmaq and the British at Governor Belcher's farm, proving that the simplistic relationships of conqueror and conquered is not supported by the text of the letters and documents of the period among Mi'kmaq and the colonialists. This paper, reprinted with permission, offers an alternative interpretation of the 1761 treaty. Through the guidance of stories told by women in her family, the paper argues that historic treaty rights must be understood within the context of relationships instead of individual or collective rights. It concludes that stories about how we, as Mi'kmaq, are to relate to one another are central to the project of nationhood.

Daniel N. Paul is a Mi'kmaw Elder and passionate advocate for social justice and the eradication of racial discrimination. The author of the seminal book, *We Were Not the Savages*, Danny shares some critical moments in his early years and early work experiences, leading to his passionate research of colonial relations and history with Mi'kmaq. He unpacks the historical experiences of racism and genocide experienced by Mi'kmaq and his direct experiences with Indian agents, with Indian Affairs. His research of Mi'kmaw history reaffirms his passion to show that racism is and has been widespread among the relations between Mi'kmaq and colonial governance and settlers and that it continues to be the critical factor in how treaties are resisted, dismissed and misunderstood.

Douglas (Doug) Brown, lawyer and nephew to Alex Denny, shares his personal background—from school, to the military, to UNSI, to law school and then, as a junior legal assistant researching a case that he encounters, a seemingly easy case involving Aboriginal food hunting rights of the Mi'kmaq that turns quite complex and long. Treaty rights to hunt for food were pitted against a Nova Scotia provincial regulation involving sporting principles for securing animals. Doug asserts that the Aboriginal right to hunt for food is one of the last remaining vestiges of the rights Mi'kmaq have exercised since time immemorial. Despite this right, white colonial settlers continue to wield the influence in the media and with politicians to counter any law applicable to them that is not also applicable to Aboriginal people.

Kerry Prosper, a Mi'kmaw leader from Paq'tnkek First Nation, writes about his life living around water where people fished in quiet, hidden from the settler communities around him that would target the Mi'kmaq as criminals if and when they exercised their treaty rights to hunt or fish. His anecdotal, humorous and poignant stories tell of his early years filled with fishing and hunting with friends and relatives, long before such rights were acknowledged by the courts, relaying how Mi'kmaq learned to dodge officials who did not believe they had a right to hunt and fish. He urges his children to honour their rights and their responsibilities they have now from the use of all the resources they have access to and that the courts have affirmed.

Victor Carter Julian is a Mi'kmaw lawyer from Pictou Landing, whose memories of his aunt's home and her dining room table draw him to the treaties and their mysteries, unlocked when he goes to university and then law school. He begins to understand the importance of those treaties to his family and his people as he stretches his understanding to the court cases involving the Mi'kmaw hunting and fishing rights, but also the hegemony, resistance and silence that is displayed among non-Mi'kmaq with regard to the treaties signed by their ancestors.

Naiomi Metallic, lawyer and daughter of Emmanuel "Manny" Metallic, a famous linguist from Listuguj, relays her personal history in "Becoming a Language Warrior." Her family's experiences with colonialism resulted in part to her father choosing not to teach her Mi'kmaw; later he came to pursue with passion Mi'kmaw language teachings, grammar and writing systems, becoming the local expert. **Naiomi's** passion for language evolved from a research project examining the Aboriginal language situation in Canada and the losses and rights that are available for Mi'kmaq to retain their language(s). She urges us all to consider what is lost when we lose our language as it affects all of these things, but also cautions us to consider how we want it regulated or legislated, if we do want that.

Eleanor Bernard explains the many changes that the Mi'kmaq of Nova Scotia have undergone in educating their children. Prior to European contact, the Mi'kmaq taught their children through oral traditions and hands-on learning but, with contact, the government and church set up schools wherein the children were taught to forget their traditional ways and made to feel ashamed of their ancestry. The day schools and provincial schools, which followed Indian Residential Schools, were similar in design and result. Eleanor closes with the return of Mi'kmaw control over education, which is increasing the graduation rates within high schools and increasing Mi'kmaw children's confidence in themselves and sense of pride in their ancestry.

Marie Battiste's family lived within treaties on both sides border of USA and Canada; their priority was their children's access to education and economic opportunities needed to succeed and led to their leaving the reserve and working and remaining in Houlton, ME, throughout all of their children's basic education before returning to their homeland of Potlotek. This education and years in Maine provided the rich experiences led to Marie's understanding of both the injustices of education in Canada for Mi'kmaq and those of diverse Native Americans in the U.S., and to working in education for Mi'kmaw learners and treaty reconciliations. This chapter is both remembrances and teachings that evolved in a life lived before treaties were recognized by the courts, and how the need for awareness of them still exists. Treaties are foundational to education for all Canadians.

Stephen J. Augustine

Negotiating for Life and Survival

The Mi'kmaw Creation story was handed down to me through my paternal grandmother, Agnes (Thomas) Augustine (1898-1998), who learned it from her father-in-law Thomas Augustine, who heard it told by his great-grandfather Michael Augustine. Michael Augustine was chief of the Elsipogtog Mi'kmaq. He was known as Michael Alguimou before he was baptized in the mid-1700s and given the surname Augustine. He signed a ratification of the first of the Mi'kmaw peace and friendship treaties with the British Empire, the 1725 treaty, at Annapolis Royal in 1726, and signed another in 1760 in Halifax.

Agnes Thomas was born on Lennox Island in a birch-bark *wikuom* on June 14, 1898. At the age of thirteen, Agnes married my grandfather (Basil Tom) Thomas Theophile Augustine, who shared his extensive traditional knowledge with her. They lived off the land and over the years moved extensively throughout Mi'kma'ki. Agnes became a living library of orally transmitted knowledge and ancient traditional teachings, values and survival skills. She was also a renowned basketmaker. As a wife, mother and grandmother of a line of hereditary chiefs, she took her responsibility toward her community seriously, always lending a helping hand. Since I was a child, and long into my adult life, she tirelessly and lovingly imparted to me much of what she knew because I was her oldest grandson (from her only son) and destined to become hereditary chief, a direct descendant of Michael Augustine. Agnes died on December 6, 1998, in Rexton, New Brunswick, at an age of more than one hundred years.

The Creation story explains my ancestors' interpretation of how the Mi'kmaw world was created and how the first Mi'kmaw people came into being. The creation story has more depth than a simple tale about our origins: since time immemorial it has been the vessel of our clan's history, our system of values, our modes of governance and our relationships with each other. In their relationships with their world, environment and geography, the Mi'kmaw forefathers evolved into seven Mawiomis, each further subdivided into seven clans, living in Mi'kma'ki. The seven Mawiomis became the seven districts of the Mi'kmaw Grand Council. That is the origin of our Aboriginal title and Aboriginal rights today. (I represent the Sikniktok district on the grand council). In addition, through spiritual ceremonies we have "negotiated" our survival with our environment, gaining our natural rights based on the natural laws of the land to which we belong.

For centuries we had casual and seasonal encounters with sailors, fishermen and whalers from across the ocean. But when the European nations started to send explorers to our territory with intention to create settlements, we entered into treaties with them, as we had done all along with neighbouring tribes. Before the written treaties with the British, we made ceremonial friendship treaties with the French, welcoming them to our shores, making an alliance. When they arrived as settlers, Europeans asked our permission to land, to build wharves and habitations and fortifications to protect themselves from "hostile tribes." Over time, the treaties eventually became written documents outlining and confirming what are today called "treaty rights." We did not surrender our sovereignty or our land. We negotiated peace and friendship, allowing various European powers to create settlements on our shores and share in the vast resources of Mi'kma'ki. We would not interfere with their conduct and they would not interfere with our way of life; the treaties were never understood as a surrender of our lands or of our Aboriginal rights. Actually, the treaties that we negotiated with the English in the 18th century had as their purpose recognition and guarantees of our indigenous rights.

When Mi'kmaq negotiate our survival on the land and waters, we engage in ceremonies as a way of giving thanks to all of Creation and to show appreciation for the gifts that we receive from Mother Earth, *ositgamu* (the surface area that we stand upon and share with all living beings is *weskit kakamulti'wk*). Our ceremonies include fasting, feasting, gift giving, drumming, singing, dancing, sweat lodges, burning sweetgrass, tobacco offering, smoking the sacred pipe and burying the hatchet. Treaty ceremonies were traditionally witnessed by the sons of the chiefs so that they would learn the protocols.

Negotiating treaties with Europeans involved the same spiritual considerations. As previously with the French, it involved negotiating with the representatives of on behalf of their symbolic "father," the English monarch, the king, as he was introduced to us. In exchange we were promised protection from European conflicts and guaranteed freedom of trade (at truckhouses, licensed trading posts) and some types of staple foods and goods, blankets and ammunition. But we did not give up our land.

The strangers that came to our shores four hundred years ago recorded that we Mi'kmaw people were very friendly. We had developed technologies well adapted to our geography and climate, such as birch-bark canoes, toboggans, snowshoes and wigwams. We used a wide variety of medicinal plants to cure ailments. We were skilled makers of fine clothing of animal skins and furs fit for our extreme climate. We made baskets and bark containers decorated with dyed porcupine quills, bows and arrows, eel spears, fish weirs, nets, carving and everything we needed to live in Mi'kma'ki. We worked hard in *netukuti'mk*, sustainable hunting, fishing, trapping, woodcutting, gathering and organizing our travels to our winter and summer villages. We shared our resources, our knowledge and took care of each other so that no one was in dire need.

All these activities reveal a structured society and a coherent system of governance. This is what helps us human beings

Stephen J. Augustine prepares for the pipe ceremony. Photo by Barry Bernard. Courtesy Stephen J. Augustine.

living together in shared territories with similar values, beliefs, language and history. We may not all believe in Kluskap (the Mi'kmaw archetype) but we all know who he is!

Other aspects of our existence are the spiritual, mental and physical realms. This is the reason we negotiated our survival spiritually, with ceremonies, feasts, gatherings and communal events. When we traded with Europeans, we also hosted feasts and pipe ceremonies (*tabagies*), exchanged gifts, and praised each other in long speeches. This idea of gift exchange, feasting and ceremony had long been the code of conduct in maintaining peaceful relationships with the neighbouring Algonquian-speaking tribes. Once Champlain learned this code of conduct from the "Souriquois" (as the French called us), he started building parallel relationships with other indigenous groups living along the St. Lawrence River. The biggest tabagie took place in Innu territory at the mouth of the Tadoussac River in 1603 (in present-day Québec). It was a gathering of of more than 3,000 Innu, Huron, Algonkin, Nippising, Maliseet, Abenaki and Mi'kmaq.

Three events illustrate the Mi'kmaw code of conduct for establishing good relations. The first is the treaty of 1678 with Wabanaki leaders at Casco Bay in the present-day U.S. state of Maine. Once both parties had agreed to the terms, the British documented the English-language terms on parchment and hosted a lavish feast (Mi'kmaw terms were undocumented, passed on in the oral tradition). Presents were exchanged: furs, meat, wampum, guns, gunpowder, lead, musket-ball moulds, blankets and more. This feast involved

Re-enactment, in 1987, of the Watertown Treaty of 1776 between the Mi'kmaq nation and the United States. (L to r) William Bulger, President of the Massachusetts Senate, Mi'kmaw Grand Council Kji Keptin Alex Denny and Massachusetts Lt.-Gov. Evelyn F. Murphy. MicMac News, 1990, vol. 20 (9): 31. vhttp://beatoninstitute.com/micmac-news-1990.

the pipe ceremony, sweat lodges, drumming and dancing. After three days of celebration the English and Wabanaki finally stood together in front of two pillars of stone called the "two brothers" (*wijiketu'k*). The men who gathered together formed a circle, linking their arms, creating a human chain around the two brothers. We called the treaty *teplutakan*, from *tep* (inside) and *elutakan* (fence), because the men formed a human chain like a fence, and agreed on the words that were shared with each other inside this human fence. As a final gesture, the Wabanaki lit a sacred pipe and shared it with the English, indicating that together they were sending their treaty words to the sacred directions. The agreement could not change unless the parties came together to take back their words. The English were asked to bury a sword and an Indian hatchet was placed on top of it. The meaning of this gesture was that the hatchet would remain buried unless the English raised their sword again against the Indians.[1] For Mi'kmaw leaders this meant that if their hatchet was exposed because of the action of the British, they could pick up the hatchet in their defence; *neskwat* means to defend oneself in Mi'kmaw. There is a dance we call *neskwat*, which is danced at the Mi'kmaw Grand Council meetings at Potlotek, Cape Breton. The person dancing holds one hand in the air as in defence to ward off blows coming toward him. This dance has been called the "war dance" by anthropologists, though this is inaccurate for it is not a dance of agression but of defence.

The Casco treaty was renewed a generation later, in 1703, by the newly arrived British governor of Massachusetts.

> At the arrival of Governor Dudley in the Year 1702, the whole Body of Indians was in a tolerable good Frame and Temper; but being animated by the French, they soon began to threaten and insult the English: Upon which in the succeeding Year June the 20th a congress was appointed at Casco, where the Chiefs of the several Tribes met, ... with about 250 Men in 65 Canoos, well arm'd and mostly painted with variety of colours, which seemingly were affable and kind, and yet in some Instances gave cause of jealousy.
>
> A tent being fixt for entertaining the Governour and Gentlemen who accompanied him, together with the Sagamores; His Excellency very kindly saluted them, saying "That as he was

Commissioned by the Great and Victorious Queen of England, he came to visit them as his Friends and Brethren, and to reconcile whatever Differences had hapned since the last Treaty."

At this they made a pause, but after a short Intermission Captain Simmo, who was their Orator arose and said "That they acknowledged his Favour in giving them a Visit as such a juncture, with so many of the Council and Gentlemen of both Provinces; assuring him, that they aimed at nothing more than Peace; and that as high as the Sun was above the Earth, so far distant should their Designs be of making the least breach between each other."

And as Testimony thereof they presented him a Belt of Wampum, and invited him to the *Two Pillars* of Stones, which at a former Treaty were erected, and called by the significant Name of the TWO BROTHERS; unto which both Parties went, and added a great Number of Stones.

This ceremony being performed, several Volleys were discharged on each side; and the Indians added their usual dancing, singing, and loud acclamations of Joy. Trading-houses in several places were hereupon engaged; and that the Price of Commodities should be stated, and an Armourer fixed at the publick charge. Many Presents were also made them, which they kindly received; so that every thing looks with a promising Aspect of a settled Peace; And that which afterward seem'd to confirm it, was the coming in of Captain Bomaseen and Captain Samuel, who informed that several Missionaries from the Fryars were lately come among them, who endeavoured to break the Union, and seduce them from their Allegiance to the Crown of England; but had made no Impression on them, for that they were *as firm as the Mountains,* and should continue so, as long as the Sun and the Moon endured. (Penhallow 1973 [1726]: 2-4)[2]

What did this treaty have to do with the Mi'kmaq, who lived further north? There was a ring of alliances at play. Penobscot Chief Madakwando's daughter Matilda was married to the French Baron de Saint-Castin, who lived near present-day Bangor, ME. Their daughter was married at Port Royal, in Mi'kmaw territory, in 1703. The officer appointed to represent French interests in Acadia in 1711 was probably the Baron's Penobscot son, Anselme, who married Charlotte d'Amours, daughter of Louis d'Amours, the Sieur de Chauffours, at Port Royal in 1707 (Murdoch 1866: 329). Mi'kmaq frequently travelled through Maine, New Hampshire and Massachusetts, sometimes joining French military forces in action against the English during the long period of imperial conflict from 1650 to 1710. Penobscot and Mi'kmaq often intermarried, and Penobscot leaders routinely represented Mi'kmaw interests in the south.

The second event that comes to mind is the treaty celebrated at Nova Scotia Lieutenant Governor Jonathan Belcher's farm near Halifax, in 1761 (Nova Scotia Legislature 1761). Belcher invited all of the official representatives of the Crown as well as the members of the Nova Scotia House of Assembly. After the terms of this peace and friendship treaty were agreed, Belcher led the Mi'kmaw chiefs to two pillars of stone he had erected at his farm, where the party gathered for the feast, burying the hatchet and smoking the pipe. This was a great day of celebration for the town of Halifax. The Mi'kmaw chiefs were feasted, honoured with gifts, and most importantly, symbolically made a *teplutakan* with representatives of the Crown.

The third event was recorded by Clara Dennis on Chapel Island in 1929. Mi'kmaq Grand Chief Gabriel Sylliboy was conducting a treaty re-enactment ceremony at St. Anne's Mission on Chapel Island. Dennis was the daughter of the owner of the *Halifax Herald*, a local newspaper. When she graduated from university in 1927 with an English degree, her father gave her a Model T Ford car that she used to explore Nova Scotia, writing about her travels, which were published in three books and several travel magazines. In her book, *Cape Breton Over*, she relates how she met Grand Chief Sylliboy at St. Peter's selling baskets and axe handles. He invited her to the St. Anne's Mission, where she witnessed a reading of the Crown treaties by the Grand Chief and Keptin Andrew Alex, who was then the putu's, the official wampum-belt reader of the grand council. Alex read the belt that recalls the 1752-1761 treaties of peace and friendship. Sylliboy then lit the sacred pipe and Alex buried the hatchet near the corner of the mission church (Dennis 1942).

Sylliboy was chosen as grand chief in 1919 after the death of hereditary Grand Chief John Denny. Grand Chief John Denny and putu's Andrew Alex were descendants of previous members of the Mi'kmaw Grand Council and were born less than one hundred years after the treaty ceremonies at Belcher's farm. Their grandfathers may have witnessed the signing of the treaty in Halifax.

I think that the re-enactment at Chapel Island in 1929 was part of our oral traditional knowledge of historical events being passed down to new generations, and follows a chain of tradition that began in 1676 at Casco Bay. These events well reflect the strength of Mi'kmaw oral traditions.

Notes

1. My source comes from my grandmother. I think the spelling should be *tplutakn* and may refer to the *tplutew*, smoke that comes from a burning fire, sweetgrass or tobacco in a sacred pipe. This would make sense because the smoke from the sweetgrass or a pipe is often referred to as sacred words or, today, as prayers. It all makes sense to me—my metaphysics, as Leroy Little Bear would say.
2. Samuel Penhallow witnessed treaty negotiations from 1703 to 1725.

References

Dennis, Clara. 1942. *Cape Breton Over*. Toronto: Ryerson.

Murdoch, Beamish. 1866. *A History of Nova Scotia or Acadie, Vol. 1*. Halifax: James Barnes.

Nova Scotia Legislature. 1761. Ceremony and Treaty—Ceremonials at Concluding a Peace with the several Districts of the general Mickmack Nation of Indians, http://nslegislature.ca/index.php/about/timeline_event/1761/25_June_1761.

Penhallow, Samuel. 1973 [1726]. "History of the Indian Wars." A Facsimile Reprint of the First Edition, Printed in Boston in 1726, with the notes of earlier editors and additions from the original manuscript. Notes, index and introduction by Edward Wheelock. Williamstown, MA: Corner House Publishers.

Pamela Palmater

My Tribe, My Heirs and Their Heirs Forever: Living Mi'kmaw Treaties

Long before Europeans created what is now known as Canada, the British Crown signed treaties with the Mi'kmaq. These were not land-surrender treaties, nor were they treaties agreeing to the relocation of the Mi'kmaq from any of the seven districts in Mi'kma'ki (Mi'kmaw territory) onto reserves. The treaties signed with the Mi'kmaq were about mutual respect, mutual peace and mutual prosperity. The colonial powers knew that they could not settle here peacefully without our cooperation because the Mi'kmaq nation has lived in Mi'kma'ki since time immemorial and has legal and cultural obligations to manage and protect these lands for our future generations. Our Elders tell us stories of other indigenous nations trying to encroach on our lands and how we vigorously defended them. It is one of the reasons Nova Scotia Governor Cornwallis issued bounties for Mi'kmaw scalps in 1749—because we never stopped protecting our territory.

The Mi'kmaq were willing to give up their lives to protect the lands in our territory—not for greed or individual wealth accumulation—but because it was essential to our culture and identity as a people, our strength as a nation, and because we had obligations to protect it. Land is an essential part of who we are as Mi'kmaq. It is the land where our ancestors were born, where we raised our families and helped grow our nation. We have sustained ourselves and developed our economies from the many gifts offered in our territories—including the waters, plants, animals, fish and birds. We were able to develop and sustain our economic activities, like trade and commerce, from the precious resources within Mi'kma'ki. The land is where we practised our customs, ceremonies and traditions, and where the Mi'kmaq came together from the seven districts to engage in celebrations, assign hunting rights and confirm treaty alliances with other Indigenous nations. The land is also where our mortal ancestors returned when they left this world for the spirit world. The Mi'kmaq nation, our culture, identity and very survival have always been tied to our land.

In order to properly understand Mi'kmaw treaties, it is essential that one understand the Mi'kmaw context and world view from which the treaties were born. Any conversation about the content, meaning and/or legal force and effect of those treaties can only be truly understood from a telling of how those treaties have been lived by successive generations of Mi'kmaw people. No understanding of our treaties can start in reference to the federal *Indian Act*, by interpreting section 35 of the *Constitution Act 1982*, or by conducting a legal analysis of recent court cases. Our treaties predate all of those laws; they predate Canada as a country, and they predate the Royal Proclamation of 1763, which recognized indigenous nations and the rights we have to our lands. That is the point of this story. Mi'kmaw people knew all along that Mi'kma'ki was ours and we made sure that we never gave up one inch of those lands. It is through the stories of lived treaties that the truth emerges. This is my story.

My Story

Kwe', ni'n na teluisi Pam. Tapusijik nijink, kitk l'pa'tujk. Pikwelkik nikmaq. Ukumuljin wijikitultiekik e'pite'sk and ne'sijik l'pa'tu'sk. Nas-wikasultiek Ogpi'ganjik(k) utank, Oqwatnuk N.B. Ninen na utanminen pas+k pkesikn ta'n te'sit Mi'kmaw. Ninen na maqmikeminen teluisik Mi'kma'ki aq wiaqa'toqol ma'w, Nova Scotia, Epekwitk, pkesiknn, New Brunswick, Tkisnuke'l Ktaqmkuk, Kespe'k aq Kepek.

Hi, my name is Pam. I have two children, both boys. There are many in my family. Eight sisters and three brothers. We are members in Eel River Bar First Nation in northern New Brunswick. Our community is but a part of the whole population of the Mi'kmaq nation. Our traditional territory is known as Mi'kma'ki and consists of Nova Scotia, Prince Edward Island, and parts of New Brunswick, Gaspé and Quebec, and in and around western Newfoundland. (Palmater 2013a: 147)

I come from a large extended Mi'kmaw family with a long history at Ugpi'Ganjig (Eel River Bar First Nation). My great grandfather, Louis Jerome, is said to be one of the last traditional chiefs of my home community and was well known for the time he put into travelling to the other Mi'kmaw communities to maintain political and social relations.

One of the first chiefs on the Bar reserve was a great leader of Louis Jerome. Large in stature, clothed in deerskin, decorated with porcupine quills.... He would journey every summer ... to meet other Micmacs and celebrate in the Indian festivities. (Palmater 2010: 5)

He and his wife had ten children, one of whom was my grandmother Margaret Jerome. She was gifted as a healer and had an extensive knowledge of the medicinal uses of various plants and herbs. She was fluent in Mi'kmaw, but the Department of Indian Affairs agents, missionaries and the education system did not condone anyone speaking Mi'kmaw, so she did not pass it on to her own children—including her son, my father, Francis (Frank) Xavier Palmater.

Frank Palmater was an exceptionally intelligent man. Though he had to leave school at the elementary level in order to work and care for his brothers and sisters, he never stopped learning. He took every opportunity to read his siblings' school books and remained an avid reader in his adult life. He also knew about and believed in the alliance the Mi'kmaq had made with the British Crown and therefore enlisted in the Second World War to help defend our territories. He didn't risk his life for the right to vote or be Canadian—he fought to protect our lands and treaties. Though he came back a different man, he always encouraged his children to be active in First Nation activism and politics at the grassroots level. This is likely why so many of my older brothers and sisters got involved in community organizations, politics and advocacy. It was at their insistence that I attend every meeting, negotiation, election, community gathering, information session, assembly and protest—that I am who I am. I didn't know why I was doing all of these things back then, but I knew it was important. Their commitment, passion and unrelenting defence of our identity, land and treaty rights were and remain a strong influence on my life. I may not have known it then, but I know now that they were making sure that I enjoyed the benefits of my treaties and also lived up to my obligation to stand in defence of them. It is for this reason—my obligation to do everything in my power to defend and uphold the treaties—that I volunteered and worked at the community level to stay informed, and help engage others on treaty research and protection. It is also the reason that my education, work and advocacy have—at their core—the exercise and protection of our Nationhood and treaty rights.

Living Treaties

My view of Mi'kmaw treaties is slightly different from what one might expect of a lawyer with a doctorate in law. My view is not based in provincial, federal or international law. My view is based on how treaties are lived. I am not a treaty signatory, nor was I there when the treaties with the Mi'kmaq nation were signed. I have never seen nor touched the original treaty documents. As a young adult, I didn't know how many treaties we had, nor did I know much about the treaties, textually, until I studied them in university. But I have lived the Mi'kmaw treaties ever since I was born.

My first real recollection of treaties came when I was in grade two. My teacher had taught us that treaties were ancient documents that had no modern-day application, and that Indians had died off a long time ago. I wasn't quite sure about what all this meant, but I knew I could ask my brothers and sisters. As soon as I told my brother Nelson, he got very angry. He told me that when the teacher used the word "Indians" she was referring to the Mi'kmaq, Wolastoqiyik and other First Nations. He said we did not die off a long time ago or we wouldn't be standing there talking about the issue. Then he said that treaties were as valid today as they were when they were originally signed. I don't remember much else about what he said after that, except that he told me to never stand up for the Canadian national anthem, "O Canada" again.

I wasn't really sure how the two things were connected, but I found out the next day when my brother came to school to talk to my teacher. He spoke with my teacher in front of the whole class and told her that I would not be standing for the national anthem unless and until Canada respected our treaties and returned the lands they stole from us. He told her that he would be back to make sure that I did not stand for "O Canada." I didn't understand how important this moment was, but I could tell from how upset my brother was, that defending Mi'kmaw treaties was an important thing to do. So, on that day, I knew that in order for me to stand up for my treaties I had to sit down during "O Canada." I did not stand for the anthem that day, or for many days thereafter.

Had a reporter been there in the classroom that day and started quizzing my brother about Mi'kmaw treaties, I am quite sure that he would not have been able to cite them by heart, offer a legal interpretation, or even reel off treaty dates. He wasn't in my classroom defending treaties as an academic or a legal expert; he was there as a treaty beneficiary and as a protector of the treaties. He knew enough about the importance of the treaties to know that he should teach me to defend them. As a treaty person, my brother was the only expert I needed to know that something important was happening, and that it related to Mi'kmaw treaties.

I don't remember learning much, if anything, about Mi'kmaw people or treaties at school for the rest of my K-12 education. I did, however, start listening very carefully to my brothers and sisters every time they mentioned the word "treaty." Every time one of my brothers would bring home lobster, salmon or trout they would mention our treaty right to fish. They would always tell me to thank our ancestors for protecting our long-held right to fish. Sometimes I would watch as my brothers or sisters prepared the fish, and listen to them talking about enforcement officials who patrolled lakes or rivers and to try to stop our Mi'kmaw relatives who didn't have government-issued fishing licences from fishing. They would be angry and talk about how unfair it was that they had to sneak around like criminals to get food to eat. Other times, they would talk about family members or friends who had fishing gear or boats seized. Sometimes my brothers would joke and say that we are the lucky ones because we were so poor the officials had nothing to seize from us. The same thing happened with hunting, though I always got the impression that our hunting rights were something unique. It was around hunting rights that my family and many other Mi'kmaw families would gather and have long discussions about what was happening to our people. As a child, I heard stories about enforcement officials seizing hunting rifles, ammunition and even people's trucks. Though not all Mi'kmaw hunters were arrested, many were harassed. Law enforcement officers would arrest and seize their equipment and then drop the charges once hunting season was over. This seemed to be very effective at intimidating people, but did not stop us from hunting.

I remember that as I got a little older I would ask some why they kept hunting when officials told them it was illegal and they risked losing their gear and vehicles. They always gave me the same answer: "We are Mi'kmaw and we have a right to hunt to feed our families. The treaties protect our right to hunt and fish as we always have." This was usually followed by my brother Frank telling me, "And I'll be damned if I let some government official tell me otherwise." Treaties recognized our rights, which seemed to be independent of whether government officials presently recognized our rights. In this way, treaties seemed to me to have a power all of their own. It was during this time that I started to see treaties differently.

It seemed that treaties represented something so important that the denial of treaty rights by individual officials—even law-enforcement officers with the power of Canadian law behind them—could not extinguish them or their power. When I was quite a bit older, my brother Nelson was arrested for hunting out of season and rangers seized his rifle. He was forced to attend court on several occasions to explain himself. He was a non-status Indian (i.e., not registered as an Indian under the *Indian Act*) at the time, and a lawyer wanted proof of his "Indianness" before they would consider a treaty defence for his hunting activities. They wanted pictures of him at powwows, letters from the Chief, and/or attestations from Elders that he was in fact "Indian." To their surprise, my brother told them that he was not "Indian," neither legally nor culturally, but that he was Mi'kmaq and would never admit to any wrongdoing in the current regard. Not surprisingly, the Crown later dropped the charges—however the process took almost two years, during which time they held his rifle. He may not have been found guilty, but the Province of New Brunswick found a way to keep him from hunting. There were even times when he feared that a ranger would shoot him for refusing to stop hunting—but he held strong to the belief in his treaty rights and identity as a Mi'kmaw man.

This kind of harassment has been part of the treaty experience for as long as I can remember. Every Mi'kmaw person I ever met could share a story about interactions with enforcement officials in the context of hunting, fishing or gathering. Cutting wood was especially dangerous for Mi'kmaq as it was often followed by mass arrests and seizures. They didn't bother us when we were gathering wild berries or fiddleheads, but anything that might interfere with business interests that utilized our resources usually meant trouble of some sort. Despite all the legal risks and potential economic losses associated with hunting or fishing under the treaties, my family never once contemplated giving up. That message was repeated over and over—in family discussions, in community meetings, in negotiations with governments and in protests. Treaty rights are forever, and we would never give up protecting them.

But treaty rights weren't always portrayed as merely hunting and fishing rights. I remember my sisters Patsy, Glenda, Phebe and Sandra, telling me that our very identity stemmed in part from the treaties. They told me that governments in Canada had tried very hard to eliminate our people. They told me stories about bounties on our scalps and abuses in Indian residential schools. While this had happened in the past, they explained, the *Indian Act*, which is still in force, was designed to legislate our people out of existence. The act's Indian-registration scheme was designed to ensure our eventual disappearance, and it was the very reason my Granny had been an Indian, then lost her Indian status, then gained it back again—despite that she had never stopped being Mi'kmaq. When I asked how this affected treaties, my sister, Patsy, said:

Treaties are for Mi'kmaw people—not Indians. Canada is unilaterally trying to redefine who is Mi'kmaq by whether or not they are Indian (i.e., registered under the *Indian Act*). If they are successful in convincing us that we have to be Indian in order to be Mi'kmaq, then that will mean we will have to prove we are Indians before we can exercise Mi'kmaw treaty beneficiary status. (Personal communication, 1989)

She explained that this is where they get us. The *Indian Act* has a disappearing Indian-registration scheme, and you must be Indian to be Mi'kmaq, then that means Mi'kmaw people will disappear just as fast as Indians are targeted to disappear. However, our ancestors protected us by ensuring that Mi'kmaw heirs and were protected forever in our treaties, which long predates the *Indian Act*.

I learned all of this from our many conversations at the dinner table. I noticed the families of my non-Mi'kmaw friends talked about the weather, sports, local events and entertainment, whereas my family only talked about our treaty life. Even to this day, it doesn't matter which family member's home I visit, we always end up talking about Mi'kmaw history and treaties, First Nation politics and governance, and Canadian and provincial politics as it relates to First Nations. Even today, we don't ever talk about anything other than the condition of our peoples and how we can make things better. But my family members were not the only influences in my life in terms of how I have come to understand treaties. Elders from Mi'kmaw First Nations all over Mi'kma'ki have shared their wisdom with me about Mi'kmaw identity, nationhood, sovereignty and treaties throughout my life, and have had a profound impact on my understanding. The Elders had a strong role to play in grounding me about treaties.

When I was upset at how our treaties were ignored or violated, they would tell me that our treaties have out-lasted every prime minister and minister of Indian Affairs has ever had, and that I should not worry about a few rangers running around the woods looking for Indians. Their perspective is one with the benefit of many years of knowledge and experience, and one that can see beyond the immediate political and legal issues impacting treaties. The Elders reminded me that our people have survived despite scalping bounties on our heads, deaths in residential schools and attempts to legislate us out of existence. In their view, the treaties are no different, surviving attempts to erase them, ignore them and litigate them out of existence—but they are still as valid today as when they were originally signed. These were important messages to ensure that government actions did not discourage our younger generations.

At powwows, community gatherings and ceremonies, the Elders always acknowledge the treaties and the role our ancestors played in protecting our rights and lands. I have heard many Elders describe our treaties as sacred agreements that were to govern how we related with the newcomers. Most of the Elders I have talked to said they have never seen nor read the treaties, but have learned what they know about them from their Elders, and their Elders before them, who passed down oral histories about the spirit and intent of those treaties. In fact, I have never heard an Elder refer to an actual treaty document, speaking instead about the way they govern a way of life. There is both knowledge and comfort to be had in the Elders' teachings about treaties and the way our treaties have withstood the test of time, court cases, legislation and government pressure to erase them.

Learning Treaties

The treaties we signed are often referred to as peace and friendship treaties, but they are much more than that. They are some of the most significant nation-to-nation treaties ever signed on this continent because the Mi'kmaq never surrendered anything in return for the treaty promises. We simply committed to refrain from war with the Crown and to live in peace with settlers. While lawyers, courts and political commentators can make treaties seem complex, when read from a common-sense perspective, many of the promises are fairly straightforward.

This nation-to-nation relationship was solidified in the treaties of 1725-1726, 1752 and 1760-1761. There are other documents considered to be part of the covenant chain of treaty agreements, but the above are the most-often cited. The treaty of 1725 is believed to be one of the first negotiated between the British Crown and the Mi'kmaq (including the Wolastoqiyik). It was ratified in 1726 by Mi'kmaw representatives, and included an agreement that:

(1) the Mi'kmaq would maintain peace between our nation and Britain's settlers;

(2) the Mi'kmaq would permit the settlers to live where their current villages were constructed at the time of treaty signing;

(3) Britain would recognize and protect all Mi'kmaw lands, liberties and properties, including beaches and fisheries (not previously sold);

(4) the Mi'kmaq would continue to hunt, fish and fowl as formerly; and

(5) the nations of Mi'kmaq and Britain would continue to trade as usual.

The ratification of this treaty in 1726 included provisions that whenever there would be quarrels between the two parties, revenge should never be taken. This was an important part of the peace process and one of the reasons Mi'kmaw people have acted peacefully in the face of aggressive and violent actions by the Crown. The treaty of 1752 contained similar provisions, assuring the Mi'kmaq that our way of life would not be disturbed by virtue of concluding Articles of Peace with the Crown, reconfirming the commitments made in the previous treaties and intended to apply to the Mi'kmaq and our heirs "forever." It included the following provisions:

(1) Mi'kmaq would always have the "favour, friendship & protection" of His Majesty [the Crown];

(2) His Majesty promised to provide "aid and assistance" to the Mi'kmaq in our defence of our treaties;

(3) Hunting and fishing would continue as usual and Mi'kmaq would have complete freedom to engage in the trade of our resources;

(4) That provisions would be provided to all Mi'kmaw families as needed on a regular basis to sustain us in recognition of our maintaining the treaty promises;

(5) That every year, on October 1, His Majesty would provide the Mi'kmaq with presents, blankets, tobacco and ammunition as part of the treaty renewal process; and

(6) That the Mi'kmaq would save any settlers who were shipwrecked.

Despite the scalping proclamation made by Governor Cornwallis in the mid-1700s, and the bounties paid to settlers for the scalps of Mi'kmaw men, women and children, our nation nevertheless met with the Crown's representatives in the name of peace again. The Treaties of 1760-1761 reconfirmed the commitments made in the earlier treaties and included some of the following additional promises:

(1) The Mi'kmaq would not disturb any of the "lawful" settlements made by British subjects; and that

(2) No revenge will be taken by the Mi'kmaq for wrongdoing by His Majesty's subjects.

The spirit and intent of these treaties were based on mutual respect, mutual benefit and mutual protection. There was no surrender of Mi'kmaw territory. There was no surrender of our traditional occupations or economic endeavours. There was certainly no agreement to surrender our sovereignty and independence to the Crown. We agreed to be allied nations and all that entails. These agreements applied to both His Majesty's heirs and Mi'kmaw heirs, forever.

However, we know from experience that the Crown has not lived up to its side of the bargain. The Crown has failed to fully respect and fulfill the treaty promises and has, at times, acted violently against us in violation of the peace treaties. The chronology below is a shameful one for the Crown, but a true sign of honourable restraint, and peaceful resistance for Mi'kmaw people.

1725-1726 – Peace treaties signed with Mi'kmaq to stop hostilities on all sides and protect hunting, fishing, and fowling;

1749 – Proclamation offering bounty for Mi'kmaw scalps;

1752 – Treaty with Mi'kmaq confirming hunting and fishing rights, and military alliance;

1760-61 – Treaty with Mi'kmaq protecting hunting, fishing and trading rights (no surrender of land or sovereignty);

1971 – Donald Marshall Jr. (Mi'kmaq) wrongly convicted of murder, Halifax, NS;

1981 – Police assault and arrest Mi'kmaw for exercising fishing rights in Listuguj, QC;

1989 – Donald Marshall Inquiry, acknowledging that racism against Mi'kmaq in justice system was behind reason for Marshall's wrongful conviction;

1998 – RCMP called in against Mi'kmaq for exercising timber rights in Listuguj, QC;

1999-2001 – RCMP and DFO ram fishing boats of Mi'kmaq for

MicMac News, vol. 18 (1): 5. http://beatoninstitute.com/micmac-news-1988.

exercising court-proven treaty rights in Esgenoopetij, NB; and 2013 – Army of RCMP assault and arrest peaceful Mi'kmaq protecting lands from hydro-fracking in Elsipogtog, NB. (Palmater 2013b)

In every instance, the Mi'kmaq have refused to give up our sovereignty, land, identity and treaty rights. In return, we have faced confiscation of hunting and fishing gear, harassment by enforcement officials, numerous arrests, protracted and expensive litigation, wrongful imprisonment, and even physical assaults for refusing to give up the treaty life. We have been labelled as eco-terrorists, radicals, militants and terrorists, but we have a lot to be proud of in our struggle, for we have always lived up to the spirit and intent of those treaties, not just in the exercise of those rights, but in our commitment to maintaining the peace.

The Mi'kmaq and British settlers have been living treaties since they were signed, beginning in the early 1700s. We have not molested them in their settlements and we have shared our resources with them. We have fought in their wars as their allies to protect these lands. We have kept the peace. We have had more than two hundred years of practice and implementation. Yet, the Crown has not lived up to its obligations and, in fact, has used both law enforcement and the courts to impede our rights. While the Supreme Court of Canada has upheld our rights in some cases, like in *R. v. Simon, R. v. Marshall* and *R. v. Sappier; R. v. Gray*, the courts have often limited rights. In other cases, like in *R. v. Bernard*, the Supreme Court has outright denied specific treaty rights. This hasn't stopped the Mi'kmaq from exercising our treaty rights, nor do I expect it will change our activities any time soon.

All of which begs the question: Since the issue of treaty rights is so important to the Mi'kmaq and to Canadians alike, why has Canada continually ignored and subverted them?

Understanding Treaties

One cannot read a treaty and claim to "know" what it means without understanding the history and context or having lived it. This is why there are so many misunderstandings about the treaties in some segments of Canadian society. A true understanding is a process that takes time because treaties between nations are relationships that are unique, organic, evolving, adapting and enduring. Any relationship changes over time. Treaty rights are not like a defined benefit from a social program found in a piece of government legislation or policy. Nor are the promises contained in the treaties akin to contract provisions subject to the laws and dispute mechanisms of the British drafters. Although represented in the parchment versions, the meaning of the treaties is first and foremost found in the spirit and intent of the treaties. This is what guides the nation-to-nation relationship—not the limited scope of the English-language text. Though some lawyers are quick to cite court cases, some forget that Mi'kmaw laws were and are still as applicable and relevant to the negotiation, signing and interpretation of these treaties as any imported British laws.

I did not begin this chapter with an analysis of documents because the spirit and intent of treaties are found outside their written form—yet they are as valid today as when they were signed, not because a court said so, but because Mi'kmaw people and settlers both have lived the treaties and have never stopped exercising these treaty rights since they were signed. For our part, Mi'kmaq continue to hunt under the treaties, despite being harrassed and arrested. We continue to fish under the treaties, despite having our boats seized or run over. For every time that a government said our treaties were "superseded by law," we kept living the treaty life. When settlers were permitted to live undisturbed in their lawful (and unlawful) settlements; we defended the settlers in their wars anyway. Every day that the settlers live peacefully on our lands they are confirming the treaties. That is the enduring nature of these agreements, in any context.

Perhaps, seeing the relationship from the eyes of the settler might better explain why treaties are so important, even today.

Dear Treaty Partner

Imagine this as a scenario:

Your family, once headed by your great-great grandfather (we'll call him Grandpa), is struggling to survive, the crime rate is rampant where they live, and there appears to minimal employment or other opportunities. Your Grandpa hears about a new place that promises wealth, prosperity and a great deal of individual freedom. So, on behalf of the entire family, he decides to move to this new place. This involves a very long trip and everyone feels a little afraid and nervous, but also cautiously optimistic about the potential for a new and better life. The trip is rough and by the time they arrive in this new place, your ancestors were close to starvation and suffering the ill effects of malnutrition. They are desperate to find food and shelter.

When they finally arrive on the shores of their new home, however, the weather is brutal and there is no shelter in sight. Having used up all the rations on the trip, their situation is desperate. Luckily, off in the distance, your Grandpa spots some men and called out for help. These men respond right away, but spoke a different language and could neither communicate in English nor understand what your Grandpa was saying. The strangers have no idea if your family members were there to harm them or not, but since your Grandpa looks so desperate, the strangers guide them off the boat and into their community to give them food, shelter and medicine until they are well again.

For years, these helpful new friends work alongside your family to help them grow stronger, build their own shelters and connect with other families like yours. They hunt, fish and gather food and share with your family. They share their medicines when your family is ill and share some of their hunting and fishing spots, and point out places to gather berries and other wild food. It is because of their kindness and generosity that your family survived in this new place. All was peaceful, for a while.

Then, one day, your Grandpa decided that he wanted to fence off the area where the best berries are found. He doesn't let anyone else enter that area, including his new friends. Your family's new friends don't appreciate this and complain about this treatment. Your Grandpa, fearful of retaliation, drafts an agreement in English (which his new friends could not read) promising that he is only going to fence off a small area and that neither he nor his family will ever bother any other lands or resources. In the spirit of friendship and goodwill, the new friends agree to this.

Then your Grandpa seeks out other families like yours and decides to fence off larger and larger pieces of land in violation of the agreement. He stops his new friends from picking berries, hunting moose and catching fish. Now his new friends must go through your Grandpa to access food. Your Grandpa continues to fence off larger and larger portions of his garden and hunting grounds and starts making so much food that he has more than his family needs. So, he starts selling the excess food to other families at a profit. Grandpa's former friends are becoming upset at this turn of events. They start to suffer the ill effects of not having enough food to eat or being able to bring goods to trade to sustain their peoples. They start to complain on a persistent basis that your Grandpa should honour the agreement made and share the food and resources which, after all, are rightfully theirs. Your Grandpa, who is quite wealthy at this point, has enough money to pay other families to attack and scalp his former friends to keep them from your Grandpa's stolen garden and hunting area.

Your family is strong and healthy as they have access to enough food to eat. Meanwhile, your Grandpa's former friends are suffering the ill effects of poor diet, lack of clean water and access to their former trade routes and economic activities. They can no longer support themselves. All they have are the meagre handouts your Grandpa provides them. After a while, your Grandpa grows tired of their different languages and ways of being and tells the new settler government to create an identification system for his former friends, round them up and stick them in schools to learn English and European history. Half of the children don't make it out of the schools alive.

As time goes by, your Grandpa's son takes over the business and starts using pesticides in the fenced garden to prevent the loss of crops to animals, birds and bugs. The chemicals are highly toxic and cause cancer, and therefore are stored far away from your family's homes. They are, instead, stored on the lands of your family's former friends—the Indians. They start to get sick and some even die from the effects of these chemicals, but your family doesn't stop storing the chemicals near their homes.

After many generations, your family has become quite prosperous, able to provide you with a good education, healthy food, lots of sports and music lessons, trips to Disneyland and opportunities to start your own career. You feel happy and believe everyone can accomplish the same things you can, if only they work hard. You don't feel any responsibility for the conditions of Indians because you personally had nothing to do with the scalpings, Indian residential schools, theft of their children, murdered and missing women, and over-imprisonment. You didn't personally fence off the garden or steal the land, nor did you personally spread the pesticides.

You forget that your healthy, prosperous life is thanks to the dispossession and oppression of your former friends, the Indians, by your family. You forget that none of your family—including you, your father, your grandfather and your great-grandfather—would be here on this land were the Indians not there to care for your great-great grandfather: feed him, shelter him and provide him with medicines to keep him healthy. You forget that the original agreement, drawn up by your Grandpa, promised to share the wealth and work together in peace. You forget that even by your own laws, how you acquired the lands and resources was a scam and that the breach of the agreement was illegal. You forget that, by your own laws, restitution, compensation and justice are required.

You can't undo what your Grandpa did, but you and your family and generations of your family benefit from it every day. Something more than a mere apology is required.

This isn't about feeling bad or guilty; it's about undoing as much of the harm done as possible. That will require more than a handshake, an apology or a memorial—it will require giving back some of the land. It will require opening the fence and allowing Indians to have some of their garden back. It will mean using the wealth acquired from Indian lands and resources to help pay for the health care they need from generations of poverty. It will mean remediating contamination from pesticides, and taking steps to save the languages your Grandpa tried so hard to remove from them.

Justice and reconciliation will require some sacrifice, effort, time and patience. It took many generations to create this unjust situation. It may take just as many generations to heal from it. But no less will suffice for a just country built on the good faith and promise of the Mi'kmaw treaties. This is the meaning of our treaties.

Conclusion

The Mi'kmaq signed treaties of peace, friendship, protection and alliance, not as subjects but as representatives of a sovereign nation. While subsequent Canadian laws and courts try to impose various ways of defining and limiting these treaties—they cannot touch the treaty itself. Even the *Indian Act*, and all of its limitations on local band powers and who gets to be considered an Indian, was enacted long after our treaties were signed. None of these measures can change our treaties—regardless of how politicians, lawyers or courts choose to interpret them. However we come to understand treaties, we must never forget the original spirit and intent, which was a good-faith agreement, filled with promise, between nations sharing this land in peace.

At this point in my life, I have learned a great deal more about treaties than I knew when I was a child. I didn't know how important it was when my brother Nelson instructed me not to stand for the national anthem until treaties were respected. I didn't understand why I had to attend countless community meetings and protests in defence of our treaties. But thanks to my family, Elders, leaders and indigenous activists, I have come to understand treaties in a variety of ways. I have learned that Mi'kmaw treaties protect our way of life, our identity and our means of subsistence. The treaties are evidence of our strength as a people and our power as a sovereign nation that has endured for generations.

There is no dividing line in my life between being Mi'kmaw, my family life, my career as a lawyer and academic, and my First Nation advocacy and activism efforts. I'm not sure when it happened, but I have come to realize that being a treaty person is not a matter of legal interpretation, academic debate or governmental program that comes with an identity card—it is a way of life. Treaties represent a unique relationship between nations that guarantees the survival of our future generations if we honour them.

Were it not for the important symbiotic relationship we have with our world—the lands, waters, plants, animals, birds and fish and, indeed, spirits—we would not exist as Mi'kmaq. Canada would not exist but for the good graces, kindness and generosity of the Mi'kmaq and many other Indigenous nations. If we have any hope at a future for our great grandchildren seven generations to come, we should protect these gifts by honouring the treaties.

References

Palmater, Pamela. 2010. *Beyond Blood: Rethinking Indigenous Identity and Belonging.* Saskatoon, SK: Purich Publishing.

———. 2013a. Matn Tel-Mi'kmawi: I'm Fighting for my Mi'kmaw Identity. *Canadian Journal of Native Studies* 33 (1): 147-67.

———. 2013b. Oh Canada! Your Home's on Mi'kmaw Land. *Indigenous Nationhood* (blog). http://indigenousnationhood.blogspot.ca/2013/11/oh-canada-your-homes-on-mikmaw-land.html (accessed June 15, 2015).

Fred Metallic

Treaty and Mi'gmewey[1]

Mi'gmaq teachings often begin with the Creation story and the "one who came first," the sun. A description of the birth of Glusgap follows that of the sun. Glusgap is formed in "dry earth"; a bolt of lightning turns dry earth into green earth giving life to the animals who in turn give life to Glusgap. Glusgap's first act upon arising was to offer thanks to the seven directions.[2] The Creator sent Nugumi, Grandmother, to guide and teach Glusgap in life. Grandmother was created from stone as an Elder whose knowledge and wisdom was enfolded in the Mi'gmaq language. Grandmother's first teaching to Glusgap was to ask for the permission of his brothers and sisters, through the martin, to consume their flesh so that they may survive. Glusgap was granted permission by his brothers and sisters the animals, and provided with song and ceremony to honour them.

> The first family continued to grow with the birth of Glusgap's nephew, Netawansum. He came into human form through the foam of the ocean, sweet grass, and the midday sun. Netawansum brought Glusgap teachings and gifts of the underwater realm as well as the ability to see for great distances. Glusgap, in honour of his nephew's arrival and the gifts he received, offered thanks and held a feast. (Retelling of Mi'gmaq Creation story)

My knowledge of treaty comes from my family. I was raised in the Mi'gmaq community of Listuguj, Québec, located within the territory of Gespe'gewa'gig, Mi'gma'gi.[3] I grew up surrounded by my extended family—parents, siblings, aunts, uncles, grandparents, cousins—and many friends. Similar to other indigenous peoples who were raised in reserve communities in the 1960s and 1970s, we lived without electricity and running water. In my early years, I attended an Indian day school on the reserve. Taught by nuns, a formal, Canadian curriculum was woven together with Catholic teachings.[4] In Listuguj, the most prominent building, which is also located in the centre of the community, is St. Anne's Church. As a young boy, I regularly attended this church and served as an alter boy. There were teachers beyond those of the school and the Catholic church that shaped my life, however. Over the years, rivers, in particular the Restigouche River, which runs alongside Listuguj, have profoundly influenced the shape of my life and my world view as a Mi'gmaq.

Fred Metallic. Photo courtesy Jaime Battiste.

My father, Isaac Metallic, taught me how to make a living from the rivers. Each season, we fished—smelts and trout in spring, salmon in summer, trout in the fall, then winter smelts. He often shared the story that when he was a young boy, he would climb on his father's back and they too would fish the river. On the river, with my father and my uncles, we spoke mostly in Mi'gmaw. I learned not only how to fish, but I learned that our family is historically connected to this territory. I learned about *ta'n tett tle'iawultieg*—how we truly belong to this territory.

There were other teachings as well. From my mother, Eunice (Wysote) Metallic, I learned how to share what we caught with our extended family. For instance, she would always remind us that we needed to share the first catch of the season. She taught us how to prepare and store salmon for use during the winter months. As she prepared the salmon for eating, she would speak about the women who taught her—her mother-in-law, Madeleine Metallic, and her aunt

Alma Jerome. Still today, my children love to hear my mother tell stories about when she was young, about what life was like, that we come from here, and that we are "made from the ground, the *maqamigew*."

From my family, I learned about what I consider to be our rights and our responsibilities to our lands and the waters that have sustained our lives. As I grew older, different people came into my life—language keepers, knowledge holders and ceremonialists. They helped to strengthen my identity, my relations, and to articulate an understanding of treaties from a Mi'gmaw perspective. One story, in particular, shaped my understanding of treaty philosophy, and that is the Creation story. There are many Creation stories, and many ways to describe how we came to be in this territory. But the story that Geptin (captain) Egian Augustine from Ilsipugtug tells (some of which I have related at the beginning of my story) has helped me understand, in a new way, what it really means to "live treaty"—to honour and respect all our relations in Creation; to live and think in our Mi'gmaw language and culture; and to share these teachings not only with those today, but with future generations.

Treaty Knowledge and Oral Tradition

Mi'gmaw children become knowledgeable about their political ecology through their experiences, observations and the teachings provided by family members and Elders. Through oral tradition, the Elders inform the children about what they need to know concerning the history of their territory. For instance, when Mi'gmaq signed the 1726 treaty of peace and friendship with the British, "an important component of treaty signing was the presence of not only elders and sakamows, but also of younger men who would eventually assume the leadership positions" (Wicken 1995: 151). For these young men to become family leaders, they would have to recite and recall oral and, later, written traditions of that treaty and assume the responsibility of keeping the spirit and intent of the treaty alive. Yet Mi'gmaw children who know the event through oral history eventually have their traditional understanding challenged and reinterpreted by the courts.

In 1928, Mi'gmaq Grand Chief Gabriel Sylliboy was charged for trapping muskrats out of season in the district of Unama'ki. He was brought before provincial court and charged with illegal trapping.

Sylliboy defended his right to hunt based on (the 1752 peace and friendship) treaty, saying that "since I was boy I heard that Indians got from king free hunting and fishing at all times" (Wicken 1995: 158). In the same court proceeding, a deputy grand chief said that he "heard that according to treaty we had right to fish and hunt at any time. I can not read, heard it from my grandfathers. Heard that King of England made treaty with micmacs" (161). The court's position was that the treaty did not affect Sylliboy because he was not a "band member" of the territorial district of Shubenacadie, where the treaty was signed. Secondly, the court added that Sylliboy would have been found guilty in any event because "the Mi'kmaq did not have the status to enter into treaty as they were not then an independent power" (145). They were, said the presiding judge, a savage people. The ruling was in favour of the province. Sylliboy's knowledge of treaty as passed on to him by his ancestors through oral tradition was no match against the legal system's Eurocentric logic—that treaties were fixed not only in time but also in place. However, in *R. v. Simon*, in 1985, the Supreme Court of Canada affirmed 18th-century Mi'gmaq treaty rights and rejected the earlier ruling. The Supreme Court noted that such jurisprudence reflects the biases and prejudices of another era in our history. Such reasoning is flawed and the language used is no longer acceptable in Canadian law.

Oral tradition as a means of expressing knowledge about ecological relations within a territory is often treated as inauthentic knowledge when compared with the written tradition. In this manner, written records are privileged over oral traditions, thus influencing how we understand our relations within the territory. Privileging the written record as the basis of political decision-making allowed people within our territory to deny our ecological relations, and justified hierarchal relationships between "man" and the land. In *Delgamuukw v. British Columbia*, the Supreme Court of Canada affirmed the use of oral tradition of the Aboriginal peoples in courts. It found that the findings of fact made by the trial judge were flawed due to his treatment of the various kinds of oral histories, and ordered a new trial.

Treaties as Covenants

In political thought, Mi'gmaq operate on the extended family system, whereby we are born into a tradition for the purpose of extending our interconnectedness and interdependency with each other—a tradition considered a sacred vow. In Mi'gmaq, we express the extending of our interconnectedness as *angugamge'wel*. When the first extended family came into being in our territory, they too had to enter into agreement with the Creator. They needed to know how to live with each other and how they could help each other realize what they had to offer as gifts to Creation. Treaty-making is a part of our sacred ordering, and every time a treaty is made we are adding to this order; in essence, we are adding to our extended family. We are all brothers and sisters in Creation. Treaties are covenants to that order and guide us in our relationships.

Our Creation story teaches that our first treaty establishes a relationship with the animals, while the second recognizes a treaty with the water beings. Each relationship requires an understanding about the context in which we live and how each being may help each other—remembering, for instance, to only take what we need and agreeing to manage our lives according to that need. The first treaty orders land tenure, while the second treaty establishes a water-tenure system. It is through this treaty process that the Mi'gmaq agree to share responsibility for the land and water. By renewing our treaty responsibility through ceremony every year at each fishing and hunting station, we secure our relationship with Creation and our way of life. According to our Elders, we have to learn how to protect, defend and live by our treaties. We protect ourselves by ensuring that the land and water systems are properly managed, that the animals and fish are not overharvested. That is our journey; we continue to seek guidance from the Creator, from Nugumi, our grandmother, and to draw strength from Netawansum, Glusgap's nephew.

Similar to other indigenous nations, the Mi'gmaq recorded their treaty relationships, proper rituals and agreements in their own symbolic literacy through wampum belts and strings. During the early encounter era, the British and French colonial powers recognized the oral and written political traditions of indigenous peoples in their written treaties and transcripts. For example, the written version of the treaty of Montreal (1701), a peace treaty between New France and forty First Nations, contains a recital of the delivery of prisoners and the giving of calumets. The transcript highlights how nations delivered calumets and wampum—both methods recognize the spiritual link to the concept of peace (Henderson and Barsh 1995). Further, for the Mi'gmaq, these proceedings were formalized and sealed by the smoking of the pipe. Elders would not agree to any treaty without the smoking of the pipe. To the Mi'gmaq, when the pipe is joined and the tobacco is lit, we are in essence unifying the physical and spiritual realms of our territory. When Mi'gmaq smoked the pipe and thereby gave life to the treaty agreement, it was understood and agreed by the parties that we were creating a new vision for the territory based on a shared legal meaning. The pipe and the agreement would create for Mi'gmaq and the rest of creation a new vision of politics within Gespe'gewa'gig.

Delegates Chosen for Treaty Negotiations: Processes of Governance

When the Elders summoned a council meeting to deal with matters (whether it was land distribution, crimes committed, or affairs of war and peace between nations), the meeting would open with a ceremony and then one of the chiefs would speak to the issue at hand. Leadership in this sense unfolded through a process established by the people present for the council. For the Elders, choosing a suitable candidate to negotiate affairs between families and nations was taken seriously. Delegates were not chosen randomly or elected by the majority, rather they demonstrated to the Elders why they would be suitable candidates.

The process of choosing a suitable candidate was observed and commented upon by Christien Le Clercq, who worked as a missionary among the Mi'gmaq in Gespe'gewa'gig between 1675 and 1687. Le Clercq noted: "the chief would name, and would cause to enter the circle, that one of the young men whom he considered the most suitable for the execution of the project" (Ganong 1910: 148). When a young man had been chosen by the Elders in council to act as a delegate, the *sagamaw* (chief) would inform him publicly of his task, reciting the proposed agreement, along with a speech to confer the terms of the agreement made by the Elders in council. Le Clercq wrote that the young delegate would then depart from the council and, upon completion of negotiations, when he returned the council would be reunited in a similar ceremony, to which he would recite his report of the voyage.

The decision-making process that Le Clercq describes in his observation of Mi'gmaw politics within the Gespe'gewa'gig district highlights key aspects of Mi'gmaw political thought. Although ideas of accountability and consensus-building are described as important political values in Mi'gmaw political thought, the processes through which we practice these values and beliefs are not often discussed. Consensus and accountability are essential when considering all those affected by our decisions. As Le Clercq observed during his stay in Gespe'gewa'gig, the business of the Elder's council and their responsibility to ecological governance has strict procedures and each individual is reminded publicly of the importance of seeking consensus and being accountable for their decisions.

Wampum protocol and diplomacy recognized the importance of patience, respect and sharing as essential values within the traditional way of governing. The delegates who were chosen by the Elders to carry the wampum or treaty messages to and from the nations were generally young. In this way, youth were instructed and educated on wampum records, procedures and protocols. Young men who demonstrated this knowledge and skill later assumed their responsibilities as *putu's* or as *samgoneese*, critical diplomatic roles necessary in the maintenance of peace and harmony within a territory.

Treaty Relations and Contemporary Protocol

The relationship between the Penobscot, Passamaquoddy, Maliseet and Mi'gmaq and the formation of the Wabanaki Confederacy is said to have begun in the mid-18th century (Speck 1915: 494). Henderson draws on oral evidence to argue that Mi'gmaq in Mi'gma'gi have been in a relationship with Mohawk people dating back 1,000 years or more. Although this raises issues about written and oral traditions, the privileging of certain "texts" and what constitutes legitimate knowledge, we cannot dismiss the point that Mi'gmaq have a unique and distinct political relationship with other nations, within their confederacy, and within the broader indigenous political community. These traditions continue today.

In 1999, the Supreme Court of Canada affirmed the treaty right for the Mi'gmaq to make a "moderate livelihood" from the resources of our lands and waters. Immediately following this decision, however, there was conflict in the community of Esgenoopetitj (Burnt Church, New Brunswick), which is located in the southern part of the Gespe'gewa'gig district. This situation has often been analyzed to illustrate the conflict between Mi'gmaq and the state; however, the events that took place also illustrate the manner whereby Mi'gmaq govern themselves and the protocols of treaty-making, both inside districts and between nations. The following is my own account of my experience having been invited by the then chief of Listuguj, Allison Metallic, to take part in the protection of Esgenoopetitj.

Mi'gmaw Treaty Rights—Standing Together in Esgenoopetitj

The Mi'gmaw leadership in Esgenoopetitj felt strongly that treaty rights and responsibilities signed with the British Crown 1760-1761 provided them with enough political protection to govern their fishery, based on local protocols and procedures. However, the representative for the Government of Canada, the minister of Fisheries and Oceans, did not agree and proceeded to impose sanctions in an attempt to persuade the Mi'gmaq of Esgenoopetitj to accept Canadian protocols and agreements as the foundation of their fishery. The following is my own account of my experience having been invited by the then chief of Listuguj, Allison Metallic, to take part in the protection of Esgenoopetitj during the summer of 2000, as member of the Listuguj delegation.

The situation in Esgenoopetitj escalated in the summer of 2000. A blockade had been set up on the highway. At this point, the Esgenoopetitj leadership called upon their brothers and sisters of Listuguj for assistance. It is protocol that when one member of the family requests assistance we are obligated to assist. However, before Listuguj could provide political and human resources, a protocol agreement had to be negotiated between the Listuguj and Esgenoopetitj leadership. The protocol agreement outlined the political framework for each community's role and responsibilities in the matter. When the situation again escalated, whereby other indigenous nations had to be called, the Mi'gmaw leadership within the Gespe'gewa'gig district asked their brothers, the Mohawks, to assist. After the Mohawk delegation arrived, the delegates of Esgenoopetitj, Listuguj and Kahnawake held a council meeting with the federal minister to discuss peace and harmony within Esgenoopetitj. After the council meeting ended without resolution, the delegates from Esgenoopetitj felt that the barricades should be removed as a symbol of good will. The Kahnawake delegation, however, reminded the council representatives that removing the "barricade from the highway" would require consent from all the delegates at the council meeting. The Kahnawake delegate spoke of political protocols that must be respected when other districts or nations are asked to intervene in local affairs. Each council within the district is obligated to respond and provide support to each other, like brothers and sisters within a nation. Just as Listuguj had to follow protocol to enter the Esgenoopetitj territory, the hosting territory must also respect international protocols when inviting outside nations. As the *sagamaw* of Listuguj said, "when one of our communities [or nations] calls for help we have a responsibility to help." This is the consistent protocol among families, districts and nations, which dates back in time. A council meeting among the indigenous nations was convened, and the decision was made to remove the barricade from the highway—as it was important to restore peace in our territory.

Conclusion

The teachings of respect, peace, reciprocity, sharing and caring remain central to our way of life, and to how we govern in our territory. Our relations in our territory—with the lands, the waters, the winged ones, the fish—all serve as the foundation to our language, our families and our way of life. These are the values that guide our relationships within our home of Gespe'gawa'gig. In our territory, we teach our children to respect and care for all beings and the importance of maintaining the well-being of our home.

By renewing and honouring our relationship with Creation, we continue to trust and believe that the land in which our ancestors are buried will continue to provide the necessary knowledge to govern in that Mi'gmewey. Many of our teachings speak about various human families and how each one is gifted and powerful in its own way. Each family has something different to contribute to the achievement of peace and harmony. Politically and spiritually, we have to get along and we are all obliged to respect each other's gifts and responsibilities. In the Creation story, Glusgap's first act upon his birth is to offer thanks in each of the seven directions—acknowledging all our relations, we remain connected; showing gratitude, we honour Creation.

Notes

1. Mi'gmawei refers to the relationship between treaty and those matters that pertain to Mi'gmaq.

2. In Mi'gmaw teachings, the seven sacred directions are: North, South, East, West, Mother Earth, Father Sky and the self.

3. This chapter uses the Listuguj orthography for Mi'gmaw terms.

4. In Canada, jurisdiction over First Nations education is that of the federal government.

References

Augustine, Stephen. 2000. *Tan-Wet-Abeg-Sol-Teagw—Where We Come From*. Gatineau, QC: Canadian Museum of Civilization.

———. 2001. Presentation for Mi'gmawei Mawiomi. Video recording. Campbellton, NB.

Henderson, James Y. Sake'j and Russel L. Barsh. 1995. International Context of Crown-Aboriginal Treaties in Canada. In *Final Report of the Royal Commission on Aboriginal Peoples*. Government of Canada. CD-ROM.

Le Clercq, Fr. Christian. 1910. *New Relations of Gaspesia with the Customs and Religion of the Gaspesian Indians*. Ed. and trans. William F. Ganong. Toronto: The Champlain Society.

Metallic, Allison. 2000. Communique to Esgenoopetitj Chief and Council. Esgenoopetitj, Gespe'gewa'gig. August 15.

Speck, Frank G. 1915. The Eastern Algonkian Wabanaki Confederacy. *American Anthropologist* 17:492-508.

Wicken, William C. 1995. Heard it from my Grandfathers. *UNB Law Journal* 44:145-61.

Patrick J. Augustine

Mi'kmaw Relations

This chapter sketches concepts of Mi'kmaw law as it is illustrated by Mi'kmaw relationships, as currently found in the academic literature. Mi'kmaw knowledge is largely experiential: embodied and acquired through both anecdotal and observational evidence. While non-indigenous writers, such as historians and anthropologists, have attempted to capture their understanding of this experience vicariously by textual analysis, they do subject many stories to their Eurocentric cultural bias or to misinterpretation. Without the oral traditions to verify these accounts, this chapter's reliance on non-Mi'kmaw writers should not be viewed as an affirmation of their work, as I do not address the biases or perceptions of the authors. What I do provide is a descriptive view as to how Mi'kmaw law and knowledge are reflected in the existing literature and provide some insights or examples of these relationships.

A short essay cannot cover the extent of knowledge concepts, especially those pertaining to the Mi'kmaq. However, it can serve as a starting point for examining such laws as are embedded in textual references to culture and Mi'kmaw relationship to the land. The phrase, "all my relations," often acknowledges relationships concepts as cultural, but there are numerous forms of relationships in Mi'kmaw law, the earliest being outlined in various Wabanaki and Mi'kmaw

Creation stories (Augustine 1996: 48-49; Maine Indian Program 1989; MacDougall 2004; Nicolar 1979; Leavitt 1991; Wallis and Wallis 1955; Sable and Francis 2012; Native Council of Nova Scotia 1994; Joe and Choyce 1997; Coates 2000; Whitehead 1988).

This essay is the result of a community presentation in Elsipogtog, New Brunswick—within the traditional district of Sikniktuk (or Siknikt) of the Mi'kmaq nation—of my heritage and relations with my ancestors who negotiated and agreed to the treaties. I will use some examples documented in non-Mi'kmaq literature and caution that much would be lost in their translation without a cultural context.

Mi'kmaq Relations and the Creation Story

As told through the Mi'kmaw Creation story, the most important relations are between the original people, L'nuk, and their environment. L'nuk is an older way of identifying indigenous people, including the Mi'kmaq. Kisulk, the Creator, made the universe (the heavens), the sun (our grandfather), the earth (our mother), human people, animal people, plant people and insect people, along with rock people, mountain people and all the various forms of people, including the Mi'kmaw archetype, Kluskap. All of these elements are permeated with the "Spirit of Creation," all are spirit. Oral traditions and semiotics, symbolism, petroglyphs, pictoglyphs, metaphor, analogy and so on, provide a Mi'kmaw world view centring on reverence of all things as sacred with spirit. The sacred pipe ceremony and the sweat-lodge ceremony replicate, or recreate, these elements. Kluskap changed the environment of Mi'kma'ki, and his marvellous feats were told while Mi'kmaq travelled the land. Everyone knew the stories of Creation; as a result, all knew their relationship with their surroundings, and their responsibilities.

Some notable Mi'kmaw values are esteem for Elders, sharing, cooperation and respect for people and nature (Johnson 1991). These various aspects were derived from the Creation story and are seen as interdependent (Robinson 2005). Familial relations were important. Amkotpigtu, the younger brother, perpetrated violence against family, which was Kluskap's responsibility to protect (Parkhill 1997), and Kluskap eventually killed him in a fight. Kluskap lived with his grandmother (Nukumi) and Marten (Apistane'wj), who changed from boy to youth to a young man according to need (Leland 1968). The Mi'kmaq maintained their knowledge and spiritual belief system when some began converting to Catholicism, creating a unique and blended form of Catholicism. Some believe this blending of tradition was a form of resistance to assimilation (Wilson 1988). Kluskap's grandmother, with her healing powers, became syncretic with St. Anne, the patron saint of the Mi'kmaq (Hornborg 2002).

Cosmology and the Six Worlds

Mi'kmaq view their cosmology as relationships between the six worlds: beneath the Earth, beneath the Water, Earth World, above the Earth, above the Sky, and the Ghost World (Whitehead 1988).

Many examples exist, in the literature of the Mi'kmaw view, of transformation between worlds. Kluskap's family arrive from the Sky World, or the World above the Earth, where the Kulu (the Great Bird) live, and beyond is the World above the Sky, where the Star People live (Whitehead 1988). A pole adjacent to the door of the wikuom was also a guide to the other worlds. A hole of the doorpost was a pathway to the World beneath the Earth and where the *jipajikámaq* (the Horned Serpents) live (Whitehead 1988). People who cross into another world have the ability to change their perspective and adopt another point of view. In such a transformation, a beaver dam becomes a wikuom, and poplar bark becomes meat. There is a spiritual unity across different types of beings, where the individual soul or spirit is the index within a larger, complex cosmology (Hornborg 2006).

There are spiritual laws involved in the interconnectedness of the six worlds and the transformations between worlds. Many have forgotten these spiritual protocols with the hybridity of Mi'kmaw Catholicism. A person can send his spirit to the *buoin* (shaman) to ask for help; a dead spirit could be determined through sleep and dreaming by the buoin, although their spirit could also lead them astray (Wallis and Wallis 1955). Fr. LeClercq, a missionary in the mid-1600s, drawing from his experience with the Mi'kmaq, described the soul as a black image of the individual, with human needs of drinking, eating, hunting and fishing (Wallis and Wallis 1955). The buoin or person with special powers can call upon the spirits for curing (Goldthwaites 1898). The buoin has a special object, which anchors them to this world but helps them to return. A buoin could change their shape into a bird or a turtle, as well as they could fly in the air or travel under the water (Wallis and Wallis 1955). A buoin can visit all worlds except the ghost world, where there is a very limited protocol for coming back. Although stories exist which mention the return from the ghost world, the return is short. In one story, Papkutparut, the guardian of the ghost world, forbids entering there alive, yet is eventually convinced otherwise by a desperately saddened father seeking to see his recently deceased son. His return is short-lived (Whitehead 1988).

Netukulimk/Harvesting

The relationship between Mi'kmaw cosmology and law with gifts or resources of the land and water was practised through a code of conduct overseeing the harvesting of resources while protecting the "integrity, diversity or productivity" of the environment (NCNS 1994: 8). The code of conduct was between people and animals, people and the environment, and among people. As the Mi'kmaq said, "We killed only enough animals and birds to sustain us for one day, and then, the next day, we set out again" (Whitehead 1991: 10).

The Mi'kmaw law on harvesting applied to the annual food cycles of the seasons (NCNS 1994), and involved certain protocols. These protocols were not to be breached for fear of offending the animal spirits, for they might not return (NCNS 1994; Whitehead 1991). Salmon bones were placed back into rivers. Moose bones were placed high into trees so that dogs would not eat them. Moose and marten bones were not to be burned in fire (Wallis and Wallis 1955). An ancestor, Arguimaut, told 18th-century Jesuit missionary Abbé Maillard: "They told us that our domestic animals must never gnaw the bones because this would ... diminish the species of the animal which had fed us" (Whitehead 1991: 17). Offerings and prayers were made prior to harvesting of plants and animals, enacting a reverence for all things of creation imbued with spirit. Animals were to be left alone if not needed (Wallis and Wallis 1955).

Mi'kmaw law emphasized sharing resources and harvest. There was an understanding to take only what was needed, and to leave for others and for rejuvenation and regrowth. "They are in no wise ungrateful to each other, and share everything. No one would dare to refuse the request of another, nor to eat without giving him a part of what he has" (Goldthwaites 1898: 95). District chiefs allocated particular lands for specific families who migrated between harvesting the gifts from the coast and inland waters and hunting lands consistent with the seasons and traditional knowledge. These hunting grounds "are nearly always arranged according to bays and rivers" (89). Provisions for hunting were provided by the chief; chiefs also mediated family and intra-band disputes (Goldthwaites 1898: 95; Nietfeld 1981). Elders settled disputes over hunting grounds (Whitehead 2001). There were protocols for those entering into the hunting or harvesting areas of others, and for those providing for the chief's benevolence: "if there any profits from the chase he has a share of them, without being obliged to take part in it" (Goldthwaites 1898: 75).

Traditional Districts

Mi'kmaw law and the literature say the Mi'kmaq nation was composed of seven districts or tribes headed by a district chief (*sakamowti*) whose settlement served as the district meeting place for the local chiefs (*saqmaq*) (Nietfeld 1981). In general, these territorial districts were related to the ocean and inland that followed drainage systems and principal river systems, forming natural and flexible boundaries (Sable and Francis 2012). These traditional districts include Kespe'k (end of land), Epekwitk aq Piktuk (cradle above water and explosive place), Sikipnékatik (area of wild potato/turnip), Kespukwitk (end of flow), Unama'kik (variation of Mi'kmaw territory), aq Ktaqmkuk (across the waves/water), Siknikt (drainage territory), and Eskikewa'kik (uncertain translation) (Sable and Francis 2012). Keptins were specialized leaders who assisted the chiefs (Nietfeld 1981; Wallis and Wallis 1955). The *Jesuit Relations,* chronicles of Jesuit missions in New France, refers to the captains as "Sagamores" (Goldthwaites 1898) or chiefs. "The chief over a district of settlements was known as *bun*.... A district chief was also the chief of his own settlement" (Wallis and Wallis 1955: 176). The grand chief headed all the district chiefs. There were intermarriages between the districts. Cooperation in warfare was obtained between them. "It is principally in Summer that they pay visits and hold their State Councils; I mean that several Sagamores come together and consult among themselves about peace and war, treaties of friendship and treaties of common good" (Goldthwaites 1898: 91).

The Mi'kmaq were involved with the Wabanaki Confederacy, which utilized its own protocol, and also involved exchanges of wampum that were "read" to disclose meaning and content (Leavitt and Francis 1990). The confederacy consists of the nations of Pannawamskewiak (Penobscot), Peskada mokantiak (Passamaquoddy), Wulastegwiak (Malecite) and Mikemak (Mi'kmaq) (Speck 1915). Wampum documented the peace and outlined details of the organization (Speck 1915). Among non-Wabanaki writers there is some debate about when the confederacy was established; however, its existence has always been part of Mi'kmaw law and is represented by a purple and white wampum belt (Leavitt and Francis 1990). "The Eastern or Coastal Algonquians, including Micmac, Passamaquoddy, Penobscot, and Abenaki, seem to have crystallized family territories in response to the fur trade" (Bobroff 2001). After a peace with the Mohawk (Kwedej), the Mi'kmaq were invited to attend the confederacy at Caugnawaga (Kahnawake) (Speck 1915).

The convention council of the Wabanaki was held every seven years with the Mohawk, Wabanaki, Ottawa and Mi'kmaq (Nicolar 1979). The western Waponahki, or Abenaki, represented the Wabanaki Confederacy in the Great Peace of Montréal, signed in 1701 between New France and many First Nations, including the Iroquois League and the Great Lakes nations (Havard 2001). The continental or extended confederacy was translated into the "Great Council of Fire" (Putuswakn) and involved the Wabanaki tribes and the Haudenosaunee, Lakes Confederacy of Ojibwa and Atikamekw Nehiywaw (Têtes de Bule) (Speck 1998 [1940]).

The Mi'kmaq recited the wampum at their national union on Saint Anne's day at Holy Family Island on Potlotek First Nation (Speck 1915). Among the nations of the confederacy there has been a current interest in renewing the confederacy for many purposes. More recently, during the 1970s, Penobscot, Passamaquoddy and Mi'kmaw traditionalists formed a loose alliance called the Wabanaki Federation (MacDougall 2004).

Historical Impacts

The early fur trade, the Mi'kmaw treaty era (1630-1779) and the Royal Proclamation of 1763 (see below) protected Mi'kmaw territory and government. However, the *British North American Act, 1867*, and the Government of Canada's *Indian Act* impacted upon these Mi'kmaw treaty relationships. Despite these, many Mi'kmaq retain the knowledge and maintain the existence of such nation-to-nation formalities. Under the recognition and affirmation of aboriginal and treaty rights of the Mi'kmaq, in sections 35 and 52(1) of the *Constitution Act, 1982*, Mi'kmaw sovereignty could be claimed under so-called treaty federalism (Simmons 2008). Under this constitutional reform of the colonial order, Mi'kmaw law and relationships exist as part of the supreme law of Canada.

Trade (1600s)

Trading has always been important to the Mi'kmaq nation and the other nations of the Wabanaki Confederation—Mi'kmaq traded with European fishermen as early as 1534 (Bailey 1969). "Sauer believes that the Micmac [who] met Cartier in Chaleur Bay were awaiting a European ship with stocks of furs, and that they had already learned to trap beyond their needs for the European market" (Nietfeld 1981: 286). The fur trade with the Europeans was an earlier impact on the Mi'kmaw relationships with the animals and the land. The commercialization of resources saw substantial changes for the Mi'kmaq involved in the fur trade (Coates 2000). "The importance Amerindians attached to trade concerned the accumulation of goods in order to honor community obligations, based on status and reciprocity" (Dickason 1984: 236). This affected the relationship with the environment, and shifted away from sustainability. Skills tied to harvesting and cultural activities fell into disuse and were lost when pushed aside for furs.

> Mi'kmaw hunters soon were concentrating their attention on animals with commercial potential, trading pelts for cloaks and blankets, for beans, peas, and prunes, and for firearms, not only to hunt game more effectively but to extend their hunting territory at the expense of other native groups. (Faragher 2005: 13)

The sacredness of spirit was pushed aside to profit.

Treaties (1700s)

Although the French wished to enter into treaties, the Mi'kmaq responded that they were not necessary and maintained that they were guests and friends. In 1630, the Mi'kmaq entered into alliances with King Charles of Great Britain and into formal treaties of peace and friendship with the British Crown from 1726 to 1761. The interrelated treaties of peace and friendship ensured trading relations and a shared justice system (Gould and Semple 1980). "What is unique about the Maritimes is that the treaties signed there did not acknowledge the cession or release by the First Nations of any rights, including perhaps Aboriginal title" (Isaac 2001: 27). The Mi'kmaw treaties retained all their ancestral territories except for some small English settlements already made or those lawful to be made in the future (Wicken 2004). The king created truckhouses (authorized trading depots) that regulated trade with the Mi'kmaq, but a royal proclamation later changed the truckhouses to free trade with the Indians, wherein the colonies regulated the traders. Justice Binnie, in writing the majority opinion of the Supreme Court of Canada in *R. v. Marshall* in 1999, said that "the surviving substance of the [1760/61] treat[ies] is ... a treaty right to continue to obtain necessaries through hunting and fishing by trading the products of those traditional activities" (*R. v. Marshall 1999a* 3: para. 56). The Supreme Court reiterated this understanding in a Marshall rehearing, in a decision known as *Marshall No. 2*, when it stated that "[t]he treaty right permits the Mi'kmaq community to work for a living through continuing access to fish and wildlife to trade for 'necessaries'" (*R. v. Marshall* 1999b: para. 4).

Royal Proclamation, 1763

The proclamation reserved all the existing land of the Mi'kmaw not purchased or ceded in the treaties and commanded that the territory of the Indian nations and tribes has to be purchased by the King's representatives at a public meeting called for that purpose (Woodward 2007). The 1761 royal instructions to the Nova Scotia governor affirmed that existing Mi'kmaw treaties were inviolable and that Nova Scotia Lt. Governor Belcher's proclamation of 1762, which partly outlined lands reserved for the Mi'kmaq (Gould and Semple 1980), implemented this. This constitutional reference protected and reserved the Mi'kmaw relationship with their traditional lands (districts). This proclamation set the standard in the imperial constitutional law of Great Britain for purchasing Mi'kmaw territory at a time when the Mi'kmaw were ever willing to sell parts of their land.

Constitution Act, 1867

Section 91(24) of the *British North America Act*, now called the *Constitution Act, 1867*, moved "Indians, and lands reserved for Indians," from provincial powers to newly created federal powers (Woodward 2007). This affected the Mi'kmaw relationship with the provinces, which was already close to non-existent. "Interestingly, there was a short-lived panic among the Mi'kmaq about Confederation, for rumours apparently circulated that the existing treaty rights would be abolished under the new dominion" (Coates 2000: 45). Previous reserve lands for Indians in the Royal Proclamation of 1763 became the responsibility of the federal government. "It was far from clear, however, what the acreage of reserved lands and the status of the claims of Indians and settlers was with respect to such lands" (Bartlett 1986: 32-33). This influenced those colonial funds and gave much reserve land to squatters. "The [land] title of squatters being incomplete and often non-existent at the time of Confederation, made the problem persist to the present day" (Gould and Semple 1980: 70). Another impact was federal and provincial governments' neglect of the Indians' social and economic well-being, marginalizing them from mainstream society. Many oppressive policies originating in the colonial period continued.

Indian Act, 1876

"Indian" as a constitutional category became unilaterally defined in federal legislation, first passed in 1876, in the *Indian Act* (Woodward 2007). "The *Indian Act* was created to consolidate administrative control over aboriginal people, their resources and property" (Podlasly 2003: 196). This affected their inherent right to self-government and instituted elected band councils. The Indian Branch of the Department of the Secretary of State of Canada imposed the band-council system in 1869 (Walls 2010). The federal government sought to replace the traditional government of the Mi'kmaq, the Mi'kmaw Grand Council, by creating elected administrative systems then responsible to the Department of Indian Affairs. "Before 1899 and a federal Order-in-Council which mandated the creation of band councils, the community's governing body had been the Grand Council" (Walls 2010: 51). The federal band system was subjected to policies and regulations derived from the *Indian Act* and were regulated by the white government agents appointed by the minister. From cradle to grave, "Indian" life was the responsibility of the minister of Indian Affairs, "the *Indian Act* grants government officials power to control virtually everything that is done on the reserves" (Cumming and Mickenberg 1972: 236). "Government policy was to move the Mi'kmaq onto reserves and to encourage them to farm so that they would one day assimilate into Anglo-Canadian society" (Wicken 2012: 133). It influenced their identity and replaced it with a legal definition, excluding any cultural, language or familial connections disconnected through marriage.

Constitution Act, 1982

Aboriginal and treaty rights were afforded constitutional protection by the *Constitution Act, 1982* (the 1867 and 1982 *Acts* are collectively known as the Constitution of Canada). This constitutional basket of rights is argued either to be empty, as asserted by the Crown, or to be full, as asserted by the indigenous peoples of Canada. The Crown's approach is to determine those case by case in court, which amounts to challenging the resources available to those asserting their rights. "Some lawyers argue that Canadian case law is incredibly thin and that the courts should be flooded with dozens, if not hundreds, of case[s] that would, over time, flesh out, clarify, and formalize the legal rights of First Nations" (Coates 2000: 92). The Mi'kmaw perspective is that all previous rights were protected by the treaties and by imperial law, and now constitutional law, and that although often threatened and stifled, they remain valid and protected by the supreme law of Canada, the Constitution. "The problem has been that the intergovernmental conferences that were to define 'treaty and aboriginal rights' never did so" (Wicken 2002: 6). Canada's approach to incorporating Indians into the mainstream is low on specifics, especially in the economic sphere. Oppressive policies continue to marginalize indigenous peoples despite international human-rights instruments that Canada has entered into.

Conclusion

The Mi'kmaq continue to assert their treaty rights and preserve their ancestral territory, relying in part on their understandings of Mi'kmaw knowledge and law. These understandings are inherent in their collective stories and memories—despite centuries of European contact and early participation in the colonial economy—which were later excluded and marginalized through *Indian Act* policies and regulations. Mi'kmaq still assert and maintain their treaty relationships, as well as more ancient relationships. "Clearly, it is the need to maintain respectful relationships that guides all interactions and experiences with community, clans, families, individuals, homelands, plants, animals, etc., in the Indigenous cultural ideal" (Alfred and Corntassel 2005: 609). Mi'kmaq will often say *m'set nogemaq*, meaning "all my relations," after participation in ceremonies, such as sweat lodges and talking circles. "All my relations" is an acknowledgement of all the ancestors, their relationships and their hardships. It acknowledges all the spirits who bear witness, and existing in the Creation story and related teachings. It reaffirms the original relationships between the Mi'kmaq and their environment, emanating from their centre outward into Creation. All my relations also respects the relationships between family, community, districts and nations, both indigenous and non-indigenous. These relationships include the relationships and Wabanaki Confederacy obligations. There is much meaning embedded in this simple phrase.

M'set nogemaq – All My Relations.

References

Alfred, T. and J. Corntassel, J. 2005. Being Indigenous: Resurgences Against Contemporary Colonialism. *Government and Opposition* 40 (4): 597-614.

Augustine, Stephen. 1996. English translation of the Mi'kmaq Creation story. *Report of the Royal Commission on Aboriginal Peoples Looking Forward Looking Back. Vol. 1: Looking Forward Looking Back.* Ottawa: Supply and Services Canada.

Bailey, A. G. 1969. *The Conflict of European and Eastern Alqonkian Cultures, 1504-1700: A Study in Canadian Civilization.* Toronto: University of Toronto Press.

Bartlett, R. H. 1986. *Indian Reserves in the Atlantic Provinces.* Saskatoon: University of Saskatchewan.

Bobroff, K. H. 2001. Retelling Allotment: Indian Property Rights and the Myth of Common Ownership. *Vanderbilt Law Review* 54 (4): 1559-1623.

Cameron, A. M. 2009. *Power without Law: The Supreme Court of Canada, the Marshall Decisions, and the Failure of Judicial Activism.* Montréal: McGill-Queens University Press.

Coates, K. 2000. *The Marshall Decision and Native Rights.* Montréal: McGill-Queen's University Press.

Cumming, P. A. and N. H. Mickenberg, eds. 1972. *Native Rights in Canada.* 2nd ed. Toronto: Indian-Eskimo Association of Canada; General Publishing Company.

Dickason, O. P. 1984. *The Myth of the Savage: And the Beginnings of French Colonialism in the Americas.* Edmonton: University of Alberta Press.

Faragher, J. M. 2005. *A Great and Noble Scheme: The Tragic Story of the Expulsion of the French Acadians from Their American Homeland.* New York: W. W. Norton and Company.

Goldthwaites, R. G., ed. 1898. *The Jesuit Relations and Allied Documents, Travel and Explorations of the Jesuit Missionaries in New France, 1610-1791.* Vol. 1-3. Cleveland, OH: The Burrows Brothers.

Gould, G. P. and A. J. Semple. 1980. Our Land: The Maritimes: The Basis of the Indian Claim in the Maritime Provinces of Canada. Fredericton, NB: Saint Annes Point Press.

Havard, G. 2001. *The Great Peace of Montreal of 1701: French-Native Diplomacy in the Seventeenth Century.* Trans. P. Aranoff and H. Scott. Montréal: McGill-Queen's University Press.

Hornborg, A.-C. 2002. St. Anne's Day: A Time to "Turn Home" for the Canadian Míkmaq Indians. *International Review of Mission* 91 (361): 237-55.

———. 2006. Visiting the Six Worlds: Shamanistic Journeys in Canadian Míkmaq Cosmology. *Journal of American Folklore* 119 (473): 312-36.

Isaac, T. F. 2001. *Aboriginal and Treaty Rights in the Maritimes.* Saskatoon, SK: Purich Publishing Ltd.

Joe, Rita and Lesley Choyce. 1997. *The Míkmaq Anthology.* Lawrencetown, NS: Pottersfield Press.

Johnson, E. 1991. Míkmaq Tribal Consciousness in the 20th Century. In *Paqtatek*, ed. S. Inglis, J. Mannette and S. Sulewski, 23-30. Halifax, NS: Garamond Press.

Leavitt, R. M. 1991. *Maliseet and Micmac: First Nations of the Maritimes.* Fredericton, NB: Micmac-Maliseet Institute, University of New Brunswick.

Leavitt, R. M. and D. A. Francis, ed. 1990. *Wapapi Akonutomakol, The Wampum Records: Wabanaki Traditional Laws*. Fredericton: Micmac-Maliseet Institute, University of New Brunswick.

Leland, C. G. 1968. *The Algonquin Legends of New England or Myths and Folk Lore of the Micmac, Passamaquoddy, and Penobscot tribes*. Boston: Houghton, Mifflin and Company.

MacDougall, P. 2004. *The Penobscot Dance of Resistance: Tradition in the History of a People*. Durham: University of New Hampshire.

Maine Indian Program. 1989. *The Wabanakis of Maine and the Maritimes: A Resource Book about Penobscot, Passamaquoddy, Maliseet, Micmac and Abenaki Indians*. Bath, ME: New England Office of the American Friends Service Committee.

NCNS (Native Council of Nova Scotia). 1994. *Míkmaq Fisheries, Netukulimk: Towards a Better Understanding*. Truro: Native Council of Nova Scotia Language Program.

Nicolar, J. 1979. *The Life and Times of the Red Man*. Fredericton, NB: Saint Annes Point Press.

Nietfeld, P. K. 1981. *Determinants of Aboriginal Micmac Political Structure*. PhD dissertation, University of New Mexico. University Microfilms International.

Parkhill, T. 1997. *Weaving Ourselves into the Land: Charles Godfrey Leland, Indians, and the Study of Native American Religions*. Albany: State University of New York Press.

Podlasly, M. 2003. Canada's Domestic Expatriates: The Urban Aboriginal Population. In *Searching for the New Liberalism: Perspectives, Policies, Prospects*, ed. H. Aster and T. Axworthy, 192-209. Oakville, ON: Mosaic Press.

R. v. Marshall. 1999a. 3 S.C.R. 456.

R. v. Marshall. 1999b. 3 S.C.R. 533.

Robinson, A. 2005. *Tán teli-ktlamsitasit (Ways of Believing): Míkmaw Religion in Eskasoni, Nova Scotia*. Toronto: Pearson Education.

Sable, Trudy and Bernie Francis. 2012. *The Language of This Land: Míkmáki*. Sydney, NS: Cape Breton University Press.

Simmons, J. 2008. *Treaty Federalism: The Canadian Experience*. Paper prepared for the international colloquium "Competitive Federalism–International Perspectives," organized by the Liberal Institute, Friedrich Naumann Foundation, Potsdam, Germany, July 3, 2008, 5-23.

Speck, F. G. 1915. The Eastern Algonkian Wabanaki Confederacy. *American Anthropologist* 17 (3), 492-508.

———. 1998 [1940]. *Penobscot Man*. Orono, ME: University of Maine Press.

Wallis, W. D. and R. S. Wallis. 1955. *The Micmac Indian of Eastern Canada.* Minneapolis: University of Minnesota Press.

Walls, M. E. 2010. *No Need of a Chief for This Band: The Maritime Mi'kmaq and Federal Electoral Legislation, 1899-1951.* Vancouver: University of British Columbia Press.

Whitehead, R. H. 1988. *Stories from the Six Worlds: Micmac Legends.* Halifax, NS: Nimbus Publishing.

———. 1991. *The Old Man Told Us: Excerpts from Micmac History 1500-1950.* Halifax, NS: Nimbus Publishing.

Wicken, W. C. 2004. *Mi'kmaq Treaties on Trial: History, Land, and Donald Marshall Junior.* Toronto: University of Toronto Press.

Wicken, W. C. 2012. *The Colonization of Mi'kmaw Memory and History, 1794-1928: The King v. Gabriel Sylliboy.* Toronto: University of Toronto Press.

Wilson, B. G. 1988. *Colonial Identities: Canada from 1760 to 1815.* Ottawa: Supply and Services Canada.

Woodward, J. 2007. *Consolidated Native Law Statues, Regulations and Treaties.* Toronto: Thomson Carswell.

Jaime Battiste

Treaty Denied:
The 1928 Trial of Grand Chief Gabriel Sylliboy

Tan wetapeksi
In Mi'kmaw, there is a term, *wetapeksin*, that does not have a precise definition or translation readily available in English. Attempts at translating this phrase would be a combination of answering the questions: Where you are from? and How you were raised? The question *tami wetapeksin*? is often asked by Elders or community members of those they have just met in the hopes of finding out what family they are from, which community they belong to, and whether or how they might be related. As a starting point of many interactions among Mi'kmaq, we attempt to understand our relationship with each other, just as it is important, when discussing knowledge, that we understand where that knowledge is grounded and how that knowledge has come to be collected. In writing this chapter, about Grand Chief Gabriel Sylliboy and his struggle for treaty recognition within *R. v. Sylliboy* [sic] (1928), I begin my narrative by situating who I am and how I have come to know what I have been given. My story, or my roots, then, is my introduction to understanding *tan wetapeksi*.

I was born long after the death of Gabriel Sylliboy, who was the grand chief of the Mi'kmaw Sante' Mawio'mi, the Mi'kmaw Grand Council, from 1918 to his death in 1964. I was born in Eskasoni, Nova

Scotia, to Marie Battiste and James Youngblood Henderson, during the era of Kji-keptin (Grand Captain) Alex Denny, who was our neighbour and friend, and who brought my parents to Eskasoni to work in the schools and in the Union of Nova Scotia Indians. I was born in the UNESCO-proclaimed International Year of the Child, 1979, gifted with the Mi'kmaw language, and raised in a proud and happy community, with relations and traditions ever unfolding. Yet, the impact of Sylliboy's teachings, and of Denny's, passed down through his family, have had a profound impact in how I came to understand what it means to be Mi'kmaq and the responsibilities that come with being a Mi'kmaw person.

The Mi'kmaw Grand Council was introduced to me at a very early age. Grand Council Kji-keptin Denny was our frequent house visitor; he was up early every morning having tea at various houses in the neighbourhood, then off to town, then back again to take his kids to school or to their sports, then back to town to work. Growing up next door, he had the greatest impact on me and, as fate would have it, I would continue the work my father did with Denny—taking the same position with Denny's son, Anlte, who became a Kji-keptin of the Mi'kmaw Grand Council when Denny passed away in 2004.

The Mi'kmaw Grand Council is made up of leaders within our communities, men who having gained respect and are recognized and thus chosen to be a captain. According to an article written by Denny, "The Mi'kmaq—The Covenant Chain" (Senier 2015: 32), the executive or leadership is made up of three positions—the kji-saqmaw (grand chief) is the ceremonial head of state; kji-keptins make up the executive of the council; and the putu's (wisdom) is the knowledge-keeper of the constitution and the treaties.

How I came to live in a neighbourhood right next door to Kji-keptin Denny and among the grandchildren of Kji-saqmaw Sylliboy is a story outside our scope here but, to summarize, in the late 1970s Denny was able to convince my parents to come to Eskasoni and help him with two of his greatest passions as kji-keptin and as president of the Union of Nova Scotia Indians: restoring and preserving the Mi'kmaw language and achieving recognition of the Mi'kmaw treaties.

My mother, a Mi'kmaq from Potlotek First Nation in Nova Scotia, had a PhD from Stanford University, where she focused on bilingual/

bicultural education, and was passionate about building programming and curricula in language education. Through Denny and the band council of Potlotek, she was hired as principal and educational director of the Mi'kmawey School in Potlotek, and later as curriculum coordinator at the Eskasoni School Board. My father, a Chickasaw from Oklahoma, had graduated with a Juris Doctorate from Harvard Law School. He too was passionate about social justice and indigenous rights. My parents believed in and were inspired and motivated by the vision of Denny, who built a house for us next door to his, on his land in the Apamuek neighbourhood of Eskasoni.

Apamuek was home also to many families closely related to Denny's wife, Janette, who was the daughter of the late Catherine (Tiannie) Paul and the daughter of Gabriel Sylliboy. Janette would become my godmother, an honoured role for Mi'kmaw people, tying our family relations even closer. This extended family would teach me, among many other values, the importance of speaking Mi'kmaw, furthering my education and having respect for the grand council as the traditional governing structure for the Mi'kmaq. Those core values and teachings helped me in developing a strong foundation for my education and passion for learning about our history and about our grand council.

As part of the continued struggle for recognition in the late 1970s, my father, Sa'ke'j (a name given to him by my grandmother Annie Battiste) Henderson, began working with the Mi'kmaw Grand Council as their research adviser. Among his many projects, he immediately began research on the covenant chain of Mi'kmaw treaties with English and British monarchs signed between 1629 and 1786. I can remember, from a very early age, sitting around the table with tea and food, listening to conversations between my father, Denny and other Mi'kmaq who would later become known as early pioneers of Mi'kmaw rights. People like Joe B. Marshall, Albert Marshall, Murdena Marshall, Patrick Johnson and Will Basque, to name a few, were frequent visitors and spent many long hours together discussing current and past events, strategies and people in the movement for change. I can also remember from a very early age hearing Kji-keptin Denny giving his yearly address to the Mi'kmaq at Chapel Island (Potlotek) during the feast of St. Anne. This feast of St. Anne has been the meeting place for the Mi'kmaw Grand Council for more than 250 years, dating at least to an 18th-century treaty-making period between the Mi'kmaq and the British Crown.

During his yearly addresses, as time would show, the kji-keptin—along with then Grand Chief Donald Marshall—would address the important issues of the day; but Denny would always talk about the importance of families teaching their children the Mi'kmaw language, and of the research, politics and advocacy work he had been doing in treaty recognition. After the speeches during the mission, it was common to be asked personally by Elders what I thought was the message that the kji-keptin gave. Probably this was to ensure that I was listening, though partly I believe this was to ensure the growth of my Mi'kmaw fluency. I would not have thought that it too would groom me for the role I would come to have as an adviser, like my father, to the grand council, which I hold today.

Growing up, I started going to schools on the reserves, first at Mi'kmawey School in Potlotek, which was grounded in Mi'kmaw curriculum and focused on our history and our language. I was taught by Elizabeth Paul and Murdena Marshall in a little school, behind my grandparent's house. In particular, I learned how to read using the Smith-Francis orthography, the official system of writing Mi'kmaw, which helped me to read and write. I did not realize until much later that my generation would be the first to learn about the Mi'kmaq as part of their formal schooling. Introduced by my mother, it was not until the early 1980s that the ability to learn about Mi'kmaw culture and language was created and used in on-reserve school systems. Thus, my beginnings were forged with a strong Mi'kmaw foundation and knowledge gained through hearing about our treaties first-hand from Elders, through conversation and as taught in schools in Chapel Island and Eskasoni.

My generation was the first to take part in Mi'kmaw Treaty Day activities in Halifax, a day of observance proclaimed by our leaders in 1986. On this day (October 1), the Province of Nova Scotia ceremoniously accepts its obligation to honour our treaties. These Treaty Day celebrations recognize and validate our treaties as affirmed by the Supreme Court of Canada in *Simon v. The Queen* (1985). Mi'kmaq celebrate it in their home communities as well, in solidarity with those in Halifax, as stipulated in terms of the original 1752 treaty, which called for annual reaffirmation and exchange of gifts.

Later, as a student within Mi'kmaw studies courses at Cape Breton University, I first learned about Grand Chief Gabriel Sylliboy and his 1928 conviction for trapping during closed season. I heard in more detail of the one-sided justice system that, in 1928, stated that Mi'kmaw treaties were not valid and that our traditional Mi'kmaw Grand Council lacked competence to bind Canada to these treaties. Despite this case, I recall how *Simon* in 1985 overturned the much earlier Sylliboy case and vindicated many leaders like Kji-keptin Denny, who could recall being told in the early 1960s that the Mi'kmaw treaties with the Crown were not worth the paper they were written on.

When I finished Mi'kmaw studies, I realized that my interests continued to follow these cases, and I completed a law degree at Dalhousie University. While attending Dalhousie, I studied Sylliboy's struggle for justice in 1928 in greater detail, and the subsequent recognition of Mi'kmaw rights in cases such as *R. v. Simon* (1985) and *R. v. Marshall* (1999).

In 2005 I was hired to teach Mi'kmaw studies at Cape Breton University. I remember looking through the case of Grand Chief Sylliboy and being fascinated by this Elder who could barely speak English, but who still asserted to the courts that he had rights as a Mi'kmaq—rights he received from the Crown that allowed him to hunt and fish as the Mi'kmaq had always done. These rights, he asserted, were not limited to hunting and trapping seasons created by Nova Scotia statutes over the intervening years.

Mi'kmaw laws and treaties resounded in the oral traditions, but were silent in the written tradition until, in 2012, historian William Wicken—a key witness for the Mi'kmaq in Supreme Court victories in *Simon, Marshall* and, in 2006, in *R. v. Sappier; R. v. Gray*—published a book titled, *The Colonization of Mi'kmaw Memory and History, 1794-1928*. This book explored in depth the knowledge that I had researched as a student, as a professor and as legal adviser for the Mi'kmaw Grand Council. I share here what I have come to learn about the grand council and Grand Chief Gabriel Sylliboy, and what he meant to his family and to the Mi'kmaw nation.

Sante' Mawio'mi

Since the arrival of Europeans, Mi'kmaq have been guided and governed by the Sante' Mawio'mi, known in English as the Mi'kmaw Grand Council. The Mi'kmaw nation has always had our own self-governing structures, embedded in customs, traditions, teachings and protocols. "Law" is a Western term, but within the Mi'kmaq traditions is the word *teplutaqn*, which means "binds together the core teachings."

While the precise date of origin for the Mi'kmaw Grand Council is unknown, Denny wrote in "Covenant Chain" that:

> six hundred years ago, the Mi'kmaq people were invaded from the west by the Haudenosaunee (the Iroquois). After a number of fierce battles, the invaders were beaten back, and a treaty of peace was concluded. With peace restored, the nation reorganized itself: all of Mikma'kik, our traditional lands, was divided into seven sakamowti [districts or tribes]. (Senier 2014: 38)

Together, the seven districts of Mi'kma'ki include the eastern seaboard of Canada from the Gaspé Peninsula in Quebec, down through New Brunswick, Prince Edward Island, Nova Scotia, parts of Maine, and over to southern Newfoundland as well. The traditional role of the Mi'kmaw Grand Council was to advise the people and defend the nation. An ancient symbol of this union can still be seen today carved into the rocks around Kejimukujik Lake, in Nova Scotia, where there is a carving of a ring of seven hills representing the seven districts, seven crosses representing the seven chiefs or leaders, which surround the sun and the moon, which represents the Creator. (See note p. 137).

While the pre-contact Mi'kmaw way of life has been described by anthropologists as that of a migratory people, Mi'kmaq have always lived in their territory, where they buried their relatives, carried out their ceremonies, and moving therein with the seasons to where food was abundant. With their sturdy canoes, the ocean, rivers and lakes of Eastern Canada were the main pathways for transportation. Among many Mi'kmaw laws, the Mi'kmaq are guided primarily by the laws of *netukulimk*, a term that, among other teachings, captures our birth rights (sustainability), what we are taught as Mi'kmaq, and our responsibilities as Mi'kmaq. Mi'kmaw governance has always been and still is spiritual, persuasive and non-coercive. The continuity and authority of this system of governance come from a common bond and common responsibilities. These responsibilities are to family, to community, to nation and to ecosystem.

Mi'kmaw Elders and our oral history has taught us that Mi'kmaq have always preserved a delicate ecological balance and travelled where the resources were most abundant, guided by principles of preserving resources for future generations. As Denny wrote in the "Covenant Chain,"

> [the] Mi'kmaq economy was based upon hunting, fishing, gathering, and farming, as well as trading surplus resources with other nations. This economic regime was founded upon the overriding principle of sustainable, responsible development to ensure long-term self-reliance and prosperity for our people. (Senier 2015: 32-33)

According to Sa'ke'j Henderson, the grand council recognizes keptins to show the people the good path, to help them with gifts of knowledge and goods, and to sit with the whole Sante' Mawio'mi as the government of all the Mi'kmaq. Keptin Noel Marshall, a respected Elder and council member from Potlotek, once said the role of the council was to "keep the faith and protect the nation." (Personal communication with Henderson)

Spirituality and faith have been important aspects of Mi'kmaw governance and continue to be to this day. This dedication balances traditional Mi'kmaw customs, as well as honouring the Mi'kmaq concordat, agreed between Grand Chief Membertou, on behalf of the Mi'kmaq, and the Holy See, in 1610. Grand Chief Membertou consecrated that relationship with his baptism and accepted Christianity as part of the agreement with the papal court. Mi'kmaw governance and the grand council continue to honour Membertou's legacy by, among other things, keeping sacred two holy days of the Mi'kmaq, Pentecost Sunday and the feast of St. Anne's, as the two dates when the grand council gathers to meet and discuss issues of importance to the Mi'kmaq.

The journals of 17th-century French lawyer Marc Lescarbot (Henderson 1997: 97), who travelled to Acadia (ca. 1606) in the era of Grand Chief Membertou, note the courage and generosity of the Mi'kmaq. He found much to praise, saying that the Mi'kmaq were "truly noble" and, probably in comparing French and Mi'kmaq leaders, wrote that the Mi'kmaw chiefs exercised restrained authority, were kind to their people and lacked "ambition, vain, glory, envy and avarice" (ibid.). The Mi'kmaw Grand Council, with its humble but persuasive governance style, practised diplomacy throughout early contact with European settlers. This diplomacy resulted in mutual understandings with the French and later negotiations with the British Crown for peace, friendship and trade. Assisted often by the Catholic priests or missionaries who helped with translation of the English language, the Mi'kmaw chiefs, delegated by the grand council, were the original signatories to the covenant chain of treaties, signed with the British Crown, between 1725 and 1786. Denny, in "the Covenant Chain," said of these peace and friendship treaties:

> The Mi'kmaq agreed not to "molest" any existing British settlements but did not consent to any new ones.... In the Mi'kmaq view, the Mi'kmaq Compact, 1752, affirmed Mikma'kik [sic] and Britain as two states sharing one crown—the Crown pledging to preserve and defend Mi'kmaq rights against settlers as much as against foreign nations. (Senier 2014: 37)

Despite the covenant chain of treaties, in which the British consistently agreed to protect Mi'kmaw rights and to treat them fairly, the years following the signing of the treaties saw the British ignoring and continuously violating the treaties, to the advantage of colonial governors and settlers. After the American Revolution, in 1776, thousands of those subjects who remained loyal to the British Crown fled the United States to come to, among other places, Mi'kma'ki, in violation of the treaties and imperial law, unlawfully occupying Mi'kmaw lands and consuming its resources. Colonial authorities made minimal attempts to ameliorate the Mi'kmaq, despite the requirements of the treaties, and despite the many requests Mi'kmaq made in correspondences to governors and monarch. Instead, governors issued "tickets of location" to the settlers, which they interpreted as forms of title to land holdings, presumably free land as a gift of the governors for their loyalty to the monarchy, which led to diminished lands and resources for the Mi'kmaq, and to even greater hardship.

With the Mi'kmaw lands and resources continually being absorbed illegally by settlers and colonizers, the Mi'kmaw way of life and sustainability of their communities, based on hunting, fishing and gathering, eroded; settlers fenced in properties and gardens, reducing indigenous mobility, and the mobility of the game they hunted. The food source became scarce and Mi'kmaq had to find new ways to live. The Mi'kmaw Grand Council petitioned many complaints with the British Crown in the 1800s regarding the lawlessness of the settlers and the violations of the treaties. According to Denny, in 1841 Kjisakamow Peminawit submitted a petition to the colonial office in London; as a result, British North America colonial officials were reminded that the Mi'kmaq had "an undeniable claim to the Protection of the Government" and that the Mi'kmaq should be compensated for any losses (Richardson 1979: 40). The colonial government of Nova Scotia responded (in 1842) by agreeing to set aside 50,000 hectares (125,000 acres) of land as "Indian Reservations" for Mi'kmaw use, a fraction of their total land base (Richardson 1979: 41).

The Mi'kmaw Grand Council continued to appeal to the Crown to honour the treaties as signed; often, if not consistently, however, their complaints and appeals were ignored. Though the treaties specifically stated that Mi'kmaq can seek redress of treaty violations in the courts—which they have done, repeatedly—the justice system was prejudiced in the favour of the colonial settlers. Denny wrote about how, in 1849, a recently created Indian commissioner for Nova Scotia asserted, in a report to the legislature, that the justice system and the political process in the colony could not be counted on to "protect" Indian interests and rights:

> Under present circumstances, no adequate protection can be obtained for Indian property. It would be vain to seek a verdict from any jury in [Nova Scotia] against the trespassers on the reserves; nor perhaps would a member of the Bar be found willingly and effectually to advocate the cause of the Indians, inasmuch as he would thereby injure his own prospect, by damaging his popularity. (Richardson 1979: 50)

Knowledge of this unjustness in 1849, and beyond, did not deter the racist attitudes of settlers or governmental institutions, however, as treaty integrity continued to be undermined, and the Mi'kmaq continued to suffer hardship and poverty as a result. Generations of Mi'kmaq began to see their way of life change, worsening, while they continued to seek justice from settler governments and the Crown. Wicken (2012: 129) writes:

By the 1850s the Mi'kmaq had come to consider the [treaties] as the basis of relationship that would steer the community's relationship with outside forces. It was both a protective barrier and a political tool."

Wicken points out that by the time Sylliboy became grand chief in 1918, the struggle for justice had gone from the Mi'kmaq seeking to protect their fishing and hunting grounds, for example, to them merely looking to protect their now limited access to such, and to hunt and fish without harassment.

The Grand Chief Gabriel Sylliboy Case

Within two hundred years of the first in the covenant chain of treaties, the Mi'kmaw Grand Council saw their authority greatly diminished, from an independent sovereign nation to having to rely on the mercy of the courts to uphold their rights. The Mi'kmaq were forced to rely on a colonial justice system that had never been sympathetic to their rights to hunt and fish according to Mi'kmaw laws, as they had done for centuries. On November 4, 1927, Grand Chief Gabriel Sylliboy was charged by Nova Scotia officials with trapping muskrat during closed season in West Bay, Nova Scotia (Wicken 2012: 30). Sylliboy elected to contest the charges in a Sydney, Nova Scotia, court. His defence argued that, according to the terms of the 1752 treaty, he had a treaty right to hunt and fish at all times; that since the 1726 treaty with the Crown, the Crown had agreed to protect the hunting, planting and fishing grounds of the Mi'kmaq. The exact reasons Sylliboy chose to fight the charges are not known. Maybe it was because the treaties stipulated that any disputes between the Mi'kmaq and His Majesty's subjects were to be settled in court; maybe it was the frustrations of seeing Mi'kmaw resources continually being taken by others. What we do know is that in 1927, after being charged with unlawful hunting, Grand Chief Sylliboy asserted that he had treaty rights recognized by the Crown, confirmed by treaty, which were superior to provincial statutes. His assertion was based on Mi'kmaw oral traditions and knowledge embedded deeply in his Mi'kmaw language.

Sylliboy was born in 1875; his father was John Sylliboy and his mother was Mary Basque. Sylliboy was originally from We'koqma'q First Nation (Whycocomagh), on Bras d'Or Lake in Cape Breton, Nova

Scotia. A day school had been set up in the Whycocomagh area, but no record is available that shows that Sylliboy ever attended. In interviews with his remaining family members (his granddaughters Murdena Marshall and Dianne Denny), they recalled Sylliboy stating that he never went to school, was largely illiterate in English, rarely conversed in English, and was passionate that the Mi'kmaq should speak primarily in Mi'kmaw.

The area of Nova Scotia known as Unama'ki (Cape Breton), and especially Holy Family Island at Potlotek, also along Bras d'Or Lake, and less than 100 kilometers from We'koqma'q, has been an area of prominence for the Mi'kmaw Grand Council for more than 250 years. In 1850, Holy Family Island was assigned the capital seat of Mi'kma'ki, moving from Malagawatj (Malagawatch); twice a year, the grand council host a gathering of Mi'kmaw and confer on a wide range of issues. It is not surprising, then, that Sylliboy would have knowledge of the treaties, recited by the putu's of the grand council every year. He would come to testify later, "Since I was a boy, I heard that Indians got from the King free hunting and fishing at all times"(Wicken 2012: 16).

In 1918, through a vote among the keptins of the grand council present during the annual gathering in Holy Family Island, during the feast of St. Anne, Gabriel Sylliboy became the kji-saqmaw (Grand Chief) of the Mi'kmaw nation, recognition of the great respect that Mi'kmaq held for him. Family members and Elders recall that when the grand chief arrived for the feast by boat, all other boats stopped until he and his family were helped to his camp. A tall, thin, elegant

Gabriel Sylliboy (right) was charged in 1926 with having fur pelts in his possession.

Grand Chief Gabriel Sylliboy (right). The other man is unidentified. Clipping (n.d.) courtesy Jaime Battiste. Source unknown.

man, always in a suit, he gave his annual address in Mi'kmaw at St. Anne's Mission to the hundreds of Mi'kmaq gathered. It was said that when he spoke, everyone was so silent that they could hear his voice move the leaves on the trees.

Many Mi'kmaq have deep, fond memories of a very kind, loving, humorous and generous family man as well. The Elders respect for him is unmatched by another person. In the community he lived, and beyond, Mi'kmaq travelled to see him and to seek his advice on many matters. He also travelled to many communities to consult on issues. He was welcomed with tea and whatever food they had. When a couple were to be wed, they would go to him, asking for his blessing beforehand.

The teachings of Grand Chief Sylliboy were numerous, but were largely in terms of identity and relations, including being proud of the ancestral language, respect for Elders, and the importance of family. However, his greatest teaching may have been defence of Mi'kmaq treaty rights, as he did in his own case in 1928. That Sylliboy could barely speak English and yet was still committed to taking a stand for the Mi'kmaq in face of the biased and prejudiced justice system of his era was indeed significant.

Experiences of the Mi'kmaq with the early-20th-century justice system showed precedents and policies that saw the Mi'kmaq as more of a nuisance than an equal partner and contributing members of society. Sylliboy would have been fully aware, for instance, of the forced relocation of the Mi'kmaq of the Kings Road Reserve, in 1915. Mi'kmaq who lived along a shoreline near downtown Sydney were moved more than a mile away from the ocean waters they depended on for travel and sustenance. In deciding to relocate the King's Road Reserve, the local court judge in Sydney, Justice Audette, stated:

> [N]o one cares to live in the immediate vicinity of the Indians. The overwhelming weight of the evidence is to the effect that the Reserve retards and is a clog in the development of that part of the city. (*Re Indian Reserve* 1916)

Despite the apparent prejudicial nature of the court system in 1927-1928, Sylliboy was determined to fight. At trial, he admitted to being in possession of muskrat pelts out of the provincial hunting season and asserted his treaty rights as a Mi'kmaq to possess the pelts, and to hunt. He turned to the courts as required by the terms of the treaty of 1752, which state that any disputes between Mi'kmaq and His Majesty's subjects would be settled within the Crown's courts with the same benefits and advantages as Crown subjects. Despite these terms, Sylliboy faced an uphill battle in court by not being legally educated or fluent in English. While Nova Scotia had access to unlimited funding to prosecute Sylliboy, the court had to appoint a lawyer to represent the indigent Grand Chief.

Surviving family members of the Sylliboy noted that the muskrat pelts in his possession were actually said to be caught by Noel Jeddore, a Mi'kmaq from Newfoundland, and friend to Sylliboy. At the time of the charges, in 1927, Newfoundland was not part of Canada, and Sylliboy feared that his friend and fellow Mi'kmaq, and his family, may be deported to Newfoundland had he not taken responsibility for possession of the pelts. This also highlights the humanity of Sylliboy, who felt it was important to help out a friend at the cost of being charged, face penalty or go to court himself, which would have been an increased hardship on any Mi'kmaw family of that era.

The idea that Mi'kmaq had different rights and legal status was known to many non-Mi'kmaq during the era of Grand Chief Sylliboy. In 1927, Wicken writes, "rural residents of early twentieth century Cape Breton, would have known that one critical difference was that the Mi'kmaq neither paid taxes, nor voted" (2012: 51). Testimony from the Crown's witness also indicates that during the hearing of the case, he pointed out that Indians "claimed the right to hunt and fish under a treaty" (ibid.).

Under the 1752 treaty, article 4 states, "it is agreed that the said Tribe of Indians Shall not be hindered from but have free liberty to hunt and fish as usual" (Article 4 1752 Treaty of Peace and Friendship; *R. v. Syliboy* 1929: 431). Despite the terms of the treaty and the allowed testimonies, the judge in *R. v. Syliboy* (1929), George Patterson, decided that the treaty was not a valid treaty, rather "it is at best a mere agreement made by the Governor and council with a handful of Indians." While Judge Patterson noted the many imperial treaties with the Mi'kmaq, he thought that they did not connect to Sylliboy, by descent or otherwise. Patterson's reasoning included that Indians were savages:

[T]he Indians were never regarded as an independent power.

A civilized nation first discovering a country of uncivilized people or savages held such country as its own until such time as by treaty it was transferred to some other civilized nation. The savages' rights of sovereignty even of ownership were never recognized.... In my judgment the Treaty of 1752 is not a treaty at all and is not to be treated as such. (*R. v. Syliboy* 1929: 436)

How the Mi'kmaq were considered savages is a mystery; they had been Catholics for many generations and had been recognized by monarchs in many treaties (Paul 2006).

Mi'kmaq leaders and law graduates have since analyzed Judge Patterson's reasoning in the Sylliboy case. When I was at university, the case troubled me. Patterson seemed to commend the Nova Scotia prosecution efforts, stating, as I remember it, that the "brief is a joy to read so complete and compact it is." At the same time, Patterson chastised Sylliboy's defence when he described: "Council for the Defendant, whose closely reasoned brief I cannot too highly recommend." Too many Mi'kmaq are left to wonder how much of a defence the appointed council raised. Were there higher powers that wanted to see the grand chief convicted of these charges? In his concluding comments, Judge Paterson conceded that the "defendant honestly believed that the treaty was valid and that he was entitled under it to kill muskrat or have their pelts in his possession at any time." Further, his sympathy for Sylliboy is evident in his closing comments, in which he recommended "waiving of both penalty and costs" despite finding Sylliboy guilty of the charge of hunting out of season.

One can only wonder what it meant to the Mi'kmaq and especially to Gabriel Sylliboy to have his lifelong beliefs and teachings dismissed by the courts. Mi'kmaw Grand Council members like Keptin L. (Mikelo) Denny have often pondered what life may have been like for the Mi'kmaq had the court recognized the treaties in that case. Would the destructive policies that followed still have diminished our livelihood, culture and language, and our ability to sustain ourselves? Would destructive policies and cultural genocide within such as the Indian residential schools—that took Mi'kmaw children away from their families partly because of "unfit conditions" and extreme poverty—still have happened? Would the attempted centralization of Mi'kmaq to two small reserves in Eskasoni and Shubenacadie, still have been put in place, further displacing Mi'kmaq from their lands and resources, forcing many, including Sylliboy, to move from their original homes? Would the Mi'kmaq have utilized their hunting, fishing and gathering rights and created sustainable economies instead of becoming reliant and dependant on government funding and welfare ("fools' gold," as Alex Denny called it)? All these "what-ifs" continue to weigh on the minds of many Mi'kmaq who would not see vindication of their rights until decades later. As Mi'kmaq, we can only look to that case as a significant blow to the our forefathers' way of life, after which we would see federal Department of Indian Affairs policies that prevented Mi'kmaq and other First Nations from hiring attorneys to present treaty rights in court, ensuring that the path for justice for Mi'kmaq would not come until years later, when visionaries like Alex Denny began the treaty imperative, collaborating with informed and allied researchers, lawyers and other leaders in an effort to pursue our treaty rights again.

Vindication and Restoration of Treaty Rights

Despite the court's refusal to recognize the Mi'kmaw treaties, Sylliboy did not refrain from believing in those treaties or in his advocacy on behalf of the Mi'kmaq. In fact, in 1937, the director of Indian Affairs awarded the King George VI Coronation Medal to the grand chief for his struggles and commitment to the Mi'kmaw nation. In 1941, he protested compulsory military service for Mi'kmaq. Sylliboy continued to represent the Mi'kmaq honourably and proudly as Grand Chief, despite the denial of treaty rights by the courts and the *Indian Act*, against hiring attorneys to advance treaty rights or land claims. The Mi'kmaw Grand Council continued to represent the interests of the Mi'kmaq and discuss issues of importance at their biannual meetings (Pentecost Sunday and the Feast of Saint Anne) and through spiritual ceremonies and events such as funerals and special masses. The era following the Gabriel Sylliboy case would consist of ongoing treaty denial and attempts of the government to assimilate the Mi'kmaq.

In 1960, eleven new band councils were created to replace the one undivided band in Nova Scotia that the Mi'kmaw Grand Council had preserved and protected. These bands introduced *Indian Act* elections to our communities and, basically, to act as administrative arms of the Department of Indian Affairs. The result was poverty and, ultimately, total dependence on alien (British) values and institutions. Such impoverishment was not consistent with the treaties of peace and friendship signed with the Mi'kmaq.

In 1969, the Union of Nova Scotia Indians was established in opposition to the federal white-paper policy of that year, which proposed to eliminate the distinct status of Indians in Canada. The union began to restore the solidarity of Mi'kmaq within Nova Scotia, and included the grand council in its advocacy. They worked together and, in 1977, made formal application for land title in the Nova Scotia Micmac Aboriginal-title position paper. While no record ever showed that the Mi'kmaq surrendered their resources or land, the government claimed Mi'kmaw rights were "superseded by law." Increased efforts at advocacy and treaty research led by provincial organizations across Canada, such as the union, were able to secure in the *Constitution Act, 1982*, recognition of the "existing" aboriginal and treaty rights and assert our human rights, too, at the United Nations (see chapter 8).

In 1985, vindication of Sylliboy and the Mi'kmaq came in the form of a Supreme Court of Canada decision (*Simon*) stating that the treaty of 1752 was indeed valid. Justice Dickson, for the court, declared that the language used and the reasoning in the 1928 Sylliboy case "reflects the biases and prejudices of another era" in Canadian history, and its reason was not persuasive. The court overturned the

MicMac News, 1985, vol. 15 (12): 5. http://beaton.cbu.ca/atom/newspapers/micmacnews/MicmacNews-1985-12.pdf

Patterson decision, and held that the treaty of 1752 was valid law. A year later, in 1986, Grand Chief Donald Marshall would declare the inaugural Treaty Day, to be celebrated from that day forward in accordance with the Mi'kmaw promises in the treaty of 1752. Fittingly, in the tradition of the grand council, it would be the son of Grand Chief Donald Marshall, Donald Marshall Jr., whose case in 1999 helped the Mi'kmaq win a great victory at the Supreme Court of Canada—the Mi'kmaq succeeded in asserting that their 1760-1761 treaty with the Crown provided a right to a livelihood through a commercial fishery.

After years, decades and centuries of petitions, complaints, court cases and activism in which Mi'kmaq demanded that imperial, colonial, provincial and federal government address violations of the treaties, finally today's Mi'kmaw leadership, including the grand council, are part of a process of negotiations with the primary mandate of seeing the reconciliation and implementation of our treaties. Yet, as of 2014, nearly fifty years after the death of Grand Chief Gabriel Sylliboy, no official pardon has been given to his family members or to the grand council for the 1928 conviction. As a matter of justice and reconciliation, the grand chief's pardon is long overdue.

References

Henderson, James (Sa'ke'j) Youngblood. 1997. *Mi'kmaw Concordat*. Halifax, NS: Fernwood Publishing.

Paul, Daniel N. 2006. *We Were Not the Savages: A Mi'kmaq Perspective on the Collision Between European and Native American Civilizations*. 3rd ed. Black Point, NS: Fernwood Publishing.

R. v. Marshall. 1999. 3 SCR 456, 1999 CanLII 665 (SCC), http://canlii.ca/t/1fqkq.

Simon v. The Queen. 1985. 2 SCR 387, 1985 CanLII 11 (SCC), http://canlii.ca/t/1fv04.

R. v. Syliboy. 1928. Canadian Criminal Cases 50 (1928), 390-1, 395-96.

Re. Indian Reserve, City of Sydney, N.S. Exchequer Court of Canada, 16 March 1916. Dominion Law Reports 42 (1916), 314-22.

Senier, Siobhan, ed. 2014. *Dawnland Voices: An Anthology of Indigenous Writing from New England*. Lincoln: University of Nebraska Press.

Thwaites, R.G. ed. 1856-96. *The Jesuit Relations and Allied Documents*. 73 vols. Cleveland: Burrows.

Wicken, William C. 2012. *The Colonization of Mi'kmaw Memory and History, 1794-1928*. Toronto: University of Toronto Press.

Stuart Killen

Memories of an ex-Indian Agent

My introduction to Mi'kmaw First Nations was in September 1960.

After a stint in the Royal Canadian Navy, in 1959, I was hired as a wills and estates officer for the Nova Scotia Trust Company in Sydney, Nova Scotia.[1] I was making $40 a week. After taking a correspondence course on wills and estates and banking through Queen's University in Kingston, Ontario, I became a trust officer of wills and estates. My salary was still $40 a week.

In June or July 1960, I noticed a Government of Canada job notice in the Sydney post office for "an exciting career working with the Mic Macs [sic] of the Eskasoni Indian Agency" as assistant superintendent. The advertised salary was $100 a week. This was more than twice my wage at the trust company. I applied.

The job interview was conducted in a room in the post office building. The main interviewers were the clerk for the Eskasoni Indian Agency, the assistant regional director from Amherst and a welfare officer from the federal Department of Indian Affairs in Ottawa. After the interview I had no clear idea of what the advertised position entailed. I actually thought it was supervising a distribution centre.

First Nations people were not mentioned during the interview, only federal policies and procedures relating to housing materials, food, clothing, "special needs" and other miscellaneous items that could have been divisions of a department store.

In mid-September 1960 I received a surprise call from the regional office of Indian Affairs, asking if I was still interested in the position at Eskasoni. I accepted, and was told to report for work in a week's time.

A year or two later I learned that I had been the government's third choice. Their first pick had refused the job. The second was Ernie Skinner, a children's aid worker for Inverness County. Eskasoni needed a welfare professional, while the regional director needed an assistant superintendent that was familiar with finances, estates and general management. So I was hired together with Skinner.

Eskasoni Indian Agency

On my first day at work I was given a big black binder: the policy and procedure manual for all aspects of Indian Affairs. I remember that it described the goal of of Indian Affairs as "the assimilation of Indians into the main stream of Canadian society." The word "assimilation" meant to me that, at some point in time, Mi'kmaq would exist no more. That disturbed me at the time, as it does today.

During the first month of working at the Eskasoni Indian Agency, I was overwhelmed by the poverty of the residents of the Eskasoni community. My first day consisted of meeting Eskasoni Band members who were lined up in the hallway of the band office. They were waiting to see the government agent—the Indian agent—to get a purchase order form for food, clothing or other household items they could buy from the Eskasoni "community store." The store was run by the Eskasoni Indian Agency with money provided to the band office by the regional office of Indian Affairs in Amherst, as part of the federal budget. It was not a community store in the minds of the residents of Eskasoni, who complained about its high prices and lack of variety.

The first person I met in my office on my first day of work was Jim Prosper, a thin man who was fifty-two years old but looked well past sixty. He looked like my father. He approached me with humility. He took off his shoes to show me the holes in the soles. He also showed me the cardboard that the previous Indian agent had given him to put inside his shoes, rather than give him an order for a new pair. I never got over that experience with Jim Prosper, and I became his friend until the day he died. I eventually convinced him he did not have to doff his hat for me.

That first day was a powerful experience. My first thought was to quit, and I almost walked away from my new job. A more powerful force told me that I could help change this dehumanizing environment by working from within. I talked to my co-worker, Skinner, the new welfare officer, and discovered that he felt the same way.

In two years we succeeded in replacing orders for rations with cheques that Mi'kmaq could cash and then use to purchase what they needed for themselves. As a result the so-called Eskasoni community store closed, and Eskasoni Band members began shopping in town where they could bargain for betters deals on food, clothing and other needs. The regional director was not happy.

One time, when the superintendent of the Lennox Island Indian Agency was ill, I was sent there to serve as acting superintendent. The island was about 400 metres from the mainland of Prince Edward Island, connected by a small ferry. In winter, some people crossed over to the mainland on the sea ice; several had drowned in the 1960s.

The superintendent had imposed a sign-in and -out system on all Lennox Island residents. At the first council meeting I attended, the band council abolished that system. They also called for construction of a bridge or causeway, citing the hazards of crossing the ice. A causeway was finally completed in 1973.

I helped the Mi'kmaq of Eskasoni and Lennox Island write complaints to members of the Canadian Parliament. I did not write those letters myself, but organized letter-writing classes. The first class at Eskasoni was at Margaret "Granny" Johnson's home and was attended by many members of the band. That did not please the regional director in Amherst, who spoke of First Nations people as "my Indians." In the paternalistic environment of the 1960s, my actions as a civil servant were considered disobedient.

Bart McKinnon, the regional director, made it his project to get me out of the Maritimes as fast as possible. He actually did me a great favour by sending me to Ottawa for a course in community development at Carleton University, taught by Professor Farrell Toombs. For six months I studied under Prof. Toombs with thirty like-minded students. We graduated as "change agents" who would not do anything for people that they could do for themselves. That seemed to be the only way to break the overt paternalism practised by Indian Affairs, then and today.

My thesis was CD=D10xP10xT10xP10 over X, a mathematical equation explained in the English language as follows: Community Development equals Definition to the tenth degree, Principles to the tenth degree, Techniques to the tenth degree and Philosophy to the tenth degree, divided by X, the unknown, which is the people. My thesis called for eventually abolishing the Department of Indian Affairs in favour of Indian self-governance: "government of the people, by the people, for the people," to borrow a familiar phrase.

Eventually, I was invited to apply for the position of regional director of Indian Affairs. At the interview I was asked what I would do if I were the regional director for the Maritimes. I said that my first action would be to abolish the office, let go its staff and establish the Maritime chiefs as the rule of law and order within the Maritimes. Needless to say, I did not get the job. Within two months I was transferred to northern Manitoba as superintendent of the Norway House Indian Agency, which had jurisdiction over area Cree and Ojibwe First Nations. That was in October 1966.

Grand Chief Sylliboy

I remember first meeting Grand Chief Gabrieal Sylliboy within two weeks of my arrival at Eskasoni. He was a tall man with bright, brown piercing eyes. When we first met, it was in the hallway of the Eskasoni Agency.

I said "Hi Grand Chief." He looked me up and down and said, "Another Scotchman?"

I said "No, Grand Chief, an Irishman!"

To which he replied, "That's worse."

We both laughed and I asked if I could buy him some chew: Old Chum. I was told he liked that brand and the community store stocked it. I remember he said something in Mi'kmaw, and only later I found out that it was *wela'lin* (thank you). From that encounter, a long friendship developed.

I would visit him at his house at least two or three times a week. I drank a lot of *pitewey* (tea). He talked about the Mi'kmaw treaties and a trapping-rights case that was lost in the courts. He said that Nova

Scotia did not have a deed for Mi'kmaw territory, and told me that what the Indian agency called "rations" or "welfare" was payment for the use of Mi'kmaw land. Grand Chief Sylliboy was familiar with the terms of the 1752 treaty with the British Crown. He knew that section five of the treaty promised the Mi'kmaq "bread, flour, and such other Provisions as can be procured." That is what he understood as "rations." He also knew that section four of the treaty granted Mi'kmaq "free liberty of Hunting and Fishing as usual."

Sylliboy had brought a trapping case to court (in 1928) in his capacity as Grand Chief and took the loss of that case personally. He felt he was somehow to blame. When he said that, it occurred to me that no case brought by a Mi'kmaq would have found judicial favour in those days. Some time later I told him that. He smiled, got up and gave me a tearful hug.

He also talked about the "centralization" program. Indian Affairs promised the people that if they moved to Eskasoni they would not have to worry; they would be looked after "like a baby." That was why he was for it, for his people. Everyone who moved to Eskasoni would be given a new house and would want for nothing. He understood the relocation to Eskasoni in relation to section five of the 1752 treaty, which promised Mi'kmaq a "truckhouse," or trading centre, where they could barter or sell their goods to best advantage and receive provisions.

The Eskasoni agency superintendent, Joe MacPherson, informed me that visiting the grand chief was not part of my job description. I disagreed. Through Grand Chief Sylliboy I had learned that the members of the grand council were the true historical leaders of Mi'kmaw communities, rather than "*Indian Act* chiefs."

My meetings with Sylliboy were responsible for my interest in treaties, Aboriginal title and Aboriginal rights. I began searching for clues in libraries, land-registry offices and the Nova Scotia Archives. When I was in Ottawa, for the community development course with Prof. Toombs, I visited the land-registry office at Indian Affairs and also the National Archives. Hugh Conn was the first person I met when I was looking through the land registry. Indian Affairs had hired him to refute the concepts of Aboriginal title and Aboriginal rights. Instead, his research convinced him that First Nations did have inherent rights as well as specific claims against the federal and provincial governments. He was a thorn in the side of Indian Affairs before he died in 1970.

I also met many chiefs at the community-development course at Carleton, and they spoke of the same issues as Sylliboy, including the racist policy of assimilation practiced by the federal and provincial governments. The perspective I gained from my talks with Sylliboy would help me in later years at Norway House, where I tested my ideas for community development, and upon my return to the Maritimes to work for St. Francis Xavier University as a community-development worker on Cape Breton Island.

Norway House Indian Agency

I drove out to Manitoba, to The Pas Indian Agency, for briefing on my new position at Norway House in 1968. The superintendent of The Pas Indian Agency was the most paternalistic person I have ever met. He, too, routinely used the expression "my Indians," and he told me that he knew what was best for them.

I had never witnessed the kind of racism I encountered at that agency and in the town of The Pas. Drinking establishments were divided into non-Indian seating and Indian seating, for example, and it was strictly enforced. I remember visiting a pub in town and sitting in the "Indian Section." First Nations people already seated there told me they would get in trouble if I stayed. The waiter told me that if I did not leave he would close down the "Indian Section," and "throw all the Indians out." Of course I left!

It did not surprise me when the townspeople of The Pas formed a conspiracy of silence to cover up the murder of a nineteen-year-old First Nations woman, Helen Betty Osborne, several years later (November 1971). Charges were eventually filed against the son of a clerk who worked for The Pas Indian Agency.

I did not stay long in The Pas, but went from there to the Norway House Indian Agency. Norway House was an isolated community at that time, with access only by chartered aircraft. I visited Norway House in 2008 and it is now accessible by road.

There were two other Indian reserves associated with the same agency: Cross Lake, to the north, and Poplar River, to the south. All were geographically isolated and accessible only by light aircraft such as Cessna 180s and De Havilland Beavers and Otters. The agency owned a Cessna and had an on-call relationship with a pilot.

Nonetheless, all three reserves were totally inaccessible for several weeks during spring breakup and fall freeze-up, and we could only communicate by radiophone. The radiophones were like walkie-talkies: when you wanted to talk, you pressed the talk button, and when you wanted to listen, you took your finger off the talk button. This became my lifeline.

I quickly realized that this community was a perfect place for becoming a "community-development change agent." The first thing I did was to visit the chief of the Norway House Cree Nation and introduce myself. He called me the *sonie uga mah* or "money boss man." I asked him to call a meeting of his twelve band councilors within a few days, and he agreed. Two days later, we had our first band-council meeting. The chief asked me to prepare the agenda, as had been the practice of the previous superintendents. I explained that I did not do agendas, and felt that was a role of the chief and council. I remember the smile on the chief's face.

At the council meeting we needed an interpreter. By unanimous vote, the council chose Alan Ross, the agency clerk, who was not a registered member of the band but who spoke fluent Cree. Alan became my right hand (being left-handed myself). I would explain why I was doing or not doing certain things. He understood I was not going to do anything for the chiefs that they could do for themselves. If they could not do something that they needed to do, it was a teaching moment. (Years later Alan attended law school, became chief of the Norway House agency and eventually, grand chief of the Assembly of Manitoba Chiefs.)

The council asked me for the agenda. I told them I was new at the job and did not know enough about the community to make an agenda relevant to their community. When Alan Ross began interpreting my message I saw confused and perplexed faces, but, as he explained it, all in Cree, I saw some smiles among the council members. They adjourned for a week. From that day forward, the council set its own agenda. The council also called a band meeting to introduce me to the community at large. This council was soon managing its own welfare, housing, special-needs and work-for-relief programs. Within six months of taking leadership of their affairs, they had deposited more than $10,000 in a Winnipeg bank.

A financial officer from Ottawa was flown in to do an audit. He told me he was sent there because I obviously could not control my Indians. The chief called a band meeting, and it was filled to capacity. The chief asked the financial officer what was the problem. He answered that under the rules and regulations of the department of Indian Affairs, bands cannot hold money saved from programs for later use.

Then it was council's turn to speak. One by one, the twelve councillors described how they had managed programs to save money. They argued that it was their money, and therefore it was their responsibility to spend it wisely. And with winter coming, they wanted to save some of the money to buy hardwood for fuel for the community's houses. They spoke in Cree with Alan interpreting. The meeting began at 7:00 p.m. and did not finish until 2:00 a.m. The finance officer left that next day and that was the end of the matter.

The people of Norway House had successfully beaten the department of Indian Affairs at its own game and directly addressed a need they perceived in their community. They were pumped! Not long after, the council of Norway House and I occupied the non-Indian section of a local pub. In time, the RCMP actually flew in six Mounties from Winnipeg, who advised me that I had a duty to "control my Indians." I asked them to go ahead and charge me with something under the criminal code, such as disturbing the peace or public mischief. Of course, they did nothing of the kind. The Norway House Band continued to administer their own affairs, and the idea spread quickly to the communities of Cross Lake and Poplar River.

Alan Ross and Don Maybe, a provincial community worker, also helped circulate information to the bands about their treaties with the Crown. The chief had old copies of the treaties and the *Indian Act*. We ordered hundreds of copies over a two-year period to show they were in fact real treaties, and that, further, self-governance is a right under the *Indian Act*.

"Control your Indians" was a phrase I heard a lot. In October 1969 I resigned from Indian Affairs, explaining that I was no longer needed on the Norway House agency reserves.

I returned to Nova Scotia the next day.

The Union of Nova Scotia Indians

In the 1960s, St. Francis Xavier University received grants for community-action projects with African Canadians and Indians of Glace Bay and eastern Nova Scotia, including the five Mi'kmaw reserves on Cape Breton Island. When I got back from Norway House I applied to the university for a position as a community-development officer, and was assigned to Sydney in the fall of 1968. Noel Doucette was also hired as a community-development officer for Cape Breton. That was when I first met him, although he had also been a student at Sydney Academy, where I went to school.

Noel and I became good friends. Many times we travelled together on visits to the First Nations communities of Nova Scotia. He felt the same about "working with, not for" the chiefs and councils. Noel Doucette and Roy Gould were co-editors of the *MicMac News*, which had been set up in 1965 with the help of Ernie Skinner of Eskasoni and another St. Francis Xavier University extension worker. *MicMac News* quickly became the voice of the Mi'kmaq as well as a critical source of independent information for Mi'kmaw people about treaties and Aboriginal rights.

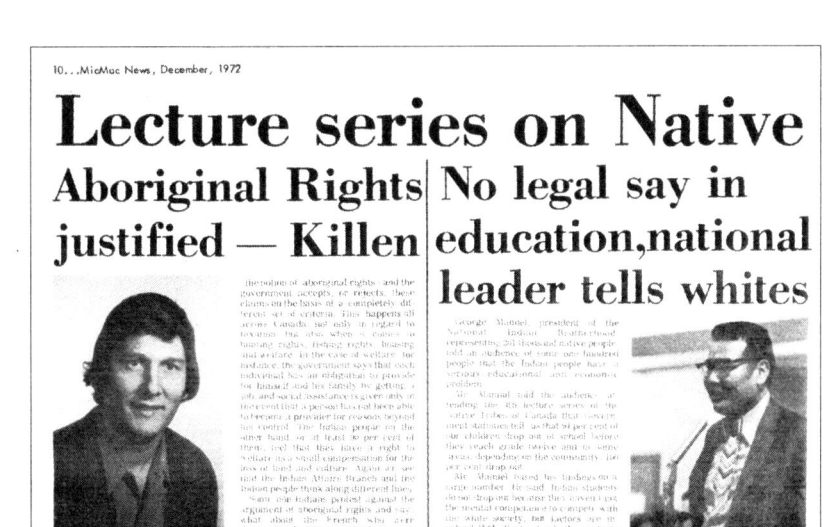

MicMac News, 1972, vol. 2 (12): 10. http://beatoninstitute.com/micmac-news-1972

During my travels Noel introduced me to Joe B. Marshall. I first learned about "Joe B" when he came home to live in Eskasoni after his tour of duty in the Royal Canadian Air Force. I had been responsible for the education portfolio at the Eskasoni agency, and Joe B applied to go back to Sydney Academy high school to complete grade twelve. Through Joe B, I was introduced to Greg Johnson of Eskasoni and to Stanley Johnson of Millbrook. They became founding members of the Union of Nova Scotia Indians.

Noel Doucette suggested that the union compete with St. Francis s University for the federal funding that had been used for community-development workers, and he organized Mi'kmaw to respond to the Canadian government's infamous 1969 white paper on Indian Affairs. We made a submission to Indian Affairs, and the community-development funds were redirected from the university to the union. Fr. George Topshee, director of the university extension program at St. FX, was quoted saying that Noel Doucette and Stuart Killen were henceforth persona non grata, a statement I wear as a badge of honour.

The union hired me as research director. My job was to carry out research on treaties, Aboriginal title, Aboriginal rights and specific land claims, with whatever funds I could garner from a new program of Indian Affairs called "specific and comprehensive claims." I also submitted a proposal to the Laidlaw Foundation, a civil-society group, for funds to research the Middle River (Cape Breton) Band's loss of lands set aside by provincial and federal authorities since before Confederation.

The Laidlaw Foundation contributed $15,000 to the Middle River project. They were concerned about a backlash from non-Indian squatters on Indian land, however, and were conscious that the land claim was in the backyard of Allan J. MacEachern, a powerful federal politician. That was the last grant we received from Laidlaw, but Middle River's specific claim was accepted for negotiation and settlement, and this led to compensation for the loss of use of the land: the first of many Mi'kmaw-specific claims to go through the resolution process that is still underway in the Maritimes and in other regions of Canada.

The union also received a five-year funding agreement with Indian Affairs for research on specific and comprehensive claims that we used to unearth the history of Mi'kmaw treaties with the Crown.

A research committee was established to work with me: Noel Doucette, Joe B. Marshall, Greg Johnson and Stanley Johnson. The committee's first response to the 1969 white paper was an essay titled "Indians and the Constitution" that they presented to a meeting of the National Indian Brotherhood, in Ottawa, in October 1970.

We employed two research assistants, Donald Julien from Millbrook and Albert Marshall from Eskasoni, together with Joan Johnson from Eskasoni, who had just returned from working with the Boston Friendship Centre as executive secretary. Together we prepared a brief on the tax-exemption provision in section 86 of the *Indian Act* that we submitted to the Nova Scotia government in March 1971. It led to complete Aboriginal exemption from provincial sales and income tax in 1973.

We published two editorials, in April 1971, which described Mi'kmaq as "citizens plus" because they have Aboriginal title to the lands and resources of Nova Scotia, plus the right to be compensated for the historical loss of their lands and resources. We published articles on the pollution of the Pictou Landing Reserve by a local pulp-and-paper company, leading to a meeting with the provincial minister of water resources, who was quoted as asking "What have we done to this place?" Legal action was taken against the province in June 1971. Matters stand today, forty-three years later, much as they did in 1971. In 1974, the Union of Nova Scotia Indians made a submission to the federal government on Aboriginal title, Aboriginal rights and treaty rights at a meeting with the minister of Indian Affairs at Eskasoni. The union's president, Alex Denny, made the presentation to the minister, and I felt the spirit of Grand Chief Sylliboy during that presentation.

The union's research department also participated in civil disobedience, such as road blocks at the Afton and Millbrook First Nations to pressure the government of Nova Scotia to keep its promises regarding the construction of overpasses where highways had dissected reserve lands, and a takeover of the Fortress of Louisbourg historic site to ensure that Mi'kmaq are employed and represented during the tourist season. I intend to write an essay on that takeover. We had hired a filmmaker but the fog on the day of the occupation was too much for the cameras of those days.

The union's research department met monthly to review its work plan, and had weekly meetings with different bands in Nova Scotia to explain what we were doing and why. I knew from my experience at Norway House that the big issue was how our research would materially advance the everyday lives of Mi'kmaw people socially, economically and culturally. I have to say that question has not been satisfactorily answered even today.

Note

1. Nova Scotia Trust Company later merged with Canada Trust and the Toronto Dominion Bank.

James (Sa'ke'j) Youngblood Henderson

Alexander Denny and the Treaty Imperative

"Take our territory without our ancestor's permission in our treaties and without the King purchasing our territory," Alex Denny declared as he drove through the territory, shaking his head. "What a ridiculous thought, much less such a thought pretending to be law!" Denny was the charismatic, strategic, inclusive president of the Union of Nova Scotia Indians (UNSI) and the kji-keptin (grand captain) of the Mi'kmaw Grand Council. He was a political and spiritual leader. He was a realist and a visionary. He combined traditional and visionary teaching with exemplary action, with decisive implications for the improvement of Mi'kmaw life. He lived by a faith in his ancestors and their teachings. He felt and understood the lessons of the treaties of the past, of the long colonial oppression of the treaties that existed as the status quo in the present, and of the important role treaties had in the future. He believed there were better days ahead because of the treaties of his ancestors. He was a man of service to community who persevered, knowing full well he would not receive all the benefits promised in the treaties, but he believed his efforts would deliver a better life for generations to follow. Presented with an enduring crisis of the Mi'kmaq, he shaped the plans, turned it into a cause, brought in the needed people and marshalled tasks through to completion.

I was one of the people he brought in to help change the situation. I am the husband of Marie Battiste from Potlotek First Nation (the Chapel Island reserve), Nova Scotia, and a member of the Chickasaw Nation and Cheyenne tribe from Oklahoma. As a law and native-studies professor at the University of California, I was a scholar of Aboriginal and treaty rights. I had finished my family projects by securing judicial re-establishment of the government of the Chickasaw Nation, resolving the land claims of the Cheyenne tribe in Oklahoma, and, with my friend, Russel Barsh, writing a book on the legal history of Indian tribes in the United States. On our annual visit for the St. Anne's Mission at Potolek with my wife, in 1975, Russell Marshall connected me with Alex Denny for a long conversation about Mi'kmaw land claims and treaties. From this conversation, we were recruited to live in Eskasoni, near Alex, and I began my in-laws' difficult family project of conceptualizing legal arguments for the recognition of the Aboriginal and treaty rights of the Mi'kmaq, and directing their entrenchment in the Constitution of Canada.

Most of our conversations and strategizing about Aboriginal and treaty rights were carried out during long rides to various meetings and conferences across Atlantic Canada in Alex's new, red, full-size Lincoln Town Car, with its plush velour interior. It served as our main office. As we travelled throughout Mi'kma'ki to respond to invitations from Mi'kmaq and others, Alex and other Mi'kmaw travellers would tell the stories related to the territory, translate the meaning of the Mi'kmaw words that named towns and regions, explain the harvesting of the ecology and clarify the boundaries of the various treaties. Our other venues were in the kitchens of many Mi'kmaw homes, where we had tea and sought advice and knowledge in meetings with chiefs; flights across Canada; meetings with government officials; and hotel rooms on the road. On sunny days at Eskasoni, we sat together on an orange bench in front of his house and continued our discussions about the predicament and the search for solutions.

Alex was a man of great energy, physically and mentally. He was liked by all who knew him for his kindness and good humour, but also for his cheerful disposition toward life, for his familiar tact and easy tone in conversations, and his unquestionable honesty. He cherished learning. No one knew better than Alex how to express simplicity and good-humoured deference for the thoughts and feeling of others. He knew that it was improper to pass judgments prematurely. Most

Mi'kmaq were delighted with his conversations and lifted up by his thoughts. He believed in the inexhaustible potentiality of the Mi'kmaq to overcome the pervasive experience of poverty and drudgery, of oppression and belittlement. These qualities had gained him the utmost respect among the people he met.

Alex led by example, rather than by sermon. His goal was to change the way Canada and the Atlantic provinces had forced Mi'kmaq to live. His visionary and exemplary action, rather than lecturing, was central to his concept of change. His actions were inspired by a view of a better life for Mi'kmaq than the present experiences allowed. He saw that Canada had established constraints that denied Mi'kmaq the vision of the ancestors in the treaties, and that federal laws had changed the way Mi'kmaq thought about themselves, creating doubts in their minds about who they were.

Alex was aware that the Mi'kmaq were faced with an intractable situation. They were mired in the worst economic and social conditions suffered by any people in eastern Canada or the northeastern United States, hanging on by the new but meagre welfare programs that left life grim and hard, surrounded by the sagging economy of Atlantic Canada as a whole. In addition to grinding poverty, the relentless political oppression of Canada's Department of Indian Affairs (now Indigenous Affairs and Northern Development Canada) and provincial governments pursuing forced-assimilation programs—from the 1969 white-paper policy to Aboriginal residential and day schools—which ignored Mi'kmaw treaties and the collective rights they had reserved for themselves in the treaties, had traumatized Mi'kmaw society. The Department of Indian Affairs, in particular, had boundless authority over Mi'kmaw life. It served as governor, banker, educator and employer, acting in unfathomable ways that fostered alienation and hopelessness. A handful of Elders and educated Mi'kmaq had grown aware of the consequences of assimilation and acculturation, and they began to question the lack of choices in their lives.

Alex's own life experience illustrated the unpredictable and unaccountable nature of the institutions and bureaucracy that controlled Mi'kmaw lives: refusal to register Mi'kmaq as status Indians because of the denial of the existence of treaties; the incremental steps to terminate treaties and Indian status and turn the Mi'kmaq into the poorest residents of the provinces; the horror of Indian residential schools; and the false promises made to Mi'kmaw families when they were relocated to Eskasoni during "centralization." Many Mi'kmaq tried life in the New England states and found it was little better. Racism, separation from families, an agonizing readjustment and hand-to-mouth existence were the price of escaping southward from the Canadian authorities.

The Mi'kmaq proved resilient; they survived the poverty and suffering, and in the 1970s most had retained their knowledge system and language. But any belief in their traditions was contradicted by the world they were forced to live in, leaving them tormented, confused and resigned. For Alex, the dominant problem was the persistent attack by government on the very idea that the Mi'kmaq had treaties with the king of Great Britain. The family that raised him shared a noble and luminous vision of the Mi'kmaw inheritance. Because his father had read the treaties to him as a child, and discussed them, he understood how the treaties could inform a greater life for Mi'kmaq.

Alex knew that Mi'kmaq had lived through periods of great strife and great struggle that tested the Mi'kmaw world view, knowledge, and the courage of convictions and the strength of relationships. Despite the divisions and disagreements among Mi'kmaq, their hesitations and their fears, they endured because families chose to move forward in response to each challenge. Mi'kmaq do not give up. They do not quit. They did not allow fear or divisions to break their spirit. Devastated by their struggle with colonization and racism, they withdrew to themselves but, as Alex stressed, Mi'kmaq persisted in their stubborn resistance and resilience in the face of adversity and conflict.

Alex believed that the spirit of the Mi'kmaw knowledge system and world view is embedded in the language, and that they were the foundations of the Mi'kmaw treaties. Because of this inherent spirit, its great decency and strength, the language survived. He saw that the Mi'kmaq were a astonishing people who had a deep faith, who lived in one of the most beautiful places in North America. However, Alex appreciated that the Mi'kmaq had to confront difficult, complex challenges. Overcoming these challenges was not going to be easy. It would be long, complicated, frustrating and disheartening at times. When you try to correct the wrongs of the past and make major change, Alex cautioned, it stirs passions and controversy with people committed to the status quo. As hard as times have been, or may become, as uncomfortable and contentious as the debates about treaties and dispossession may develop, Alex was committed to helping the Mi'kmaq get serious about fixing the obstacles in their path toward prosperity and dignity. That's just how Mi'kmaq are.

Alex responded to the 1969 white paper on Indian affairs by entering into politics. He tried to end the divisiveness, factionalism and indifference of Mi'kmaw families through a daunting but persistent strategy: break the department's domination over the Mi'kmaq by reasserting the ancestral rights to the land and waters of Mi'kma'ki, secured by their treaties; achieve treaty federalism within Canada and a strong, fresh start as an economic force in the Atlantic region; reassert Mi'kmaw knowledge and language within the Eurocentric educational system; and escape the abyss Mi'kmaq feared would result from a termination of the lifelines of social welfare.

He painstakingly and patiently attempted to build a creative and inclusive movement against the power of the status quo. His movement was not for power, but for justice. Alex often told Mi'kmaq, "standing still in our situation was a curse, if our generation refuses to unite and win this struggle, it will be our last stand with our ancestors, and our children will face a totally distinct struggle to live as someone they were not meant to be." If that occurred, "being Mi'kmaq, our knowledge, traditions, and language would be a relic of the past." He warned that "if Mi'kmaq did not unite under the treaties, then Canada will force complete assimilation on our children to make them live as white people." He did not believe that Canada had any plan other than incremental forced assimilation. The Mi'kmaq had to develop an alternative plan based on the teachings of their ancestors.

Scattered throughout Atlantic Canada on small reserves, and small in number, he argued, Mi'kmaq could only count on their own ancestors and current families to prevent cessation. While the most pressing issue among Mi'kmaq was daily survival—to build adequate housing, put food on the table, pay the bills, find opportunities to get ahead and, most of all, to give their children opportunity for a better life—all this would depend on uniting for the treaties against governmental policy and against flawed components of the federal *Indian Act*.

Alex built on the shock of the decision by the Supreme Court of Canada (in 1973 in *Calder et al. v. Attorney-General of British Columbia*) that affirmed that Aboriginal title exists in Canada even though the Government of Canada and the provinces had denied such existence. In response to the judicial decision, Canada pledged to negotiate with native peoples concerning their traditional interests in land, and to redress grievances arising from the Crown's "lawful obligations" under treaties and the 1763 Royal Proclamation. The *Calder* decision and new federal policy left open the status of Aboriginal title in the Atlantic Provinces, however, which comprised most of the land reserved by the Mi'kmaq under their treaties. Canada acknowledged that no treaties of "surrender" (i.e., cession of territory) or purchases of their territory had ever been signed with the Mi'kmaq, leaving the possibility that Aboriginal title and rights still existed without limitation, protected by the imperial treaties and laws. Alex used *Calder* to build a team, in conjunction with the UNSI, to restore Mi'kmaw Aboriginal and treaty rights, with the underlying goal of restoring Mi'kmaw knowledge, language and life.

The Mi'kmaw Grand Council, Elders and his family taught Alex that treaties are covenants interrelated to the other sacred covenants of their knowledge system and spirituality. They were part of the sacred covenants that informed Mi'kmaw law, values and beliefs. They were the covenants that informed the possibilities of an emerging future. Because of his experiences with ineffective and insincere provincial and federal laws in generating a better life for the Mi'kmaq, Alex developed the idea of the inviolability of the various treaties with the seven districts or tribes of the Mi'kmaq nation as a solution and guideline for Canadian legislation. The meanings of the treaties were not his vision alone, it was the accumulated vision of many ancestral chiefs, grand captains and teachers. He had been taught that the treaties had been made orally, and that their terms could be found in the oral traditions and symbols of his ancestors.

Alex was aware that the Canadian governments were conscious, or at least half conscious, of their denial of, or bad faith toward, the imperial treaties with the Mi'kmaq. He knew that the government operated without confronting its problematic disobedience to the treaties. He often stated that generations of politicians under the guise of democracy viewed the imperial treaties as a conspiracy that could affect the privileges of the colonists and settlers, and their descendants. He knew that politicans were ideological manipulators who deceived the Canadian public for generations. He argued that, indeed, some Canadians wanted their politicians to keep the imperial treaties secret, to misrepresent them as complex, inaccessible or obsolete, or to deny their validity altogether. Yet he knew that, as a consequence of the manipulation, other Canadians were ill-informed or not conscious as to the existence or meanings of the treaties. He had to expose the collective denial/unconsciousness with respect to the true nature of the Mi'kmaw treaties to generate awareness of the treaties to both Mi'kmaq and Canadians.

Alex understood that because of the denial of the treaties by governments and courts, most Mi'kmaq lived in a halfway house of treaties—between belief and doubt. Yet most had learned about the treaties directly from their families. Their doubts and illusions about the treaties existed because of government denial of the treaties, the traumatic effects on the residential-school experience and the powerful grind of Mi'kmaw daily life. Alex thought that once the confusions of the halfway house could be corrected, the Mi'kmaq would take seriously the sacred vision and voice of their ancestors.

Alex rejected the idea that the written copies of treaties in the archives were comprehensive or correct; they offered only a partial, English perspective alongside Mi'kmaw orally transmitted knowledge and law. He taught us not to wholly trust the written documents in the archives as they were only the British, English-language version of the treaties. He cautioned the legal and research team never to say that the Mi'kmaq "signed" the treaties, because that would privilege the written document over understandings of the sacred obligations undertaken by the Mi'kmaq and the British monarchy. The Mi'kmaw perspective is embedded within the treaties, which affirmed continuity with Mi'kmaw law, he explained, and this would be revealed when both the oral and written records were combined, and we had to bring the records to light.

The Mi'kmaw treaties with the British kings did not bestow upon the Mi'kmaq any rights, he clarified; rather, the Mi'kmaq gave certain rights to the British king for the benefit of British settlers in Mi'kmaw territory. As such, the settlers had unlawfully benefited more from the treaties than had the Mi'kmaq. The Mi'kmaq then already had everything they needed to be self-sufficient. Neither the British nor the French had anything essential for the Mi'kmaq, as their ancestors had told the European missionaries and colonists.

Alex attempted to show how the Mi'kmaw treaties were not only part of the foundation of Canadian law, but they also had to be read as the reverse of subsequent Canadian law. In the rest of Canadian law, he taught, everyone had to be granted powers and rights by the mystical Crown. In the treaties, however, Mi'kmaq retained sovereignty, law, their knowledge system, freedom of religion and their territory for themselves; they never granted the kings any power over those ancestral rights. The settlements, trade and dispute-resolution processes in the Mi'kmaw treaties were a limited delegation to the British Crown. Provincial and federal legislation violated the limited delegation and thus could not be considered lawful or justified; such legislation was, in fact, unlawful. This situation created a legal quandary between the Mi'kmaq and the settlers, who came to call themselves Canadians.

Alex comprehended the Mi'kmaw idea that the treaties would never come easy for Atlantic Canadians, who had been mostly landless refugees from Great Britain, other colonies and Europe, who were seeking new opportunities in a "new world": in this case, Mi'kmaw territory. They knew little about the Mi'kmaq or their history, and were ignorant, ambivalent or indifferent to the broken promises of the Crown that created the injustices. Alex argued that "white people" really believed in the Canadian government's illusory claim that Canadian laws had created the Mi'kmaw communities and reserves, and could just as easily re-define or terminate them.

Alex appreciated how much the overwhelming power of the status quo would be an obstacle to treaty recognition and implementation. The Department of Indian Affairs continually coerced the Mi'kmaw chiefs and band councils, and actively resisted and undermined change. Because of funding, the department was still a powerful force, and the chiefs buffered the grievances of the community. Alex reminded us that government would resort to dirty tricks and misinformation to try to maintain their power over the Mi'kmaq. These tricks would be directed at him and the team. The government would spread the idea that Mi'kmaq regularly received large government cheques, paid for by Canadian taxes, yet were refusing to become "real" Canadians. This misrepresentation understandably made many Canadians angry, and a great deal of energy was expended proving it false.

Alex realized that to protect the Mi'kmaq and their knowledge system, he had to rely on the imperial-era treaties and their legal obligations and rights. He believed that no federal legislation or policy would offer a sufficient or sustainable foundation for rebuilding Mi'kmaw society, since it could always be amended or repealed. He knew the Mi'kmaq had to enshrine their treaties with the kings and their ancestral sovereignty in the constitution of Canada.

Federal and provincial politicians and bureaucrats told Alex that his focus on Aboriginal and treaty rights was impossible, impractical and too ambitious; it would be too contentious and controversial for Canadians, in any case—Aboriginal justice would best be put on hold. Mi'kmaq cannot turn the clock backward, they argued, with a metaphorical vibrancy that exculpates those who broke the treaties and dispossessed the Mi'kmaq from the lands reserved for them in the treaties. To this, Alex responded that the time for justice was now, that the time of injustice and excuses had passed. When he spoke, his words wise beyond his years, he had the ability to bend the past and generate a new vision of the future for his listeners. His graciousness, his smile, his sense of humor, his style in dressing, all helped Alex effortlessly wear the heavy burden of leadership and expectations.

The politicians and bureaucrats asked Alex potentially insurmountable questions: Why are contemporary Mi'kmaq entitled to ancient treaty rights? Why are Mi'kmaq special? Why should Atlantic Canadians, who (they said) were not responsible for the dispossession, have to provide a remedy for the past? While Alex pondered the argument that correcting the mass dispossession of the Mi'kmaq was im-

MicMac News, 1988, vol. 18(10): 5. http://beatoninstitute.com/micmac-news-1988.

possible, his typical response was that Mi'kmaq are special because of their treaties with the king, the only foundation for Atlantic Canadians being in Mi'kmaw territory. No Canadian has such a treaty with the king—they, in fact, were dependent on the king or parliament for their powers and rights. That is what made the Mi'kmaq and other Indian nations special in the Constitution of Canada. He embodied a politics that was not small, and would respond to the excuses of the government officials: How long should we wait? How long should Mi'kmaw families delay their future? Who benefits from our patience? Why are those who benefit from Mi'kmaq land acting so innocently?

Alex refused to wait. He led by example, unravelling the governmental blind eye toward the treaties. He encouraged progress by seeking out ideas, partnering with people to make things happen. He assembled the team via the UNSI to pursue his vision of restoring Mi'kmaw Aboriginal and treaty rights to create a better future for the Mi'kmaq. He was convinced that Aboriginal and treaty rights could generate a new way for those who had lost their traditional way of life through wrongful dispossession of their land by the colonists. The rights he sought would enable Mi'kmaq to prevail in their struggles against racism and prejudice and find new ways to regain prosperity.

Alex and his team knew that the oppression of the Mi'kmaq relied on concealing and degrading the treaty relationship between the Mi'kmaq and the colonizers. Written evidence of the treaties had supposedly disappeared; oral traditions and historical accounts became suspect. Alex continually returned to surviving oral traditions. He told the research team that the treaties of the ancestors speak to the needs of the living and those of the future. If the treaties had been observed and implemented in the first place, he said, the Mi'kmaq and their descendants would not have suffered the injustices they did. The colonists and their governments had performed an amputation on the Mi'kmaw future, he said, diminishing the lives of the dispossessed Mi'kmaq and their heirs, as well as the dispossessors and their heirs. The heartbreak and smouldering, corrosive effect of injustice persisted in Mi'kmaw consciousness, however. The corrosion can only be overcome by taking collective responsibility to make amends, which was the purpose of land claims and treaty litigation.

Alex proposed a two-stage process. To address racism and colonialism, we had to reconstruct an identity separate from the status-Indian identity of the *Indian Act*. At the same time, we had to negotiate with Canada, and with Canadians on many levels, to restore an understanding of Mi'kmaw nationhood and treaties. The research team had to recreate some of the past from the archives and then check it against oral traditions of the Mi'kmaq to formulate an Aboriginal-rights position paper for Canada. After about two million hours of archival research, and more than four hundred band meetings, the research team assembled the documentation to be used in asserting Aboriginal rights and found the treaties the Mi'kmaq had been party to. The archival documents affirmed Mi'kmaw knowledge of the treaties as acquired in consultations with Elders, the Mi'kmaw Grand Council and the bands.

Alex coached the research team in what he called "legal jiu-jitsu." Canada simply avoided the treaties, relying on the inertia of the status quo. Alex determined to animate the archival research. He determined to use our research in fighting various hunting and fishing charges, for example, against individual Mi'kmaq. He believed that each generation has to seek to eliminate injustice to improve Mi'kmaw life. After much pondering and discussion, he decided to test how the courts would respond to the Aboriginal- and treaty-rights argument. It was a tiny ripple of hope on which to build a current of justice. He was convinced that political processes would never give back the stolen land or honour the treaties; the only chance was the courts' concern with justice. This was a difficult and risky strategy, because defending individuals in the courts would be one-sided: non-Mi'kmaw lawyers and judges would decide what are acceptable arguments and outcomes. If justice could not be found in court, Alex suggested, non-violent protests and politics would be the only options.

Advancing Mi'kmaw Aboriginal and treaty rights in the courts required months of analyzing and organizing the archival material and existing law for the various lawyers that participated in each round of trial and appeal. Alex recognized that the central problem was the contrived, socially constructed idea of the Mi'kmaq as nomadic savages living in an indeterminate state of nature. This popular belief lay at the foundation of systemic racism in Canada. In Grand Chief Sylliboy's 1929 prosecution for hunting during closed sesaon, the stereotype of Mi'kmaq as savages was the central tenet of the judge's rejection of the 1752 treaty central to Sylliboy's defence. Mi'kmaq were unworthy of being a territorial sovereignty. The same stereotype was used to justify the illegal and unjust dispossession of the Mi'kmaq.

They were falsely conceived as a dying, vanishing people in the face of European civilization.

The Mi'kmaw Grand Council's traditions and the UNSI research into the British and French archives contested this image. This revealed that the British and French monarchies regarded the Mi'kmaq as worthy of partnership and legal protection as a territorial nation. From the perspective of the treaties and their written clauses, the colonists and their descendants, and indeed their representatives, were responsible for violating the treaties, and present-day residents are responsible for ameliorating the effects because they continue to enjoy the fruit of injustice.

The research team employed the archives as a form of counter-memory of the nationhood and treaty relationships that had been suppressed, ignored or edited out of Canadian law and history. Alex understood that treaty litigation was contentious; many of the chiefs, under the influence of Indian Affairs, were against using "the white man's courts." He worried about the treaties being construed as evidence that Mi'kmaq had become part of Canada, rather than as a Mi'kmaw framework as a partner with Great Britain, colonial Canada, and confederated Canada. While Alex believed that impartial judges could be enlightened and persuaded to rethink Canadian history, he was aware that litigation is dangerous because judges' prejudices could prevail. Finding the right cases was essential to the success of treaty litigation.

Alex believed that the courts were supposed to be as adaptable and flexible as the needs of justice. The courts provide a forum through which Canadian society can give effect to what is perceived as just. Nonetheless, land claims under the treaties and imperial law would be the most complex litigation imaginable, with incredible potential costs that the Mi'kmaq had no ability to finance, and with enormous potential economic and social consequences for Atlantic Canada.

At the same time, the Mi'kmaw chiefs and families leaders did not yet understand how much power resided in the treaties. They knew that Grand Chief Sylliboy had decades ago lost his treaty hunting-rights case, and some felt that he had done a great deal of harm in pursuing it. After the Sylliboy case, some Mi'kmaq were afraid even to talk about the treaties after Indian Affairs officials had scolded them, saying that the treaties meant nothing. The chiefs and band councils were not focused on using treaties as guidance, but rather focused on obtaining funding under the *Indian Act*, funding which Alex called fool's gold. Alex thought the Mi'kmaq had little to lose by going to the courts in an effort to protect the Mi'kmaw way of life. The alternative was appealing to Canadian politicians, who often had no understanding of the treaties and who were unlikely to accept responsibility for treaty commitments, or violations of the treaties, or for the taking of Mi'kmaw land that, after all, continued to benefit their constituents.

The first case to go forward concerned the application of Nova Scotia provincial law to Stephen Isaac's hunting on Chapel Island reserve lands (Potlotek). The trial court at Port Hawkesbury convicted Isaac of illegal hunting on reserve land, as per provincial statutes, and Alex arranged for Bruce Wildsmith to take an appeal to the Nova Scotia Supreme Court. There, Chief Justice MacKeigan reversed the conviction, finding that Indian hunting on lands reserved for them was a use of Indian land and its resources within the meaning of the federal *Indian Act* and, as such, was beyond the legislative power of Nova Scotia. In reaching this decision, MacKeigan conducted the first judicial review of what Mikmaw Aboriginal and treaty rights are protected by the *Indian Act*. He affirmed that Mi'kmaw treaties existed, and reasoned that Mi'kmaw customary rights to the use of their traditional lands were confirmed by the 1763 Royal Proclamation, and reconfirmed by the *Indian Act*, which precludes the application of provincial game laws on reserves. He expressly overruled the contrary 1929 opinion of Judge Patterson in the *Syliboy* case, and ruled that the rights of the Mi'kmaq to reserved lands had never been extinguished by treaty or surrender.

Based on the reasoning in the *Isaac* case, Alex led the grand council, through the UNSI, to submit a comprehensive land claim for Nova Scotia to the Department of Indian Affairs, in 1977. Their position paper argued that the whole administration of Mi'kmaw lands, from 1763 to the present day, violated the Mi'kmaw Aboriginal right to the land protected under their treaties and British imperial law.

Alex viewed the administration of Mi'kmaw territory by Canada and provincial governments as a conspiracy by settlers to evade the imperial rule of law and the Crown's obligations to the Mi'kmaw people. The position paper reasoned that under the terms of the 1763 proclamation, neither Canada nor Nova Scotia ever had legal authority to deprive the Mi'kmaq of lands reserved by the treaties, or of the right to gain a livelihood from the territory reserved for the Mi'kmaq, including for profitable work and for an adequate diet. Mi'kmaq never lost *de jure* ownership of their original national territory.

In 1978, a little over a year and a half after the submission of these arguments, the Department of Indian Affairs rejected Mi'kmaw land claims in Nova Scotia on the advice of the Department of Justice. Federal lawyers argued, contrary to the ruling in the *Isaac* case, that "law" had "superseded" all Indian title in Nova Scotia. They contended that the actions of successive pre-Confederation and post-Confederation governments in opening Mi'kmaw lands to settlement had the effect of superseding Indian title in all areas other than Indian reserves.

Alex was not surprised or discouraged by the decision. He knew we would never succeed in correcting injustices when dealing with politicians and bureaucrats. He was also amused by the government lawyers' blatantly racist theory, pointing out that they were saying that individuals, as long as they were white, could freely disregard historic treaties and acts that protected non-white people. The law was merely a camouflage for racial politics. He stayed true to his ancestors' teachings and vision. He would not grow discouraged, but was fortified by his faith in the oral histories and imagined what could be. He requested that Ottawa submit the legal issues to court, which Ottawa refused. He asked how they could ignore the *Isaac* case, and asked for a more reasoned elaboration of "superseded by law." He directed us to submit specific land claims to Indian Affairs, but noted that the team should not expect anything more than endless meetings with little results on the claims.

Alex felt that the entire federal strategy was "stall, talk, and delay, and hope that we die." Alex insisted that Mi'kmaq become organized, educated, strategic thinkers, like our ancestors. He directed the team to focus on affirming the Aboriginal and treaty rights of the Mi'kmaq in the proposed constitutional amendment bill. He viewed the constitution reforms of Canada as a site of the cumulative transformation of Canada. He viewed the treaty imperative as similar to music in that it was a succession of steps and the cadence that finished the scheme that began with the Mi'kmaw treaties with the king. He saw that the affirmation of the treaties would make Mi'kmaw life less one of imprisonment on reservations.

Our first initiative was the publication of "Maple Leaf, or Fig Leaf: What is Canada Hiding?" a comprehensive guide to including

Mi'kmaq specifically, and other Indian nations and tribes generally, in the proposed Canadian constitutional reform. Alex insisted on working with the national Indian organizations, gaining leverage by bringing Mi'kmaw skills and perspectives to the national stage. He was deeply troubled by the way Canada continued to ignore the treaties in constitutional reforms and speak condescendingly of Mi'kmaq as "our Indians." The team had much work to do, which included not only sitting down and talking with the Department of Indian Affairs but with the first ministers of Canada as well.

As part of the constitutional initiative, Alex wanted us to lobby for a conference on treaty fulfillment, and to find a way to launch a lawsuit in the United Kingdom to protect the imperial treaties with the Mi'kmaq. Short of funds, we partnered with the Alberta Indian Association. Together, we filed documents through British barristers so that neither the United Kingdom nor Canada knew exactly how we were involved. The English Court of Appeals, Lord Denning, in *R. v. Secretary of State for Foreign and Commonwealth Affairs, ex parte Indian Association of Alberta* [1982] 2 All E.R. 118 (C.A.), refused to grant an injunction against approval of the *Canada Act* (which patriated Canada's constution) because it affirmed and recognized Aboriginal treaty rights. However, he concurred in our view that the treaties remain valid, and that no parliament or legislature can change the terms of the treaties unless at the Indians' request. This was eloquent constitutional support for our perspective from a highly respected jurist.

Also related to the constitutional initiative, and what with the United Kingdom and Canada's ambivalence to the treaties, Alex asked our team to take the inherent right to self-determination of the Mi'kmaw treaties to the United Nations. He believed we could help create a new, if relatively slow, path toward self-determination, through international legislation of human rights, international public opinion and, perhaps, diplomatic pressure. At least in part through our efforts, the right of indigenous peoples to self-determination and implementation of their treaties was finally enshrined in the 2007 United Nations Declaration of the Rights of Indigenous Peoples.

Meanwhile, reckless provincial prosecutors sought to thwart our treaty rights, before the *Constitution Act, 1982* was enacted, by charging more Mi'kmaq for fishing- and hunting-statute violations, forcing them back to welfare. In 1982, the Nova Scotia courts, in the Cope fishing case and the *R. v. Simon* hunting case rejected the Mi'kmaw treaty defence that "free liberty of Hunting & Fishing as usual" as contained in the treaty of 1752, which precludes provincial regulations. Nova Scotia courts ruled that any right which the Mi'kmaq may once have had to harvest wildlife outside of reserves was extinguished "by Crown grant to others or by occupation by the white man"; that is, treaty rights are superseded by the actions of government employees. The Nova Scotia Court of Appeals also stated that the treaty was effectively terminated in 1753, when some Mi'kmaq attacked some Englishmen.

The Supreme Court of Canada allowed an appeal in the *Simon* case and affirmed the right to hunt under the treaty of 1752. It held that the treaty continues to be in force and was never extinguished, soundly rejecting the reasoning of Nova Scotia courts since the 1929 *R. v. Syliboy* decision. The Supreme Court agreed that hunting was an Aboriginal right that existed since before the treaty, and shielded Mi'kmaw hunters from Nova Scotia laws. They did not address the question of the effect of the recent amendment (1982) to the Constitution of Canada that protects "aboriginal and treaty rights" from infringement. Alex saw the *Simon* appeal as a tipping point, but the gvernments of Canada and Nova Scotia ignored the decision and retaliated by attempting to break up Alex's team. This generated another level of crisis, but Alex was determined to make government officials respect the ruling of Canada's highest court to the letter and end their estrangement from justice and adherence to the supreme law of Canada.

In 1999, in *R. v. Marshall*, the Supreme Court found that the 1760-1761 treaties affirmed the right of the Mi'kmaq to continue to provide for their own sustenance by trading the products of their hunting, fishing and other activities for what in 1760 was termed their "necessaries." Significantly, the justices shared Alex's perspective that the individual Mi'kmaq treaties were interconnected and were verbal, and were not limited to the written texts on the Crown's side. The "real treaty" is the understanding of the parties, as reflected in the context underlying the negotiations, as opposed to the surviving written record which, the court ruled, is simply one more piece of evidence of the parties' intentions. In this spirit, the court held that the 1760-1761 Mi'kmaw treaties intended to include rights that were part of an earlier Wabanaki Confederacy treaty, which included the Mi'kmaq, that served as a framework for later treaty discussions.

This decision resulted in a dramatic backlash in Atlantic Canada. On a motion for a rehearing by non-Mi'kmaw fishers, the Supreme Court took the extraordinary step, in *R v. Marshall* (No. 2), of explaining the regulation of the treaty rights, which was an issue not addressed in its original *Marshall* decision. The justices explained that the "necessaries" provision in the 1760-1761 treaties was essentially limited to acquiring food, clothing and housing. It did not extend to income-generating activities such as logging or developing offshore natural-gas deposits or a commercial fishery, although the justices left open the possibility of submitting persuasive historical evidence and arguments in future cases. Nonetheless, Canada has had to expend roughly half a billion dollars to indirectly implement the *Marshall* decisions, providing access to the regulated fishery for Mi'kmaq under federal authority rather than treaty rights.

The Supreme Court's caution in *Marshall* did not stop the Mi'kmaq from asserting the right to commercial logging in Nova Scotia and New Brunswick, both of which joined in charging Mi'kmaq under provincial legislation, forcing Mi'kmaq to defend themselves in provincial court. Alex worried that the defence lawyers were combining too many complex constitutional issues in fighting these matters. He had consistently advocated an incremental approach that presented the courts with one legal issue at a time. He also worried that public reaction to *Marshall* would pressure the judiciary, and he was concerned that overly broad Mi'kmaw interpretations of the original *Marshall* decision had contributed to the Supreme Court of Canada ultimatey narrowing its ruling.

Alex felt the time was not right to try to go beyond *Marshall*, but the Mi'kmaq had to be defended against the charges. In its consolidated cases in Stephen Marshall (no relation to Donald) and thirty-four other Mi'kmaq in Nova Scotia and Joshua Bernard, a Mi'kmaq from New Brunswick (*R. v. Marshall; R. v. Bernard*), the Supreme Court concluded in 2005 that the trading clause in the 1760-1761 treaties did not extend to commercial logging or the right to harvest and dispose of trees. The justices ruled that the treaties only protect the right to practice traditional 1760s-era trading activities in the modern context. They said the Mi'kmaq had not proven by evidence that they were engaged in commercial logging at the time of the treaties. The court noted that this interpretation did not preclude the possibility of treaty rights evolving as a result of changes in the economy or new technology.

In the *Sappier/Grey* case (*R. v. Sappier; R. v. Gray*), the defence returned to Alex's incremental approach. The Supreme Court affirmed here that the Mi'kmaq and Maliseet enjoyed Aboriginal rights, as communal rights, to engage in logging on Crown lands for "personal use" as opposed to commercial purposes. The court stated the neither Nova Scotia nor New Brunswick had convincingly shown that pre-Confederation laws had extinguished this Aboriginal right. While narrowly focused on harvesting timber for personal use, this decision implicitly rejects the argument against Mi'kmaw land claims that Ottawa has relied on since 1982: that any Aboriginal rights have been "superseded by [post-Confederation] law."

According to *Sappier/Grey*, any power to extinguish Aboriginal rights rested in the imperial Crown during the colonial period. There was no clear evidence that colonial legislatures had ever been granted this power. In any event, the legislation relied upon by the Crown as proof of extinguishment was regulatory in nature and did not meet the high standard of demonstrating a clear intent to extinguish the Aboriginal right to harvest wood for domestic use.

In response to these Mi'kmaw victories, the governments of Nova Scotia and New Brunswick attacked the procedural fairness of Mi'kmaq litigating constitutional issues in summary-conviction proceedings initiated under provincial regulations. While the provinces themselves had instigated these criminal proceedings, they argued that the rulings on appeal, upholding Aboriginal and treaty rights, were prospectively clouding the property rights of non-parties, which is to say non-Mi'kmaw people.

As Alex stressed, this strategy was another form of the political argument, based on race and colonialism, that attempted to vindicate colonial governments' failure to maintain the Crown's promises in the treaties with the Mi'kmaq, and unjustly and unlawfully granting property rights to non-Mi'kmaq without the Crown purchasing the territory from the Mi'kmaq. The provinces were pretending to be concerned about justice and fairness but had no qualms about re-victimizing Mi'kmaw people by prosecuting them for trying to feed themselves and make a livelihood. Alex observed that all of these criminal cases, and the growing expenditure of money and time on litigation, could have been avoided by Canada accepting the Mi'kmaw land claim and sitting down to negotiate a comprehensive settlement.

Some justices of the Supreme Court of Canada noted that these Mi'kmaw cases have little to do with the criminality of the accused and might be more proper subjects of civil actions. Justice Louis LeBel suggested that, in future, when constitutional-rights issues arise in the context of summary-conviction proceedings the provinces should consider seeking a temporary stay of the charges to allow the Mi'kmaq to litigate the underlying issues as a civil matter. However, Aboriginal and treaty rights continue to be asserted by placing the freedom of individual Mi'kmaw defendants in jeopardy—because the provinces prefer to criminalize Mi'kmaq, many of whom are impoverished—awakening from their diminished existence and understanding what they are entitled to hope for and realize in their lives.

Against the power of the federal and provincial governments to absolve Canada of its treaty obligations to the Mi'kmaq, Alex Denny in his lifetime had achieved much of his strategy to an astonishing magnitude, generating a most important episode in Canadian and Mi'kmaw history. He was a great leader, full of empathy and friendship, able to walk in other's shoes and see through their eyes. He mobilized Mi'kmaq to seize the initiative collectively, conceptualized their grievances and proposed solutions. He guided Mi'kmaq through protests, historical research, matters of language and identity, litigation and the political system, to create a constitutional framework within which a new future for the Mi'kmaq could be realized. More often than not, the forces Alex marshalled accomplished the profound change they dared to seek—creating a larger existence of Mi'kmaq by justice and law in the present, toward an emerging future.

It is often said that politics is the art of achieving the possible. Alex invented the art of transforming the seemingly impossible into a legal reality. Many Mi'kmaq, and very few Canadians, understand just how far-reaching Alex Denny's incandescent influence was on the national and international indigenous movements from 1960 to 2000. His intriguing movement that combined spirituality with constitutionality has not been commonly understood by Mi'kmaq or Atlantic Canadians, because the treaty imperative has had to overcome serious setbacks and governmental obstacles that resisted acknowledging Mi'kmaq treaty rights and giving them a chance to thrive. The treaty imperative had to overcome the contrived misinformation campaign of governments. The responses of Canada and the Atlantic provinces to the Supreme Court's decisions on the treaties echoes J. M. Coetzee writing, in *Waiting for the Barbarians*, that "one thought alone preoccupies the submerged mind of Empire, how not to end, how not to die, how to prolongs its era."

Alex Denny's treaty imperative movement transformed the United Nations, Canada and the Mi'kmaq. He transformed the Constitution of Canada and the human rights of the United Nations. He sporadically opened the eyes of humanity to the great injustice Atlantic Canadians had concealed. But he knew that none can or should expect a transformation overnight; he urged everyone to think of the treaties as living treaties. Finding justice was complex and hard for everyone. There were no shortcuts. "Whatever solution we find," Alex said, "will necessarily be incomplete in our lifetime." He urged that Mi'kmaq can never be allowed to lose their way again or slip into a comfortable silence or settle for symbolic gestures with injustice. Mi'kmaq had to struggle with uncomfortable and inconvenient truths about racism, colonialism and prejudice that infect Canadian thought for lasting and living change.

Mi'kmaw leaders who created a trail for others were called *atwigen* or *niganawitgen*. Alex Denny cherished the trail of ancestors in the treaties and embodied a renewal of that trail for the Mi'kmaq nation in his lifetime. The current generations of Mi'kmaq do not fully understand the Mi'kmaw knowledge and law that is foundational in generating the treaty-rights framework. Defiant governments have attempted to prevent the passionate and informed determination of the Mi'kmaw to explain the treaties to their electorates, and denied the need to constitutionally reconcile the treaties and create better lives for Mi'kmaq. Thus, many challenges and problems remain to complete his journey and the treaty imperative. In this journey, knowledgeable Mi'kmaq will carry a heavy load to educate about the Mi'kmaw treaties. But the spirit and passion of Alex Denny will be a constant colleague in such journey. And that will be a wonderful experience, and a precious and extraordinary gift.

Russel Barsh

The Personality of a Nation

I vaguely remember picking wild raspberries with my grandmother. Perhaps I was four years old. The tart aroma of the raspberries is still with me, along with my memories of my grandparents: two quiet, mannered Victorians born in the 1880s; one to a comfortably established small-town cloth merchant whose eldest son trained horses for Polish aristocrats, and the other to impoverished peasants too poor to afford shoes or own a family home, who slept with their cows and chickens for warmth. Both families fled the land of walnuts and cloudberries between Vilnya and Minsk to escape poverty, serfdom, ethnic purges and conscription into a colonizing foreign army. They left behind all but a thin shadow of their ancestors' belief in a benevolent, patriarchal God, but retained a fierce and unyielding preoccupation with social justice.

My fascination with ants and beetles made me train to be a scientist and a teacher, but when my grandfather died during my senior year at university, I decided that pursuing a career in social justice needed to come first. The following year, beginning law school (to the dismay of my science professors), I met Sa'kej Henderson, and that is where this story begins.

In September 1981, I was drafted by the Mi'kmaw Grand Council to attend meetings at the United Nations in Geneva, and to investigate the possibility of enlisting European support for Mi'kmaw assertions of Aboriginal and treaty rights in the Atlantic region. For the next twenty years, working around European capitols and U.N. offices in Geneva and New York, I had an unusual vantage point to reflect on the Mi'kmaq national movement, compare it with indigenous peoples' movements on other continents, and try to interpret it to the representatives of other states and peoples.

All cultures and peoples are not alike, notwithstanding our essential humanness, and national movements are not alike, too. They may invoke the same principles of law and essential justice, speak from similar histories of colonization and repression, and aspire to the same broad goal of meaningful collective self-determination, but political movements are made of people—people speaking different languages, digesting their experiences in somewhat different ways, and imagining each their own kind of promised land. This is the greatest strength as well as the greatest weakness of nationalisms. Nationalisms are collective dreams, but who are the dreamers? It is the hearts of the dreamers that beauty and nightmares can be born from the same laws and histories.

We can begin with the treaties between the Crown and Aborinial peoples that are now enshrined in Canada's constitution. It is tempting, but misleading, to regard them as mere exchanges of pecuniary promises, like shopping lists or purchase orders. So what if they appear on paper. So what if they tend to be read by the courts. "Spirit and intent" must be more than an exhortation to read the text of treaties liberally. At their best, treaties were made by people that agreed, often reluctantly, to live together. Whatever words are written on paper, the results depend largely on the ability of the parties to live together. "The treaties are about love and kindness," I heard a Dakota traditional scholar explain. For that very reason, the same words on paper mean something different on Cape Breton Island than in Brantford or Vancouver Island. Not necessarily more or less, but they may speak to a different relationship because a treaty, in essence, assembles a marriage of different peoples.

I would contend, for the same reason, that implementing treaties means nothing if it does not reach into the everyday lives of Aboriginal and Euro-Canadian people. Kindness and friendship at the grocery store and the hockey rink mean more, in the long term, than tax breaks, building codes or property lines—and what is more, the humanity of our regard for one another is essentially what makes it possible to get along with different tax and rule schemes. Self-government or autonomy thrive amid goodwill and neighbourliness.

But if the historical agreements that formed the landscape of Canada are only as meaningful as the neighbourhoods people build, the realization of treaties is as different as indigenous peoples are different. Why would the free development of Mi'kmaw society in Nova Scotia or the Gaspé Pennisula be the same as (for example) the free development of Blackfoot or Kainai society in southern Alberta? It is problematic that Canadian leaders still seem to think that treaty relationships with Aboriginal peoples can be standardized, or deliniated like shopping lists. Shopping lists are not human relationships.

In the same spirit, different Aboriginal peoples have imagined/interpreted their treaties differently and, as a consequence, organized and directed their treaty-rights efforts in different ways. They can be rich in legal arguments and financial demands, led by lawyers and accountants; they can rely on restoring historical memory, on cultural and linguistic renewal, or economic recovery; they have been top-down, bottom-up and (some would argue) mixed up. Central to each indigenous national movement, however, is a challenge of faith: faith in its legitimacy and, equally important, faith that its members can build a better society for themselves if they are given the freedom of opportunity.

Mohandas Gandhi once remarked that every people has the right to govern itself, no matter how badly. They must be free to make their own mistakes. All nations are struggling to achieve their dreams in the fog of human imperfection. Self-determination is not a guarantee of a happy result. Rather, it is an opportunity to make the best of ourselves, and possibly fail. This is fundamentally a human process for every nation, an amalgam of history, culture and, most of all, of the minds, efforts, genius and limitations of individuals.

Nations do not free themselves and flower just because they are real or just because they are right. They are works of art shaped by many hands. The Mi'kmaq nation is what it is today because of individual life stories. Or, we might say, the treaties are the copyright to the great novel that is Mi'kmaq.

—

It isn't enough to be correct on facts and law. Nations ultimately rise and fall on imagination: belief in themselves, belief in their existence and legitimacy recognizedby other people. This kind of belief does not arise from knowledge alone, moreover. It is a human emotion of faith and confidence, and ultimately one of hope.

People may dream of their past, but they live in their present, and are uncertain, if not anxious, about their future. It is far easier to accept the present as the future than it is to imagine a future that traces a different line from the past. Dreams can be beautiful and inspiring, but people do not trust mere ideas. Unless they are utterly destitute or desperate (not a secure starting-point for envisioning a new society), people are most likely to believe each other: the neighbours they love, that tease their children and make them laugh. Great nations are inspired by ideas but are built of personal relationships. They must really exist, in people's experience of one another, before they can exist as institutions.

Not all national projects are benevolent or nourishing. Old nationalisms have recently re-emerged in Europe with unquestionable historical legitimacy but tainted contemporary motives, led by suspect men and women. They may succeed and produce nations that aspire to rob and dispossess their neighbours. Whatever the legitimacy of their underlying nationalistic cause, a new or renewed nation is shaped fundamentally by its prophets and advocates—perhaps, I should say, like religions.

A great nation aspires to improve itself, to discover and cultivate its own genius, to contribute freely and generously to the peace and well-being of other nations, to add and not subtract from the great and mysterious puzzle that is humanity. Great nations, as Rabindranath Tagore and Gandhi believed, must be imagined by great souls. A nation's historical identity and nominal legitimacy are no guarantee that it will succeed in liberating itself, respecting and nourishing its citizens, or refraining from using power to oppress others.

It was the good fortune of the modern Mi'kmaq nation to have Alex Denny as its most dedicated believer.

In the 1980s, archival spade work was rapidly unearthing much of Mi'kmaw history, in particular the circumstances of 18th-century land-and-sea warfare between the Mi'kmaq, their French allies and the British, and the eventual peace settlement between the Mi'kmaq and British that opened the Maritimes to peaceful co-existence with British settlers.

Most Mi'kmaq would have none of it, however. The idea of a pre-British, indigenously literate, Christian, Francophone, seafaring state was too outlandish. Indeed, the assertion that British authorities would so respect Mi'kmaq tenacity, and so value the friendship of this small native Atlantic nation, as to respect its borders and extend British passports and cooperation, seemed to many 20th-century Mi'kmaq so outlandish as to be comical folly.

Residential schools, ignorant politicians, misguided bureaucrats, rising Canadian nationalism, neglectful scholarship, inadequate books and biased mass media had all eroded Mi'kmaw memory and self-confidence to a point that even the evidence of public archives could not shake the conviction that federal and provincial governements must be right: there were no treaty Indians in the Maritimes, if indeed there were Indians at all.

I began assisting Alex in 1978, and I remember Mi'kmaw people laughing at him. "There's no treaty," people said. "You can't fight the government, Alex." Hopelessness, reinforced by disinformation and abysmal education.

The harder people insisted on the historical inevitably of the status quo, the more Alex teased them, often profanely—always with gorgeous turns of phrase in the Mi'kmaw language, rude and clever at the same time, like the clowns in Shakespeare's plays. In fact, there is an ancient tradition of clowning in tribal cultures. I first appreciated the role of tribal clowns when I was studying traditional agriculture in the highlands of Viti Levu, Fiji, in 1970. In the communities where I lived, widows often became *wediwedi*, or clowns, that ruthlessly shadowed and teased snooty chiefs, stingy farmers and snotty adolescents with farcical gestures and noises. (I was teased for my canvas backpack of scientific gear.) No one was too powerful or mean spirited to miss the point.

In the same way, Alex relentlessly teased his detractors and inspired his admirers and friends. To be sure, this was ostensibly a question of evidence, facts and documents: a matter of recalling history from forgetfulness. But feelings lay at the heart of the matter. Mi'kmaw people, like long-marginalized people everywhere, had been silenced and made to feel stupid. When they criticized their Euro-Canadian neighbours, they were ridiculed, dismissed like ignorant children, until they no longer felt courageous in their own beliefs and sense of injustice. Reason and evidence are not powerless in the face of peoples' well-learned distrust of themselves, but can be terrifying in the absence of laughter. It can be easier to laugh at our own ignorance, our own clumsy efforts to be human, than to go to confession (as it were) before a sombre judge.

There is a subtle truth behind the ways that most oppressed peoples joke among themselves at their own expense (and are outraged when their "inside jokes" are repeated by others, outside of their community). Humour can be a distillation of pain and longing, a way of sharing distress—and, in the same breath, sharing hope for justice. Confronting an inebriated neighbour with the words "you're a drunk" is a statement of power, superiority, a challenge to a duel. Saying "have you heard the story about the drunk who..." is an act of love and empathy.

And so it was that the treaties came back to life through laughter and love rather than reason alone. A purely legalistic revival of Mi'kmaw identity without the self-deprecating humour may have been possible, but I do not believe that it would have produced a similar social or cultural result. Laughing your way back to self-respect reinforces your sense of humanity and humility. You can better appreciate the hurt that others feel, even the fear and bewilderment of your former oppressors. Legal arguments and judicial victories, by themselves, can make the victors self-righteous and more likely to turn their newfound power against their neighbours and supposed enemies.

I learned during my years in diplomacy abroad to avoid political movements that had humourless leaders. The strong, silent types were the ones that were just waiting for the opportunity to string up their opponents. Leaders that could laugh at themselves and tease their critics, that saw irony and absurdity as well as tragedy in their own histories, were to be trusted with the future.

Thus, for me, one of the defining moments of the Mi'kmaw campaign for political recognition overseas was the 1983 meeting of Mi'kmaw Grand Council Kji-keptin (Grand Captain) Alex Denny and the Austrian Chancellor Bruno Kreisky, in Vienna, which I had painstakingly arranged over two years of briefings with Austrian academics and officials. It was a breakthrough in "optics" insofar as a well-respected European leader was receiving a Mi'kmaw leader, publicly and with great fanfare, at a head-of-state level. It would also have had important material consequences, had Kreisky's Social Democratic Party not lost power just months later; economic and cultural exchanges were on the table.

But for me, the meeting was most memorable for the moment when Alex placed a collar of *ulnapskok* beads over the chancellor's head and discovered that it was just a bit smaller than required. "Well, boy," the kji-keptin exclaimed, "you've got the same problem that I do: your nose is too big!" Both leaders laughed heartily.

That shared laughter convinced me of the capacity of Mi'kmaq to achieve what Keptin (Captain) Noel Denny imagined when I was first sent abroad. "It's about time," he told me, "that Mi'kmaq make its contribution to the community of nations."

"So," the reader may think, "I suppose it's comforting to know that world leaders are human, after all." But it is more than that. Leaders who that do not take themselves too seriously are healers, not strongmen. They inspire change, and do not break backs. Only this kind of leader can rebuild a people's confidence in governing itself, with justice.

—

Physical evidence played a curious role in the gradual transformation of Mi'kmaw self-consciousness. Abundant archival corroboration of the British treaties had already been unearthed by 1980, but as every Aboriginal person in Canada knows, paper can lie. The memory stones surrounding Kejimikujik Lake are more difficult to dismiss.[1] Hence the re-discovery, partial decipherment and renewal of Mi'kmaw "hieroglyphs" has been as much a contribution to Mi'kmaw political self-consciousness as the publication of 17th-century French diplomatic letters and 18th-century British treaties with the Mi'kmaq.

I recall very vividly a visit I paid to Keptin John Joe Sark nearly thirty years ago. He had been told of the discovery of a memory stone in the brush near a railroad track, so we went to look. After some thrashing and slashing along the abandoned track, we found it: a small boulder, too large for us to lift, engraved with Mi'kmaw ideograms, a sailing ship, and an 18th-century date. "Just think of it," John Joe said, reverentially, as we sketched the inscription. "My ancestors' hands touched this stone, centuries ago."

In the same spirit, Alex Denny directed much of our attention to confirming the existence of a beaded Mi'kmaw wampum belt—mentioned ever so briefly in a forgotten scholarly journal article—in the possession of the Vatican. A grainy printed photograph was enough to reconstruct its most likely purpose and meaning. When (in my formal diplomatic capacity) I first communicated with the Vatican about the belt, the papal secretary of state did not deny its existence—only its legal significance. But the physical object itself grew into something of an icon of mythic proportions for Mi'kmaw historical legitimacy, in which faith alone was not enough.

Alex fundamentally understood the power of objects, symbols and mass media to elevate an assertion of historical identity into an incontrovertible modern-day truth. The most important difference between contemporary Mi'kmaw nationalism and the modern experience of many other treaty First Nations in North America, I believe, is the breadth of its cultural and intellectual foundations. The treaties are poles in the frame of this national wikuom, but they are only a part of what holds it up. Mi'kmaw nationality is not derived from, or defined by, British law, Crown treaties or Canadian constitutional law.

The issues for Alex, appropriately enough (but so often missed in movements for redemption of historical nations and peoples), was that Mi'kmaq both believe in themselves and believe in the *best* of their historical legacy: to believe in themselves so that they would be armoured against the myriad excuses that Canadian society invented to justify the disappearance of Mi'kmaw society; to believe in the best of being Mi'kmaq so that they would become a healthy nation with a contribution to make to the world.

To achieve this, external recognition was paradoxically essential. A people that has been demeaned by the authorities for generations finds it difficult to see beyond the caricatures and smears that have been applied to them. They feel the injustice, but are awash in rationalizations enunciated, confidently, by people more powerful and successful than themselves. Like a confessional in church or in a psychotherapist's office, the process of self-liberation begins with a witness—an authority—that can say, unreservedly and with complete conviction, "you are right, after all."

And this requires participation in the wider world: for Mi'kmaw people at the end of the 20th century, sharing in governing the Atlantic provinces and defending the lives and freedom of others—

from children of the conflicts in Ireland to the indigenous peoples of other continents. A nation that looks outward is stronger than one that thinks primarily about its own needs and complaints.

After pressing the case for treaty partnership in Canada with grudging results, the Mi'kmaw Grand Council, the Sante' Mawiomi, resolved in 1981 to look abroad for recognition and justice. I was sent to Europe for reconnaissance with a loosely organized delegation of mainly Haudenosaunee and Lakota diplomats that crisscrossed the continent visiting universities and government offices, attending conferences, speaking wherever local groups had arranged a forum or a media interview. In four months I visited ten countries, often sleeping on night trains. The Swiss city of Reinfelden treated us to a formal state dinner complete with guardsmen in medieval uniforms. Our hosts in Milan turned out to be anarchists. In Berlin, the venue was a solitary chair placed on the Kurfurstendamm—akin to New York City's Fifth Avenue—beneath a handwritten cardboard sign inviting passersby: *sprechen Sie mit den Indianern* (speak to the Indian).

My initial assessment was that there was a long, long way to go before European leaders would even contemplate recognizing indigenous nations politically, thereby potentially antagonizing Canada and the United States. Popular interest and sympathy for American Indians was widespread, but laden with misconceptions, romanticism and stereotypes. Like celebrities, indigenous people were expected to be glamorous and entertaining, not carrying briefing notes in attaché cases. Public enthusiasm generally did not extend into pragmatic, legalistic government offices, which on the whole regarded Aboriginal people as semi-literate, naive and certainly misguided to think they could do any better than be Canadian and American citizens.

Nonetheless, the United Nations Commission on Human Rights (as it was known then) was concluding a ten-year global review of the status and conditions

Russel Barsh at the United Nations in Geneva, September 1981, at the conference on indigenous peoples that, eventually, led to the UN declaration and permanent forum. It was his first meeting representing the Mi'kmaw Grand Council. Press photographer unknown. Courtesy Russel Barsh.

of indigenous peoples, and European human-rights organizations and academics were generally confident that this would soon become a focus of international policy and programs—not necessarily in North America, where Aboriginal peoples enjoyed relatively favourable economic conditions, but certainly in developing countries, where mass destruction of indigenous peoples continued.

It quickly became apparent to us that Mi'kmaw people were neither as glamorous as the Lakota (in European eyes) nor as urgently threatened with violence as indigenous nations in Amazonia or Indonesia. The kji-keptin reasoned that Mi'kmaq could nonetheless gain credibility and recognition by working for the survival and liberation of indigenous and tribal peoples elsewhere in the world. A critical first step in this direction was our effort to organize and coordinate a U.N.-accredited non-governmental organization (NGO) that could offer an umbrella for other Aboriginal nations to attend and advocate at international meetings. The United Nation's Four Directions Council made its debut at Geneva four years after the first Mi'kmaw mission.

Recognition must be earned. Alex appreciated that this meant behaving always as a responsible, generous and intelligent nation in dealings with states and peoples—taking a constructive role in a wide range of social-justice issues globally. To achieve this, it was essential that we develop a network of diplomatic relationships to acquire reliable and up-to-date information on issues discussed at U.N. meetings, consider issues carefully before making public statements, and be cautious of associating with particular governments or organizations. Our goal was to grow into "middle power" status such as Ireland, Portugal and Australia enjoyed at the time: small nations that were broadly regarded as unbiased, independent, principled and helpful.

Middle-power status is hard work. A successful middle power is an elder brother to less fortunate nations and a referee in conflicts between weaker and stronger states. With successful mediation comes prestige, diplomatic favours and greater responsibility. A poor choice of issues and allies leads to political isolation.

During the years that I coordinated Mi'kmaw influence in Geneva and New York, we were frequently urged to make alliances and embrace causes that posed hard choices and involved great risks. Do we accept public support of the African National Congress? What about the Palestine Liberaton Organization, Cuba or the Soviet Union, all of which were eager to align with the cause of indigenous peoples?

A case in the 1980s nearly divided the international indigenous movement irreparably: the armed conflict between the indigenous peoples of Nicaragua's Atlantic coast and that country's revolutionary leaders in the capital, Managua. Many North American Indian activists were attracted to the anti-capitalist ideology of the new Nicaraguan governement, and the ruling Sandinistas were delighted to reciprocate for U.S. and Canadian Indian support by taking a strong stand on Indian land and cultural rights at U.N. meetings.

There was only one small problem: Managua was speaking out internationally on Indian rights while taking military action against some of its own indigenous peoples. At the same time, the Miskito and other Indians of the Atlantic coast of Nicaragua were not entirely unblemished. They were taking financial and military aid from the U.S. Reagan administration, which viewed Nicaragua's dissident Indians as a convenient wedge against what Washington conceived as an upstart communist government in America's backyard. Which side should Mi'kmaw delegations befriend and defend?

I was in contact with both Miskito and Sandinista leaders, but the deciding views were those of Guatemalan, Honduran and Panamanian Indian spokespeople who told me that the Sandinistas were more naive than hypocritical, and argued at the same time that it was important to oppose killing Indians, regardless of U.S. meddling. We took the middle ground—a very uncomfortable position at the time—and criticized Managua for violence publicly while maintaining friendly conversations behind the scenes with leaders on both sides. I would like to think that we helped some Nicaraguan political leaders see the Miskito side of the conflict, and to back down from their belief that the Atlantic rebellion was solely due to CIA *agent provocateurs*.

Another kind of difficult situation involved deciding who was indigenous. Many different groups found their way to the U.N. Working Group on Indigenous Populations, as it was then called, after its establishment in 1982. Indians of the Americas were only the beginning. Tribal peoples from Africa and Asia presented a wider range of situations and histories. What about "ethnic groups" in Russia (then still the U.S.S.R.) and China; or the ethnic, linguistic and religious "minorities" of Europe itself? Are these really comparable? Are they genuine? And what of the power of their states to hurt our cause by moving from support to opposition? The Ainu people of Hokkaido, Japan, were a particularly interesting case in point. Japan had not recognized the Ainu as a distinct ethnic group, much less an indigenous people with some degree of inherent rights to their historical territory. For five centuries, the Japanese state had underscored the ideal of a single, undivided Aboriginal Japanese people and language (the "Yamato race"), within which the Ainu were simply backward and poor northerners. Coincidentally, a former university student of mine, Takemasa Teshima, had studied the history of Japanese policy toward the Ainu, and the Ainu leadership had recruited him as an adviser and translator. As so often is the case in politics and diplomacy, personal connections offer a bridge of trust. I met with Ainu leaders and concluded that they were not only genuine indigenous people, but a reliable and respectable ally that would not embarrass Mi'kmaq.

Our office sponsored the Ainu at their first U.N. meetings, politely answered some exaggerated protests from Tokyo, and had the satisfaction not only of seeing the Ainu be recognized, somewhat reluctantly, by the Japanese government, but also of watching Ainu leaders use their superior economic resources to support indigenous movements in many developing countries.

Another difficult call was the Roma, or "gypsies," of Eastern Europe, concentrated mostly within Hungary, Bulgaria and Romania. Roma human rights activists were immediately attracted to the indigenous movement, which they regarded as philosophically consistent with their own culture and aspirations. We did not fully appreciate, at the time, how Roma are descendants of a thousand-year-old tribal diaspora from northern India. They appeared to be very European outwardly, but Aboriginal in spirit—not entirely unlike the Sami of the Nordic countries, who had helped establish the World Council of Indigenous Peoples in the 1970s. While we debated what position to take, Roma intellectuals decided to pursue a different course (as a "minority") under European human-rights conventions.

At times, help at a critical moment came from an unexpected but suspect corner. The first clients of the Mi'kmaw international initiative were Labrador's Innu. Displaced by mining and North Atlantic Treaty Organization (NATO) military bases, marginalized and impoverished by official neglect, Innu were neighbours and cousins, speaking a language closely related to Mi'kmaw. It was impossible to ignore them, although there were endless issues with representation and the Innu leaders who emerged on the international stage were more extreme in their views of Canada than the kji-keptin. We found ourselves, as a disillusioned treaty partner of the Crown in Canada, assisting the cause of non-treaty cousins that did not feel the slightest bit British or Canadian. There was little we could do except create opportunities for Innu to speak for themselves.

Things came to a head over expanded NATO training flights that were believed to be scattering and stressing the caribou herds upon which many Innu families still relied to supply their meat. For Canada and Europe, this was a military matter that superseded any issues of land rights or subsistence hunting. We promised to secure a speaking slot for the Innu at the next meeting of the U.N. Commission on Human Rights. Their two spokesmen arrived on schedule, somewhat dazed from the transition to Europe, then languished in Geneva for two weeks while U.N. member states monopolized the commission's agenda, delaying the few hours of speaking time reserved for NGOs. The Four Directions Council was fourth or fifth on the NGO speaking list, but each day of meetings ended with a growing priority list of government speakers.

Frustrated, the Innu delegation informed me that they had to leave that same night. No further delay was possible. They were homesick and disappointed. As the hours passed, I realized that there was simply no way that the government speaker list would be finished before 10 p.m., when U.N. interpreters ordinarily went home. It was already late; several diplomats were returning to the meeting hall from a supper of cold sandwiches and coffee in the delegates lounge. At best, we had two hours to give the Innu their "day in court."

Desperate situations call for desperate measures. Which government remaining on the speakers list might be persuaded to trade its slot for two tired Innu caribou hunters? It would be unprecedented in any case, since governments had absolute priority for time on the agenda and I was unaware of any exceptions made in the past. Argentina? Nigeria? Syria? It was probably not worth asking. Western European countries on the list would be sympathetic, but they had their instructions, and would be unable to contact their foreign ministers in time to get approval, even if they wanted to help. No, it had to be one of the smaller countries that did not take the United Nations too seriously and had very little to gain or lose.

At that moment, I caught the eye of the first secretary of the Bulgarian delegation, a cordial but reserved young woman that I had kept at a discrete diplomatic distance, like all of the Soviet satellite countries of that time, which we considered low value and risky. She nodded and I walked over to her flag and sat behind her. "So," she said very softly, "what is it that you need?" "I need ten minutes for some Indian hunters from Labrador to speak," I said. "Well," she said without hesitation, setting aside the cigarette that always seemed to be on her lips (this was before the U.N. banned smoking from its meeting halls), "Bulgarians like Indians." She got up and walked to the desk where the speakers list was kept, crossed out Bulgaria and wrote in "Four Directions Council." A little after 9 pm the Innu were called upon to speak (after the secretariat confirmed the unusual decision of Bulgaria to cede its slot on the list), and at 9:40 p.m. they were in a cab to Geneva airport.

The Kanesatake (Oka) crisis in 1990 required a different kind of angle. I was in Geneva when the Mohawk confrontation with Québec provincial police and Canada's military began, and I learned about it in a 3 a.m. conference call with the kji-keptin and Aboriginal leaders from other regions of Canada. Mi'kmaw leaders were advocating a peaceful diplomatic response in the face of many appeals for more violent action. The upshot of the discussion was my assignment to extend all possible assistance to a Mohawk delegation that had already boarded a flight to Geneva.

Mohawk journalist and activist Ken Deer and I met at the Palais des Nations—the former League of Nations complex of the 1920s that is now the U.N. Office in Geneva—after breakfast. We agreed that our goal was to get Canada to explain its actions to the U.N. human-rights meetings that were then in session—not the commission, but its advisory sub-commission, a technical body of twenty-six individual "independent experts" (more or less, in both respects) attended by hundreds of human-rights NGOs. Securing a speaking slot for the Mohawks would be easy but relatively unprofitable, since the experts themselves would need to vote to "invite" the Canadian government to answer questions on the record. It would be far better to get one of the experts to broach the issue and suggest the invitation.

There was a Cuban expert on the panel, with whom I had worked in my capacity as one of the technical consultants to the U.N. working group on indigenous populations. I was certain he would help, but opposed to asking him. It would simply antagonize U.S. and Canadian diplomats, and unproductively; for them, Cuba would then become the issue, instead of Kanesatake. There were other sub-commission members with personal interests in the situation of indigenous peoples, but we did not necessarily want to expend their goodwill on a single conflict in Canada. We needed them to complete the drafting of the Declaration on the Rights of Indigenous Peoples, and for that they would do best to avoid confronting Canada at present. What we sought, and found in the Moroccan expert Halima Warzazi, was a very credible, moderate voice that had the respect of Canada and Europe, and no particular ties to indigenous NGOs or peoples.

Halima was well known for her key role in hammering the two U.N. Conventions of Human Rights through the U.N. Economic and Social Council in New York nearly two decades earlier. A pro-Western, humanist and feminist Muslim, Halima was very careful to avoid favouritism and ideology. I introduced her to Ken, as the representative of our Mohawk "elder brothers," and suggested that our goal was to keep Canada talking at the United Nations in the hope that that would reduce the likelihood of any shooting at Oka. She agreed. Just hours later, Halima took the floor at the sub-commission, and in the most friendly, positive terms possible, praised Canada's human-rights record and suggested that, surely, Canada would want the help of the United Nations in resolving the Oka crisis peacefully.

The next morning, the Canadian ambassador made the first of a dozen reports to the sub-commission on the evolving situation at Kanesatake, and answered the questions we had suggested to the expert members of the sub-commission. Everything was very polite and non-confrontational, but the point was not lost on Ottawa, and may have, in part, cost Canada its middle-power status at the United Nations—a privileged position that Ottawa could have saved if it had been more flexible and cooperative. I knew we made our point when an Indonesian government observer—a rather disturbing character who seemed to have the main task of denying genocide in Papua New Guinea—sidled over to my flag at the sub-commission, sat beside me and said, "how comforting it is to discover that your government [Canada] is as bad as mine."

The sub-commission voted to send a special observer to Oka. Québec authorities intercepted the U.N. envoy and detained him, creating a whole new incident for the world community to digest as it reassessed Canada's internal politics. I do not believe that the Oka crisis was necessarily resolved because of international criticism; however, it is very clear that international criticism of Canadian Aboriginal policies increased after Oka, and has become a lasting factor in Canadian politics, for better or worse.

Ten years later, I was at the U.N. General Assembly in New York, listening to a speech by the president of the International Monetary Fund about the new global economic order, when I felt a soft touch on my shoulder. It was Halima. "It is so good to see you," she said, "but this is all so very depressing."

―

Conflicts over strategy were commonplace among the indigenous organizations active on the international stage. Broadly speaking, there were three groupings of NGOs: indigenous organizations from non-democratic, mainly developing countries, where lands were still being confiscated and leaders shot or imprisoned; activists from the wealthiest Western countries, where indigenous people enjoyed the privilege of relative safety and legal protection, and were determined to seek "nationhood"; and a very small minority of indigenous peoples that were moderately secure, struggling for genuine partnerships with the states in which they lived, but willing to forego some of their own interests for sake of peoples less fortunate than themselves. It would not be inaccurate to refer to these groups as front-line, hard-line and moderate.

Mi'kmaq found themselves in the third group, together with many other Canadian Aboriginal people as well as the Sami and Ainu. Most leaders of the hard-line cluster were from the United States, Australia, Canada and New Zealand. Naturally, these two tendencies were over-represented at international meetings because they enjoyed greater personal freedom and financial resources to travel. Indeed, had elected U.S. tribal councils taken a greater interest in international affairs, they would have controlled the U.N. indigenous movement as much or more than the U.S. controlled the economic and military arms of the United Nations as a whole. But U.S. tribal councils were preoccupied with fiscal transfers, mining and casino expansion at home, so that nearly all American Indians attending U.N. meetings used AIM (American Indian Movement) or universities as their base. (Two U.S. tribal-council presidents that tentatively ventured into international politics and quickly distinguished themselves for their pragmatic views were both recalled by their own constituents for wasting funds on "junkets.")

Two interrelated strategic issues repeatedly divided the indigenous caucus at U.N. sessions: the relative priorities to be given political autonomy and socioeconomic needs; and the choice between an "all-or-nothing" position in negotiations and progressive steps. Our hard-liners wanted recognition of the full measure of international self-determination without limitation, including the possibility of independent statehood, and they wanted to make this a precondition for negotiating the terms of international instruments protecting indigenous peoples. Front-line indigenous nations sought as much

MicMac News, *1989, vol. 19 (10): 7. http://beatoninstitute.com/micmac-news-1989.*

physical security, local autonomy and international economic assistance as they could get, and were prepared to accept "half a loaf" as long as they could continue negotiating for more. Long-established players, such as anti-apartheid and women's rights organizations and U.N. operational (aid) agencies, supported the front-line viewpoint, while hard-line advocates argued that such was selling-out and would leave indigenous nations with minimal legal rights.

Matters came to a head during last-minute negotiations on the text of the revised International Labour Organization (ILO) convention on indigenous peoples, 1989, which resulted in references to the right of indigenous communities to "self-government" rather than "self-determination"; and to an obligation of states to obtain indigenous peoples' "informed consent [in] good faith" prior to any development of lands or natural resources, instead of an absolute right to territorial sovereignty and integrity. Moderates joined front-line indigenous nations in accepting the ILO (a U.N. agency) convention as a step in the right direction. Hard-liners walked out, opposed member states' ratification of the convention, and walked out again when a U.N. working group discussed acknowledging the convention as a relevant source of law.

We consulted with our front-line counterparts from Latin America and Asia at the meetings, and joined them in supporting the ILO convention. This attracted considerable ill will, on political and personal levels, for years. The convention is still unpopular with North American Aboriginal leaders, although it has become a critical legal lever in Latin America—not the least because it established a broad legal basis for inter-governmental agencies to provide technical and financial assistance directly to indigenous communities. A U.N. aid program is not a bulletproof vest, but I am convinced that lives were saved, and communities' health and security improved, by the greater international presence that the ratification of the ILO convention facilitated in many countries.

In this case and others, Mi'kmaq did not act out of self-interest, but from a sense of international responsibility in the spirit of Keptin Noel Denny's vision of a confident, generous, outward-looking Mi'kmaq nation. One sign that the Mi'kmaq were achieving visibility as a middle power, rather than merely as another victim of oppression, was our assignment by the "south group"—a consortium of third-world NGOs—to be their spokesman at the U.N. Commission on Human Rights one year: the Fourth World for the Third World.

—

A well-spoken and respected middle power has friends when it needs them. While the victim of outrageous oppression can appeal for assistance in the name of justice, it is better to rely on friends than the pity or sympathy of strangers. While Mi'kmaw chiefs and councils were negotiating and litigating treaty issues at home, the Sante' Mawiomi was making friends abroad. How much Mi'kmaq international initiatives affected Ottawa, I do not know, but I was aware that some of Canada's closest trade partners and socioeconomic allies were asking uncomfortable questions of Canadian diplomats.

Personality is an important part of politics, and even more so in diplomacy, where trust is the major currency. Systematic information gathering and patient networking with the representatives of other nations are indispensable, of course, but at the end of the day, a nation is known, in diplomatic circles, by the character of its representatives. It did not help the United States that State Department officials were almost uniformly impatient, uncooperative and condescending. Many countries admired American culture but utterly distrusted American diplomats. For a number of years, one of the most influential countries at the U.N. Commission on Human Rights was Portugal, chiefly on account of two young career diplomats—both women of humble origins—that were absolutely sincere and hardworking. (Indeed, this was a factor in the successful effort to liberate East Timor from Indonesian rule.) Nigeria and Senegal were consistently the major power brokers for sub-Saharan Africa, not because of wealth or military might but on account of the extraordinary people they sent to the United Nations, some of whom (ironically) were dispatched abroad to keep them away from power at home.

Mi'kmaw people were also fortunate in their leaders, and in their culture. Making a good impression was easy for the kji-keptin, and for other high-level leaders such as John Joe Sark, who often joined me at Geneva. Our team was naturally attracted to Ted Moses and the Grand Council of the Crees of Québec; like Alex Denny, Ted was a delightfully outgoing, magnetic personality who showed as much interest in global affairs and world peace as in the immediate circumstances of his homeland on James Bay. Once, when Erica-Irene Daes was making her opening remarks as the chair of a U.N. working group on indigenous populations, in her unmistakable, Greek-accented English, she made a point of expressing a warm welcome to "Mr. Ted Moses, Grand Chief of the Grrrees." Ted, who was seated next to me in the audience, cheerfully asked, rather loudly, "did she say *Greeks*?" It was a moment worthy of Alex.

Guatemalan activist Rigoberta Menchú and Timorese professor José Ramos-Horta were other members of a circle of indigenous people that shared growing moral influence at U.N. meetings for more than a decade. Menchú and Ramos-Horta both later won Nobel Peace Prizes, and Ramos-Horta became president of East Timor. Our mentor was Augusto Willemsen-Díaz, who had joined the United Nations in the 1940s as an idealistic young Guatemalan lawyer—and was the real author of the famous José Martínez Cobo-attributed report on "discrimination against indigenous populations" that launched the U.N. working group (I helped him compose the manuscript), as Cobo himself admitted carelessly at the U.N. sub-commission when he publicly thanked Augusto, "who completely, ah, well, who almost completely wrote my report for me." When he uttered those words, Augusto, who was in the audience beside me, slapped his forehead and cried, "Oh brother!" He preferred being quietly and effectively in the shadows.

The Mi'kmaw cause also benefited from many personal friendships among the government delegations, as well as poor policy and personnel choices by Canada. Under Prime Minister Pierre Elliott Trudeau, Canadian diplomats were an experienced, professional elite, and it would be fair to say that we learned a great deal about gaining and sustaining our middle-power status from Canada's example. Trudeau's U.N. representatives disagreed politely, lunched with us and worked hard to find compromise positions that we could share. To a certain extent, as professionals, they understood that Canada looked even better overseas when it treated its dissident indigenous nations with respect.

Everything changed with the accession of Brian Mulroney as prime minister in 1984. By the time the U.N. Human Rights Commission met in 1985, the middle ranks of Canada's foreign service had been pruned away and replaced by Conservative Party faithful, following the policy of the U.S. State Department to elevate ideology and political loyalty above experience in foreign affairs. The Canadian diplomats we encountered henceforth were uncooperative at best, and frequently hostile. They wanted to win, not to build consensus. Leadership in the field of indigenous rights quickly shifted from Canada to Australia (which switched to Labour when Canada turned Conservative), leaving Canada more vulnerable to public criticism. In the early 1990s, Mexico, Bolivia and Colombia each exercised a few years of significant positive influence on the development of U.N. indigenous policy because of individual diplomats such as Colombia's Ana Botero and Martín von Hildebrand.

—

Paradoxically, Mi'kmaw Catholicism played some role in developments around the U.N. system. We made a point of maintaining the best possible relationships with the representatives of the Holy See (a U.N. member state), consulting with them on a formal basis with frequent reference to the ulnapskok or wampum concordat, mentioned earlier. The Vatican had its own reasons to take an interest in indigenous issues: millions of Catholic indigenous peoples in Latin America, which has become the stronghold of world Catholicism (and to judge from the current policies of Pope Francis, the foundation for a return to the social roots of Christianity that accord very well with Mi'kmaw culture and theology). The kji-keptin and I were certain that the Vatican had an important role to play in our international strategy, and the work of Keptin Sark, Joe B. Marshall and Sa'kej Henderson on recovering the ulnapskok from the intellectual attic of the Vatican was keeping papal officials conscious of Mi'kmaq.

On the morning of the final up-or-down roll-call vote of the ILO conference on its draft convention on indigenous peoples, I met Martín von Hildebrand in the corridor on my way to the main conference hall. He was agitated: Venezuela had met with some other Latin American government delegations at breakfast and persuaded them to break their commitment to the policy compromise on lands and self-government reflected in the draft text. All the key Latin governments except Colombia were now agreed to vote "no" and this would defeat the convention. What to do, with barely an hour before the roll-call vote began? We walked together to the conference hall where hundreds of delegates were already taking their seats, and positioned ourselves near some Australian trade unionists that were taking bets on the outcome of the vote. "Bad luck, mates," they said, when we explained the situation. At that moment, the monsignor head of the Vatican's delegation swept by and smiled at us as he moved toward his seat.

"I have an idea," Martín said. We followed the monsignor to his flag, giving him a brief summary of the situation. "I will take care of this," the monsignor replied. As we returned to the back of the hall, we saw him rise and stride purposefully over to the flags of five or six Latin American countries—all of the rebels, except Venezuela. At each flag he whispered just a few words in the ear of the head of delegation, then moved on. Each head nodded. Then the voting began. The first of the Latin American governments to be called was Argentina: "Yes." We listened carefully for the next Latin delegation. Bolivia: "Yes." Then Brazil, and Chile. "Yes." When the secretary of the conference finally got to Venezuela, there was a brief hesitation, then: "Yes."

"I wonder," Martín mused after the votes were counted, "what he told them." We may never know. The ILO convention is now in force in twenty countries, including most of Latin America.

But to return to culture (of which Catholicism is an element in many parts of the world), it can be easier to sympathize with the victims of oppression than to like them or seek their friendship or enjoy investing in their prosperity. All cultures are interesting to an inquiring mind, although we admire and emulate only some of them. Cultural contacts and exchanges of artists (another component of the Mi'kmaw international program) can alleviate tensions and, by humanizing others, build trust. As we get to know one another better, however, we may also discover things we dislike. This is to say that a nation may attract sympathy without love or respect—or, like Ireland or Japan, great appreciation and respect, despite historical episodes of poverty, internal repression or violence.

Here, again, the Mi'kmaw campaign for international recognition was fortunate. Our Haudenosaunee neighbours could inspire respect for their historical power and laws, and the Maori for their extraordinary (and sometimes intimidating) art and music, while Mi'kmaq— This can best be told as one final story.

I was attending a high-level national meeting of chiefs in Ottawa some twenty years ago, and during the evening social event I found myself sitting across from a large, tall, very serious Cree gentleman in a broad Stetson hat. He asked me who I was. "Micmacs," the elderly gentleman said thoughtfully. "I knew one once. Happy-go-lucky people."

In expressing their historical identity, personality and generosity, Mi'kmaq have presented themselves to the world as the kind of people that other nations would enjoy as friends and neighbours. While a strong international outreach program could have made a "cause" of Mi'kmaw rights, and attracted sympathy and concern, only Mi'kmaw arts and culture, combined with the humour and civility of leaders such as Alex Denny and the evidence of concern for the welfare of other peoples around the world, can make a modern nation.

Postscript

On 9 May 2016, Indigenous Affairs Minister Carolyn Bennett announced that Canada would withdraw its objections to the UN Declaration on the Rights of Indigenous Peoples, ending nearly a decade of official resistance to the principles for which the Mi'kmaw Grand Council had fought at international meetings since 1981. It remains to be seen how this reversal in public policy translates into concrete legislative and fiscal measures strengthening Mi'kmaw institutions and families.

Note

1. Kejimkujik is a popular national park in southwest Nova Scotia. For centuries, this particular part of Nova Scotia was a place of Mi'kmaw encampments, fish weirs, hunting territories, portages, trails and burial grounds. The presence of petroglyphs on geological formations in the park lend silent voice to the lives of those who made their home in this area. Source: http://www.pc.gc.ca/eng/pn-np/ns/kejimkujik/natcul/cul/cul1.aspx

Joe B. Marshall in conversation with Jaime Battiste

Treaty Advocacy and Treaty Imperative through Mi'kmaw Leadership: Remembering with Joe B. Marshall

Since 1969, Joe Benjamin ("Joe B") Marshall, a member of Membertou and Eskasoni First Nations, has participated in organized treaty resistance against assimilation and cultural extinction. As a champion and an advocate for Mi'kmaw rights, especially those derived from the treaties, he has invested more than sixty years into learning, sharing his knowledge and skills with Mi'kmaq in the Maritimes, and being a conduit for extraordinary change. His knowledge, wisdom and calm, deliberate manner have been important forces for change for Mi'kmaq as well as his skill in being a diplomatic agent for the Union of Nova Scotia Indians (UNSI) and their transformative organizations. Fluent in both Mi'kmaw and English, he has been a hard-working, focused and perseverant servant of his people, following in the footsteps of his mentor, Alex Denny. His soft and knowledgeable voice demonstrates the confidence of an Elder, veteran, hockey player and coach, actor, patient teacher, modest mentor, and a catalyst for positive change. These qualities have not gone unnoticed; he was awarded the Grand Chief Donald Marshall Sr. Memorial Elder Award and the Role Model Award for his contributions to communities over their lifetimes. Also, in an extraordinary tribute, the governments that he fought against for Mi'kmaw rights have respected his style and knowledge and have awarded him the prestigious Order of Nova Scotia and the Order of Canada. Mi'kmaq know him affectionately and simply as "Joe B."

This chapter brings together the reflections, ideas, opinions and historical research from conversations and papers written by Joe B. With such valuable wisdom still available to us, the chapter thus attempts to capture the story of his commitment and work with Mi'kmaw treaty rights—part reflection from Joe B (as told to me in several interviews over the summer of 2015), and partly what I have come to know from and of Joe B. With his permission, I present his thoughts, his reflections and the history of UNSI, and how they have created a better understanding of Mi'kmaw treaty rights in Nova Scotia.

For respected Mi'kmaw Elders like Joe B, reflecting on the treaty relationship involves a long life as a Mi'kmaq, living among Mi'kmaq, and working beside some of the most notable Mi'kmaw politicians and statesmen, all of whom taught him how to understand treaty meanings and relationships. When talking or writing about Mi'kmaw treaties and the shared treaty relationship, it is first important to understand how to read the treaties and their significance to the past, the present and the future. Most significant is how Mi'kmaq have come to know and understand the power of Mi'kmaw intentions before the treaties were agreed upon, and how the British Crown did not bestow new rights to the Mi'kmaq; it was, rather, the Mi'kmaq that gave certain rights to the British, and thus to the people (and Crown) of Canada. From this perspective, one can see how the treaties establish some of the core Mi'kmaw teachings about how they were to live, what they could expect, and how they could maintain independence and build an empowered economy alongside the settlers'. These teachings have been passed down throughout the generations, independent from the treaties with the British Crown.

—

Joe B's early years were grounded in a settler society that denied acceptance and even knowledge of the terms of the treaty—it was an era of denial. The colonizers' government of the day, both Canadian and Nova Scotian, had come to rely on Mi'kmaw poverty as a condition of their silence and their impotence, thus limiting what Mi'kmaq were able to do, where they were able to live, gather, who they were able to gather with, and, more than anything else, controlling their day-to-day lives. Joe B still recalls a great barricade fence that the federal government erected at the entrance of the Membertou reserve that prevented people from the community from entering or exiting after certain hours. This fence was used to segregate and control the Mi'kmaq in their specific communities; it was common practice across federal reserves. On each side of the entrance of the road to the reserve read a sign: "NO EXIT." Indeed, this was the core message that the government wanted to impress on all those who entered.

Like many of his generation, Joe B was forcibly put into the Shubenacadie Indian Residential School, in Shubenacadie, where his educational journey, in English, would begin. In his understated manner, he relayed that Indian residential schools "were not great places of learning." After leaving the residential school, he was told that he could go on to grade nine at the nearest provincial middle school, close to the Membertou reserve in Sydney. There he met another fence. Within twelve weeks of his attending that school (Sydney Academy), the vice principal gathered all the Mi'kmaw students and told them they were no longer able to attend the school, and sent them home to the reserve. It was explained that the Membertou reserve was not considered part of the city of Sydney, despite being surrounded by the city and, in fact, the city being on Membertou land. Because the members of the reserve did not pay taxes to the city, they could not attend the provincial school that was subsidized by city taxes. The explanation enraged Membertou council and citizens, who were the original citizens of the land, leading to several meetings with delegates from Indian and Northern Affairs Canada (INAC, now Indigenous and Northern Affairs Canada) and the city and school administrators. Finally, the school and INAC reached a settlement, wherein INAC agreed to pay tuition for the attendance of the Mi'kmaw students.

Feeling unwelcomed at provincial schools was to continue. Joe B spent much of his first years of high school feeling like an outsider to the curriculum. He did not learn about the history or contributions of the Mi'kmaq within the curriculum. After only a few years in high school, he left without a diploma, disappointed that the school system presented more obstacles for Mi'kmaw youth than opportunities. At that point in his life, Joe B decided to join the military and he spent a few years with the Canadian Air Force. He eventually returned to high school, but not before serving in the military, coming home and getting married. Joe B laughs, remembering that he was the only married man in grade eleven in Sydney Academy. His determination to finish high school was to ensure his education could continue—as it did at the Coady Institute, St. Francis Xavier University, where he focused on community development. His interest and knowledge of community development would provide the basis of his work in improving Mi'kmaw communities in Nova Scotia within his role as a leader of more than forty years of service with the UNSI, a lobby organization for Mi'kmaq.

It would not take long before Joe B realized another goal, attending and graduating from Dalhousie Law School, becoming one of only a few Mi'kmaq with a law degree at the time. Though he would not use this degree to practise law, he did use this education to support his service and advocacy of Mi'kmaw rights in Nova Scotia. Among those years of service were in teaching at Cape Breton University as a professor of Mi'kmaw studies and political science, a teaching term that lasted eleven years, during which he was instrumental in the formation of the Mi'kmaq College Institute and the creation of Mi'kmaw studies as a disciplinary subject. During those years, the number of Mi'kmaw students rose, and he was be the source of inspiration for many Mi'kmaq, including myself, continuing their education in fields of teaching, law, health, politics and community service. He taught courses in Aboriginal and treaty rights, Mi'kmaq governance, and contemporary Mi'kmaw issues, all of which are still taught at the university. In 2005, he retired from teaching and returned to treaty advocacy.

—

Since the 1960s, the UNSI has been integral in developing the research, the litigation, and the overall movement toward treaty recognition and implementation. While many Mi'kmaq are aware of the importance of these victories in the courts, and while they have witnessed the Mi'kmaw resistance in their lifetimes, very few are aware of the story of the UNSI and how it came to be. In the creation of this account, Joe B gave me his recollections, from his early years of working beside Alex Denny at the union's inception to becoming its executive director.

The initial stages of the Mi'kmaw treaty imperative and resistance began in 1964, with INAC agreeing to provide funds for a secretary to record the meetings of chiefs and councils on reserves. In 1967-1968, INAC asked the chiefs to form into the Maritime Advisory Council for Nova Scotia, New Brunswick and Prince Edward Island. The advisory council was to consult with INAC on various topics such as housing, social assistance and economic development within the communities; however, when the initial meeting of the advisory council took place, the discussion soon turned to the long-term sustainability of the Mi'kmaw people.

Joe B recalled some of the first discussions with members of the initial organizing committee of the advisory council and the founders of the UNSI, which included himself, the late Kji-keptin (Grand Captain) Alexander Denny, of the Mi'kmaw Grand Council, former chiefs Noel Doucette, Stanley Johnson and Reggie Maloney, as well as Gregory Johnson, John Knockwood and Roy Gould. The organizing committee was initially tasked to be an advisory group to INAC, but they soon saw the imperative to formally unite the Mi'kmaq of Nova Scotia and to pursue treaties as a way creating self-sustaining Mi'kmaw communities.

Many challenges existed for the founders of the UNSI that had to be overcome in attempting to get the federal government and provinces to recognize and implement the Crown's promises made with their ancestors. It is significant to note that it was Joe B's generation, and their quest for the recognition and restoration of the treaties through the courts, that saw to the implementation of constitutional rights that the younger generations enjoy today. These rights include: the acknowledgement of Mi'kmaw hunting, fishing and harvesting rights under the treaties, both on a commercial and subsistence basis; the yearly celebration of Treaty Day, on October 1; and the present-day ability of Mi'kmaw students to study traditional Mi'kmaw knowledge and language within the curriculum in elementary, secondary and post-secondary institutions.

The perseverance of Mi'kmaq, in part led by Joe B and many other Mi'kmaw politicians and advocates, has generated Mi'kmaw treaty resistance as exemplified by collaboration, cooperation, research, advocacy, education, litigation and implementation of the court's directives to overcome the obstacles and hardships of governmental denial of treaties, and to raise the consciousness of and belief in treaties as being part of the supreme law of both the Mi'kmaq and Canada. These important concepts provide the substance of this chapter, drawing on core teachings from Joe B. They also reveal the ironic history of Mi'kmaw treaties with the Crown, and highlight the modern struggle and key moments within the creation, implementation and delivery of treaty obligations in Canada. We aim to show how treaty denial was achieved for more than two hundred years (1780-1985) and continues in different forms today. Within the last generation of Mi'kmaq, over the past fifty years, say, a resurgence resulting from Mi'kmaw treaty research and litigation—and hard-fought court battles—has emerged in order to implement the true spirit and intent of the treaties, and create a better way of life for future generations of Mi'kmaq.

Ankukamkewel: Treaty-Making Period

Prior to the Europeans' arrival, Mi'kmaq dealt with neighbouring nations in trade and friendship alliances that were based on mutual respect. Joe B, in his report *The Secular Ulnapskok*, and in his classic essays "The Covenant Chain of Treaties" and "Hunting and Fishing Rights of Mi'kmaq" (Marshall 1991), has written that the proper starting point for a discussion of treaties begins with understanding Mi'kmaw perspectives and concepts of their treaties with the indigenous and European nations. The Mi'kmaw concept of *ankukamkewel* (plural), or *ankukamewe* (singular), refers to the notion of many things being brought together, combined, or built upon. Joe B infers by the structure of this concept that the king of Great Britain was looking to join with the various districts or tribes of the Mi'kmaq nation, which existed in Mi'kma'ki for thousands of years. Mi'kmaw law thus is the overarching framework that connects the various treaties and refutes the perception that the treaties are separate entities.

Mi'kma'ki refers to the homeland of the Mi'kmaq, which includes territories of Nova Scotia, New Brunswick, Prince Edward Island and parts of Maine, Québec and Newfoundland and Labrador. Within Mi'kma'ki, there are seven recognized districts, or what some Elders have described as ecological zones. When King Charles I of Great Britain requested, in 1630, an alliance with the Mi'kmaq, the small, coastal settlements were considered English reserves within the districts of Mi'kma'ki. As the treaty alliance spread, the treaty became conceptualized within Mi'kmaw knowledge as extending to the kingdom of Great Britain, the British Isles becoming the ceremonial eighth district of the Mi'kmaq nation, as were the Holy See, France and other Catholic nations. Mi'kmaw art and historical pictographs lead us to believe that the eight-pointed star had a special significance to the Mi'kmaq, representing this eighth district.

To the Mi'kmaq, treaties are covenants that protect their ancestral livelihood and have been passed down through each generation since. Joe B recalls that many Mi'kmaq of his generation would have heard from their fathers, grandfathers and relatives about the importance of treaties as a method of ensuring the survival of the people. The interlinked treaties constituted imperial and Mi'kmaw law, each treaty becoming enveloped within the Mi'kmaw family dynamic and the values and responsibilities associated with them.

While Mi'kmaq contact with Europeans began in the 16th century, it is noted, in a 1607 report, that when Mi'kmaw Grand Chief Membertou came into contact with the Catholic French explorers, he taught them how to survive the harsh winters in the Port Royale area. Grand Chief Membertou was a central figure that helped to establish a mutual respect, symbolized by his baptism into Christianity, in 1610. This alliance would create a compact with the Holy See and the supreme leaders of the Catholic nations, such as Portugal, France and Spain.

As a result of conflicts between the nations of Europe, hostilities broke out between New France and New England that would affect as well relations with their allies and among the nations of the Wabanaki Confederacy, which included the Mi'kmaq nation. Both the French and the English wanted to negotiate treaties of peace and friendship with the nations to ensure Mi'kmaw neutrality in their war. By 1717, at least eleven treaties were negotiated within the southeastern nations of the Wabanaki Confederacy. These treaties were nation-to-nation and included many nations and tribes. However, the Mi'kmaq refused to enter into these treaties, though they were witness to them, preferring to remain neutral to French-English conflicts.

In November of 1725, the Wabanaki ambassadors from the Penobscot, Maliseet and Passamaquoddy, representing the nations of the Wabanaki Confederacy, entered into a proposed peace treaty with representatives of the British Crown in Boston. This treaty combined the terms of the existing treaties with the Wabanaki Confederacy.

In 1726, at Annapolis Royal, after negotiating at length several versions of the 1725 treaty, the elikewake treaty (the king in our house), Mi'kmaq chiefs agreed to ratify the proposed treaty within their Mi'kmaw protocols. The Cape Sable (Kespukwitk) Mi'kmaq and about a hundred of the chiefs and leaders of the seven districts entered the treaty, including chiefs of the Annapolis Royal, Chignectou, Minas, Shubenacadie, La Have, Shediac, Richibucto, Cape Breton and Newfoundland. Representatives of the Penobscot, Passamaquoddy and Maliseet nations were in attendance as witnesses for the Wabanaki Confederacy.

In the elikewake treaty, the Mi'kmaw chiefs recognized that the European Treaty of Utrecht transferred the French king's claims to the British king, and the French agreed not to interfere with existing British settlements at Canso and Annapolis Royal. The British king promised that the "Indians shall not be molested in their persons, hunting, fishing, and planting grounds nor in their lawful occasions by His Majesty's subjects or their dependents," and they were promised the freedom of religion. The treaty also provided that if any British subjects or their descendants injured a Mi'kmaw person, the Mi'kmaq "shall have satisfaction and reparation made to them according to his Majesty's law, where of the Indians shall the benefit equal with His Majesty's other subjects" (English to Indians, Treaty 1726).

Despite the terms of the treaties, the colonial authorities ignored the foundation and core messages of the treaties. They created their own perception of how to live with these treaties; to Mi'kmaq, it was a very distorted view of power relations. Their colonial settlers rarely obeyed the mandates and terms of the British Crown's treaty with the Mi'kmaq. Historical research and archival records show how colonial authorities very often confronted Mi'kmaq inhabitants in one district when supposed offences were committed against them by Mi'kmaq in another district, and accused them of violating the treaties they had signed.

In 1749, the British king established the colony of Nova Scotia, and the royal instructions and commission ordered its governor, Edward Cornwallis, to make peace with the Indian nations. Cornwallis was instructed to travel to Annapolis Royal, which was the only lawful British settlement in Nova Scotia under the 1726 treaty; however, in one of the ironies of history, the fate of the Mi'kmaq was literally tossed to the wind when Cornwallis went directly to the great bay, or Chebuctou, and established a new and unconsented post, Halifax (McNutt 1965). Cornwallis's deviation from the approval plan set off a chain of events that led to further conflicts within Mi'kma'ki.

In the fall of 1749, a letter from the Mi'kmaq protesting this new settlement was sent to Governor Cornwallis, requesting that the British vacate the settlement at Chebuctou and comply with the terms of the 1726 treaty. The letter was written in both French and Mi'kmaw to a British officer at Port Toulouse (St. Peter's, NS). Fr. Maillard, a French mission priest, was the translator who wrote the letter that asserted Mi'kmaw jurisdiction and dominion, and objected to British authority outside Annapolis Royal. The letter, translated into English, stated the following:

> The Place where you are, where you are building dwelling, where you are now building a fort, where you now wish to establish your authority, this land of which you now wish to become the absolute master, this land belongs to me, I have come from it as surely as the grass, it is the proper place of my birth and my residence, this land belongs to me, the Indian, yes I swear, that it was given to me by God to be my homeland in perpetuity.
>
> Let me first tell you how I feel in my heart about you, because it is not possible that what you are doing at Kchiboutouk (Chebuctou) does not alarm me....
>
> ...Your residence at Port Royal is no longer a great threat for me, because for a long time now I have left you in peace there. But now, by the theft that you wish to perpetuate on me, you force me to speak. I will go see you soon to see you, perhaps you will receive well what I shall say to you; if you listen to me and if you speak to me as you should, and you carry out your flowery promises, I will know by that you seek only the good, so that all things will turn out well: I will say no more about this in order to not deafen you any longer with my talk. I take leave of you my lord. (*Le Canada Francais* 1888)

The letter made by the Mi'kmaq was a plea for justice according to their understanding of the 1726 treaty. Cornwallis interpreted and later described the document as a declaration of war by the Mi'kmaq. He characterized the Mi'kmaq as "bandit, Ruffians, or rebels," rather than treaty partners (NSARM, RG1, vol. 40a). Despite the instructions of King George and the Lords of Trade (British Board of Trade) to make peace with the Mi'kmaq, Cornwallis refused to comply with the existing treaties' requirement of dispute resolution and began hostilities against the Mi'kmaq. Cornwallis placed a bounty on scalps of Mi'kmaw men, women and children in what became known as the 1749 "extirpation policy," now termed genocide (NSARM, RG1, vol. 40b; Akins 1869: 162).

Cornwallis's efforts were unsuccessful, as the Mi'kmaq were a formidable fighting force in their own territories. Cornwallis's rangers scoured the surrounding woods, but rarely encountered Mi'kmaq, whose traditional strategy continued to be containing the colonists in their forts. Every time colonists sought to establish an activity outside the settlement they were attacked and killed. This inability to rid himself of the Mi'kmaq created great frustration for Cornwallis, who, among other things, recommended that Mi'kmaq be killed off in their entirety.

By October 1749, the Lords of Trade began actively questioning Cornwallis's handling of the Mi'kmaq and urged him once again to create alliances instead of trying to exterminate them. The imperial authorities understood that military extirpation would create a "dangerous spirit or resentment" among their treaty allies (Murdock 1866: 169). In a last attempt to show he was capable of governing, Cornwallis, in the summer of 1751, sent a peace ambassador, Colonel Jean-Paul Mascarene, to a treaty conference with the Wabanaki Confederacy at Fort St. George; however, this would prove to be too little, too late in the eyes of the Lords of Trade, who saw Cornwallis's policies as costly failures that brought no money or trade value. In 1752, King George II quietly ended Cornwallis's term as governor and replaced him with Colonel Peregrine Thomas Hobson, who had royal instructions to negotiate a treaty of peace with the Mi'kmaq (UK PRO).

Renewal of Peace and Friendship Treaties

In the fall of 1752, Grand Chief John Baptiste Cope, a representative of the Mi'kmaw Grand Council, arrived in Halifax to establish the terms of peace with Governor Hobson, and called for an end to the British war against the Mi'kmaq. Grand Chief Cope's exclusive term for the renewal of peace was for the king to compensate the Sipekne'katiki Mi'kmaq for the new settlement. Hobson ignored this demand and renewed the existing peace and friendship provisions, adding a few items of trade and gifts. Cope confirmed that he would communicate the proposed renewal treaty with his people and inform the other districts of the renewal offer of peace. He agreed to return within a month to bring back their answer, which was finalized as the agreed-upon treaty on September 16, 1752.

The terms of the satisfactory proposal for renewing the "Peace, Friendship, and Protection" treaty were recorded by the new Governor-in-Council, but without the treaty negotiations or deliberations, which was a stark contrast to the 1725 negotiations. A shroud of silence about the deliberations at the time continues to hide any further understanding of the intent of both parties in the formative stages of the 1752 treaty. Furthermore, we are only left with one side's English-language text of what was agreed to in the treaty, and not how Mi'kmaq understood or explained to their people their understandings.

The English text of the treaty of 1752 renewed the existing treaties. In none of these was there a consideration of land transfer. As well, the British Crown never purchased any Mi'kmaw land, for past or future settlement, only promising, in October of each year, to provide provisions that would be given to Mi'kmaw families to reaffirm the peace. It also acknowledged to the Mi'kmaq their free liberty to hunt, fish and trade, and their agreement to allow the safe return of any shipwrecked goods of his Majesty's subjects.

After the British war with France in Atlantic Canada, 1759-1761, the chiefs continued to renew the treaties of peace and friendship with the British king. These renewal treaties were based on the 1726 treaty. In 1759, the king commanded his military governors to assure the Mi'kmaq that the peace ensures that Mi'kmaq "will enjoy all your possessions, your liberty, property with the free exercise of your religion" (Schomberg à Maillard 1759), and to make a new provision for trade at the king's truckhouses (trading posts) to ensure treaty implementations. In article 40 of the articles of capitulation of Montréal, 1760, the British king promised the French king:

> The savages or Indian allies of His Most Christian Majesty shall be maintained in the lands they inhabit, if they choose to reside there; they shall not be molested on any pretence whatsoever. (Journals 1847)

In 1761, King George III affirmed, in royal instructions to Nova Scotia, that the existing treaties with the Crown were inviolate. The king stressed that the peace and security of the colonies depended on "a just and faithful Observance of those Treaties and Compacts which have been heretofore solemnly entered into with the said Indians by Our Royall Predecessor Kings & Queens of this Realm." The king and Privy Council (the British high court) declared they were "determined upon all occasions to support and protect the said Indians in their just Rights and Possessions and to keep inviolable the Treaties and Compacts which have been entered into with them" (McNeil 1982: 285-86).

In 1763, King George III affirmed Mi'kmaw sovereignty and tenure in the North American colonies in the form of a royal proclamation. The proclamation declared to the colonial authorities that the Mi'kmaq, who lived under the protection of treaties with the king, "should not be molested or disturbed in the possession of such parts of our dominion and territories as not having been ceded to or purchased by us." These unpurchased and unceded territories were "reserved to them, or any of them as their hunting grounds," (Royal Proclamation 1763).

The Mi'kmaw treaties, and the 1761 royal instructions to Nova Scotia, had already recognized the Mi'kmaw territory in Nova Scotia as reserved lands. The 1763 proclamation affirmed that all unceded and purchased land acquired by the Treaty of Paris were reserved as hunting ground. This hunting ground belonged to the Mi'kmaq, and if the Mi'kmaq chose freely to dispose of said lands, it could only be purchased by the Crown and not by British subjects, unless they had special licence from the Crown.

In the decades that followed, more treaties would build on what is now known as the Mi'kmaw covenant chain of treaties. The metaphor of a chain link is used since each treaty is built on a relationship and is considered one link in a chain. Different districts within Mi'kma'ki built upon the 1726 treaty and ratified and affirmed the terms of peace, protection and friendship, and brought together all the ancestral territory of Mi'kma'ki. Yet, with the Mi'kmaw treaties, and various other proclamations and guarantees from the Crown or governments, the next two hundred years would see Mi'kmaw treaties ignored, denied and prosecuted almost out of existence. Almost.

Treaty Denial

Within a few generations of the Mi'kmaq signing peace and friendship treaties with the British Crown, they experienced the negative effects of colonial disobedience to the Crown in the denial of treaty terms. The unjust loss of their land and rights to their livelihood would continue to frustrate Mi'kmaq, leading to their growing poverty and disillusionment. After the American Revolution and the War of 1812, thousands of British loyalists from America were given Mi'kmaw land, further displacing Mi'kmaq, and thus also denying them their full hunting rights. With these unlawful settlements in Mi'kma'ki, in 1841, the Mi'kmaw Grand Council petitioned the king for compensation for the losses. In 1849, a Nova Scotia governmental report explained to the Crown the failure of the rule of law in Nova Scotia and why no compensation or reparation every occurred for the Mi'kmaq:

> Under present circumstances, no adequate protection can be obtained for Indian property. It would be vain to seek a verdict from any jury in this island against the trespassers on the reserves; nor perhaps would [a or any] member of the Bar be found willingly and effectually to advocate the cause of the Indians, inasmuch as he would thereby injure his own prospect by damaging his popularity. (Qtd. in Henderson 1985: 210)

This left the Mi'kmaq very much at the mercy of an unjust system that violated the terms of the treaty that said Mi'kmaq would be provided with equal protection of the king's law in disputes with colonists. In a period from 1867 through to 1967, the Mi'kmaq also experienced the following:

- The establishment of the *British North America Act, 1867*, which transferred provincial responsibility for implementing the Mi'kmaw treaties to the newly created Canadian federal government, which would exercise unchecked powers over treaties, Indians and lands reserved for them without any consultation with Mi'kmaq.
- The unilateral establishment of a federal *Indian Act*, 1876, amended several times, giving increasing powers to the federal government over Aboriginal land, peoples and their future. The Government of Canada would attempt to termi-

nate the Mi'kmaq nation as an on-going entity and would create band councils under the control of federal agents, so-called Indian agents, controlling their election processes and regulating the day-to-day life of Indians.

- They would unjustly prosecute our grand chief, in 1928, based on judicial denial of the validity of Mi'kmaw treaties, thus creating doubt and confusion among Canadians, the Mí'kmaw Grand Council and in our Mi'kmaw governing systems.
- With the judicial denial of Mi'kmaw treaties, the federal government and the Christian churches would forcibly remove Mi'kmaw children from their homes and into religious residential (boarding) schools, beginning in 1929 and through the 1950s and into the 60s that were meant to "kill the Indian in the child." Without their families, the love and nurturance of their homes and communities, and in punitive care, they suffered profound physical, sexual, mental and emotional abuses that have been described as cultural genocide.
- Beginning in the 1940s, while many Mi'kmaw men were fighting in the Second World War, Canada established a policy for the removal of Mi'kmaq from their lands under a centralization policy that would relocate them onto three overpopulated and under-resourced reserves, at Eskasoni, Shubenacadie and Big Cove. On these centralized reserves, Canada continued the heightened overregulation of the people and their governance.
- With the failure of centralization in the 1960s, Canada began establishing, or re-establishing, *Indian Act* reserves. The resistance of Mi'kmaq to centralization and some Mi'kmaq choosing to remain in their homelands forced Canada to create smaller reserves with the same band-council management scheme controlled by Indian agents.
- Canada sought to end treaties by turning over their responsibilities to the provinces in the 1969 federal white paper on Indian affairs, which is explained further in the next section.

Generating the Mi'kmaq Treaty Imperative and Resistance

Joe B said that the Maritime Advisory Council for Nova Scotia, New Brunswick and Prince Edward Island sought to end the denial about treaties but instead pursued—through collaboration, research and litigation—the Mi'kmaw treaties as a strategy to address their dire political, social and economic situation. INAC rejected this approach and reminded the council that they were merely advisory—not decision-makers. INAC's stance frustrated the council and annoyed the chiefs, who had lived under the controlling patriarchal regime of the federal government long enough; they set in place a new course of action, to work together to form their own unified organization, the UNSI, to support treaty imperatives and build resistance to Canada's perceived role and control over Mi'kmaq.

In 1969, a momentous shift occurred across Canada with the introduction of a proposed white paper from Prime Minister Pierre Trudeau's Liberal government, aimed at ending the special status of Indians, as under the treaties. The paper proposed ending the federal government's role in implementing the treaties, and end providing services, benefits and exemptions to Indians on reserves. As part of the proposed policy, there was funding offered to organizations to help promote the policy to Canadians and inform communities within each province. The newly formed UNSI took advantage of the funding offered to put together their own proposal to organize and inform communities of the government's plans, and build their own platform for researching Aboriginal title and treaty rights.

Mi'kmaw *Indian Act* chiefs agreed to work together as chiefs and leaders of their communities and as members of a newly created board that would oversee the UNSI organization. The chiefs firm commitment to be a unified force began with the slogan that "united we stand and divided we fall." It wasn't an easy sell to the government (that the chiefs could organize and deal with government together, united).

Joe B recalls that several decades had passed since the 1928 case in Nova Scotia against Grand Chief Gabriel Sylliboy that, in essence, ruled Mi'kmaw treaties were not valid. Despite those decades of being told that there were no valid Mi'kmaw treaty rights, many Mi'kmaq insisted that their ancestors—their nation—signed treaties with the British Crown and that descendent governments had refused to uphold the law. Some of Joe B's early mentors, including Ben Christmas from Membertou and, then in his later years, Kji-keptin Alex Denny, continued to assert that not only were Mi'kmaw treaties valid, but that they would lead Mi'kmaq from poverty to prosperity. Denny and Joe B, together with many others, would use this understanding of the treaties to generate the treaty imperative.

These understandings had a long oral tradition derived from closely guarded Mi'kmaw relationships. Great orators and leaders also helped to sustain the traditions of the past in the Mi'kmaq. Joe B told of how this knowledge was transmitted by Grand Chief Sylliboy, Putu's Andrew Alex, Mi'kmaw families, and the Mi'kmaw Grand Council at their annual gatherings at the capital of Mi'kma'ki at Chapel Island. These events included Lapatko'tikimk, in May, and the feast of St. Anne's Mission, in July, when the grand council also held their own Niskawtimk meetings. He notes that while the Mi'kmaq had retained their language, covenants and teachings, they had lost many of the rituals and ceremonies belonging to the grand council during the treaty denial.

Joe B pointed out that they had lost the Niskawtimk ceremony that began the grand council meeting with the keptins and chiefs. During this ceremony, a fire was made in front of the grand chief's wikuom and Mi'kmaw dignitaries—such as keptins of the grand council who had travelled from afar, or any councillors or chiefs who had special requests—would be invited to sit and each in turn dance around the fire, and as per protocol, each would share their title, their family lineage, and give the background of their achievements in song and chant as they danced in a circle. Once they had completed their introductions, they would then be invited into the *kji'wikwam* (great wigwam) to take their seat among the grand council. The putu's, or knowledge keeper, had a special role that would ensure that the council had a record of the major transactions. The putu's would be the first on the agenda when he would ceremonially speak of the alliances and treaties and meanings of the 'lnapsku (covenants of the wampum belts) previously enacted and agreed to as to ensure the continuity of the oral traditions. During the government's centralization of the Mi'kmaq, the forced removal of Mi'kmaq from their familial gatherings in their communities in the 1940s, this tradition waned, then disappeared. However, the dance circle is still visible today at the designated heritage site called Holy Family Island, or *miniku*, in

Potlotek, along Bras d'Or Lake, along with the stories and memories of some of the Elders to this ancient tradition.

While the protocols around Niskawtimk have faded from the memory of many Mi'kmaq, the teachings about the covenants of the wampum belts and the Mi'kmaw peace and friendship treaties remain. Joe B recalls that Alex Denny often shared that, when he was a child, the old man who raised him would retell the English-language version of the treaties to him as bedtime stories.

So, in the 1970s, despite being told by INAC and other government employees and lawyers that Mi'kmaw treaties "weren't worth the paper they were written on," the Mi'kmaq knew better. They would not rely on the government's arguments and the opinion of the judiciary in the Sylliboy case. They had tradition and oral history that assured them that they indeed had a valid treaty. Yet this would not be enough, and the UNSI chiefs decided to search out other avenues to prove their argument. In this regard, UNSI hired Stu Killen (see chapter 6) as research director, along with young Mi'kmaw researchers, such as Millbrook's Don Julien, Eskasoni's Albert Marshall and Potlotek's Russell Marshall, to look through the British and Canadian archives to establish, in the common-law tradition, the evidential validity of our treaties. Also hiring Sa'kej Henderson, the UNSI began to put together a comprehensive analysis of the research and, based on this research, established a position paper on a Mi'kmaw land claim.

By 1976, the UNSI's position paper was finalized and presented to the then minister of Indian affairs, Warren Almond. After a year of waiting, the government concluded that the position paper and the rights of the Mi'kmaq under the treaties "had been superseded by [colonial] law." How Mi'kmaw treaties and rights in imperial constitutional law had been "superseded" by colonial law was never explained in detail. Rather, Joe B recalled that after submitting thousands of pages of documented proof of their assertions, and a collected report of those findings that was nearly four inches thick, their efforts were denied by a singular assertion: that colonial power was greater than royal directive. This disheartening outcome led to growing resolve among the chiefs and the grand council to find other strategies to correct the imbalance of power. Could reason by way of litigation prevail?

Despite Canada's rejection of the extensive and thorough research and historical evidence brought forward by the UNSI, the Mi'kmaw leadership persevered. This began the Mi'kmaw treaty imperative:

Caption reads: Mr. Allmand (left) receives gift from Union of Nova Scotia Indians president Alex Denny (centre) and Grand Chief Donald Marshall. Fitzgerald Photo, 1977. MicMac News, 1977,vol. 7(5): 1. http://beatoninstitute.com/micmac-news-1977.

resistance to Canadian policy through various advocacy and lobbying efforts, and using the Canadian courts to have rights slowly recognized. Canada responded first by using the power at its disposal, pulling back on the funds for the organization and other forms of harassment.

Kji-keptin and then UNSI President Alex Denny invited James (Sa'kej) Youngblood Henderson, a Chickasaw man and Harvard Law graduate who was teaching at the University of California, to help in the cause. Henderson was married to Potlotek Mi'kmaw, Marie Battiste, and together they were invited to help on several fronts—Battiste in education, and Henderson with the UNSI legal research in the preparation of treaty rights and land claims for the UNSI. Joe B recalls meeting Henderson, who eventually moved to Eskasoni, where Alex built the couple a house beside his own.

After many conversations about the interpretation of Mi'kmaw treaties and how the government continued to minimize the meaning of the peace and friendship treaties, Joe B recalls how a new logic of treaties began to unfold that formed the basis of the research that Mi'kmaw treaties were meant as a means for Mi'kmaw survival and sustainability. Joe B stated it was through these discussions he realized that the Mi'kmaw treaties were meant to open doors for the Mi'kmaq, not to close them. The treaties were a starting point for the relationship between the Crown and the Mi'kmaq, and that any rights that were not ceded with the treaties would be retained and preserved as inherent ancestral laws and powers, or Aboriginal rights, that would enable them to move forward as Mi'kmaq, not as assimilated peoples. The men also discussed the many ways in which they could gain recognition of these treaties through both international and domestic processes.

The UNSI supported the legal research that went into the ongoing litigation and eventual victories in the Steven Isaac case (1976) on hunting on a reserve; however, this case was not based on treaties. Rather, it was focused on specific provisions within the *Indian Act*. It was the historic James Simon case (1985) that would validate and acknowledge that the 1752 Mi'kmaw peace and friendship treaty was valid and had never been superseded by law. This victory at the Supreme Court of Canada validated the position of the Mi'kmaw Grand Council (and of Grand Chief Gabriel Sylliboy in 1928) and the decades of research the UNSI had gathered and continued to advocate for. A year later, in 1986, through the advocacy work and collaboration with the grand council, the annual Treaty Day was announced, organized by the UNSI, which remains to this day a major event for Mi'kmaq across Nova Scotia.

UNSI and the Pursuit of Treaty Implementation

For the past fifty years, the UNSI has succeeded in achieving several major outcomes involving recognition and validation of treaties and rights of Mi'kmaq in Atlantic Canada. These would not have been possible without the research, the litigation, and collaborative creative work of many Mi'kmaq and their allies that led to the reassertion of Mi'kmaw rights within Nova Scotia. Joe B Marshall has been involved

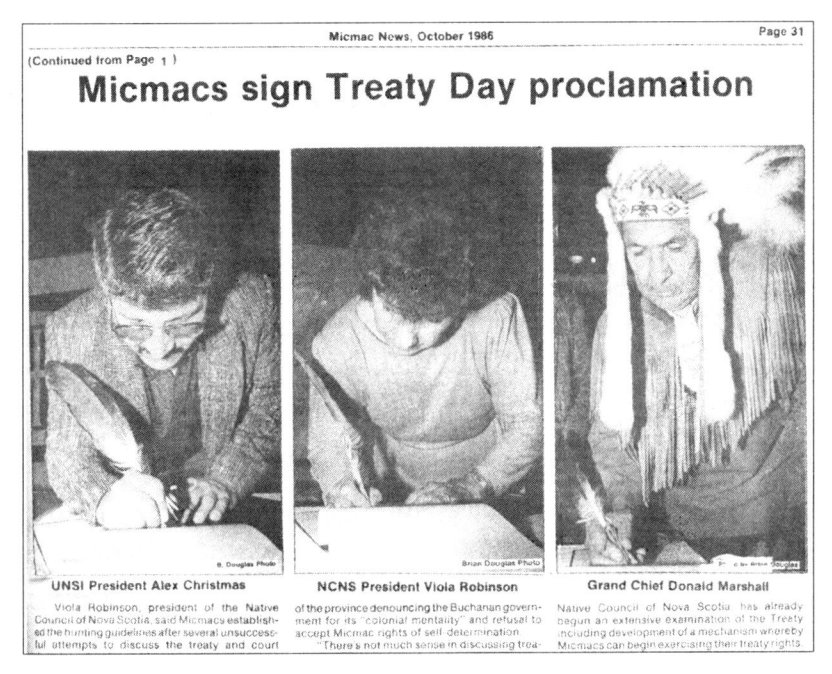

MicMac News, 1986, vol. 16(10): 31. http://beatoninstitute.com/micmac-news-1986

in almost every major movement, and a key strategist for treaty recognition and implementation. One of the key achievements of Joe B and the treaty resistance was having inherent Aboriginal and treaty rights recognized as part of the supreme law of Canada. Section 35 of the *Constitution Act, 1982* "recognizes and affirms, existing aboriginal and treaty rights." Article 25 of the Canadian Charter of Rights and Freedoms continued the constitutional protections of the reservation of unceded and unpurchased Mi'kmaw territory, and the exclusive requirement of a purchase of these lands by the Crown. These sections were implemented and to be read with section 52 of the *Constitution Act*, the supremacy clause, which states, "the Constitution is the supreme law of Canada, and any laws that are inconsistent with that law is of no force and affect." This clause ensures that federal and provincial laws have to be consistent with Aboriginal rights preserved in the treaties. While this was not fully explored during the successful Simon appeal at the Supreme Court—because the 1982 act was drafted *after* the initial evidence and arguments were presented in the case (Simon had been convicted in Nova Scotia in 1980), these constitutional affirmations of the treaties would later become the focus of Mi'kmaw efforts at treaty litigation.

To change treaty denial by Canada, Joe B stressed, UNSI made litigated treaty recognition an important objective. In late 1978, UNSI hired Bruce Wildsmith, a law professor at Dalhousie Faculty of Law, to become their lawyer. Wildsmith was subsequently successful in the *Isaac* and the *Simon* cases at validating the treaties. While the treaties were validated in *Simon*, the UNSI focused on those inherent rights preserved for the Mi'kmaq in the treaties, which were now called "Aboriginal rights." These rights were understood as Aboriginal law or power as practiced by indigenous nations prior to the settlement of Europeans or European assertions of sovereignty. Most of the struggles over indigenous rights in Canada have been in places where Aboriginal nations have not entered into treaties with the Crown. In the Mi'kmaw treaties, these Aboriginal rights were preserved for the Mi'kmaw people and protected by imperial law. The treaty-denial era of colonial Nova Scotia, and later Canada, had ignored and hidden their obligations to both Aboriginal and treaty rights through their assumed control of power over their settlement governments, institutions and courts. This reasoning did not hold up in the Supreme Court of Canada.

Joe B noted that the first test by the UNSI of the Aboriginal rights of the Mi'kmaw took place within a case brought forward based on an inherent Aboriginal right to fish for food in the case of *R. v. Denny* (1990). While in 1982 the UNSI had lost the treaty fishing case in the *Cope* decision in Nova Scotia court—the reasoning of the court was rejected by the Supreme Court of Canada in the companion *Simon* case in 1985—*Denny* was successful in establishing that Mi'kmaq food fishery was a priority Aboriginal right, as their ancestors had practised for centuries. This case would later be confirmed in the Sparrow decision, wherein the Supreme Court concluded that the Nova Scotia Court of Appeal was correct in affirming the Aboriginal right of the Mi'kmaq to fishing.

—

Another significant movement spearheaded by the UNSI in collaboration with the Mi'kmaw Grand Council that Joe B recalled was the Mi'kmaw-treaty moose-harvesting case, in 1990, in which several

Mi'kmaq were charged with hunting moose because of Nova Scotia's failure to implement the *Simon* decision. During the trial stages of court, when Nova Scotia realized the weakness of their case and likelihood of their losing the case given the *Sparrow* decision, Nova Scotia walked out of court and left the Mi'kmaq with another victory in defending their constitutional rights.

The UNSI and grand council had also collaborated with freeing Donald Marshall Jr. from his wrongful conviction in the murder of Sandy Seale in Sydney in 1971. Later, in 1999, Joe B said the most significant victory for Mi'kmaw treaty rights was when the Supreme Court of Canada decided that Donald Marshall Jr. had a treaty right to commercial fishing under the 1759-1761 treaties. The Supreme Court also recommended to Nova Scotia that rather than continuing to litigate against Mi'kmaw rights, negotiation with Mi'kmaq was a preferable goal toward treaty reconciliation. This case was monumental in creating an enriched economy among Mi'kmaq, with jobs within the commercial fishery, a fishery that, for the most part, Mi'kmaq had been excluded from for generations.

During this time, Joe B additionally spent more than a decade as a professor of Mi'kmaw studies, educating the next generations of Mi'kmaq

MicMac News, 1989, vol. 19 (4): 3. http://beatoninstitute.com/micmac-news-1989.

and others on Aboriginal and treaty rights, Mi'kmaw history, and the need for unity and self-determination based on constitutional rights. Joe B was a cherished professor who was always available to answer students' questions about history and contemporary relations. Joe B recalled that during this time he had many students and professionals call upon him for advice and with questions about treaty rights, history and law. Joe B would do his best to answer their questions, but if he couldn't answer them, he would offer other ways and people to answer them. These questions inspired him to continue to research and learn so that he could stay informed for them, then and in the future. After eleven years as a professor, he asserted, you come to learn and research a lot of different areas of Mi'kmaw rights and develop new courses with that knowledge. Joe B's passion for helping Mi'kmaq achieve justice was supported by Cape Breton University, where, as a student and a teacher, he would learn "in university, you learn how to learn."

Prior to the *Marshall* fishing decision, Joe B recalls sharing with students that he was afraid of what would happen if the Mi'kmaq lost this case, but also he feared what might happen if they won. This statement was puzzling to many of his students at the time, but after the initial *Marshall* decision was revealed and the Atlantic fishing industry went into a rage over Aboriginal rights to commercial fishing—leading to the unprecedented "clarification" of the decision by the Supreme Court—we understood the depth of his understanding of the situation of Mi'kmaq in Atlantic Canada.

The court's affirmation of Mi'kmaw rights to fish commercially under the treaties and the supremacy of law met with enormous resistance within Atlantic Canada by politicians and citizens, as well as by the federal Department of Fisheries and Oceans, which had to implement the decision. Atlantic Canadians complained that if the treaties between Mi'kmaq and the Crown granted them commercial fishing rights, denied for generations, it would ruin the fragile fishing economy of the region through overfishing. Implementing the treaty right for Mi'kmaq thus would ruin the non-Aboriginal commercial industry. The dramatic resistance to constitutional supremacy led to heightened racial tensions on the docks between Mi'kmaw fishermen and non-Mi'kmaw fishermen, with the Department of Fisheries and Oceans watching but not intervening on behalf of Mi'kmaw rights holders. Rather, a union of fishermen from Nova Scotia, not a party to the *Marshall* case, petitioned the Supreme Court for a rehearing the initial decision. In light of what was staged as a raging war on the waters, the court released an unprecedented clarification of their original decision, in what is now known as *Marshall* No. 2.

While the court did not reverse its decision, it did bend to the pressure of Atlantic Canadian politicians, media, and the general public to assert new guidelines that Mi'kmaq would have to meet in order to pursue commercial fishing. The case illustrated how difficult implementing its decision would be in this context. The public resistance to the treaties illustrated Joe B's correct understanding of the dilemma facing treaty-rights assertion in Atlantic Canada. It would cost Canada more than $5 billion to implement the *Marshall* decision. Joe B further noted that, through research, position papers and leadership from the several presidents and vice presidents of the UNSI, they have, under the treaty imperative, been able to improve the living standards for Mi'kmaq on reserve for the past fifty years.

In the years following *Marshall*, the Atlantic provinces have sought to overturn the Supreme Court decisions by continuing to charge Mi'kmaq who relied on their Aboriginal and treaty rights for fishing and hunting. The UNSI continues advocacy at court as well negotiating and consulting within the political sphere to help increase the standard of living on reserves.

Witnessing the growing strength of Mi'kmaw self-determination and advocacy through their organizations, INAC sought to limit UNSI's capacity to advocate and to adequately research the treaties by reducing its funding and creating division among the Mi'kmaq in Nova Scotia and Canada. Joe B reflected that among the challenges facing UNSI was preserving unity and strength. This was difficult when, in 1986, six of the thirteen Nova Scotia Mi'kmaw bands broke away to form their own organization, the Confederacy of Mainland Mi'kmaq. Yet, despite the split, in 2002 the provincial Mi'kmaw chiefs saw the need for their being reunited after the *Marshall* decision and treaty implementation, and they established the Assembly of Nova Scotia Mi'kmaq Chiefs. In 2004, Joe B was brought on board to be senior constitutional adviser to the assembly, a role he continues to hold. Joe B continues to guide the Mi'kmaq and the Assembly of Nova Scotia Mi'kmaq Chiefs as they proceed through the negotiation of Aboriginal and treaty rights with the Province of Nova Scotia and the federal government.

Over the years of his service to the Mi'kmaq and Canada, Joe B has been the calm voice of reason for Mi'kmaq who continue the journey toward treaty implementation and reconciliation. Joe B has always asserted his understanding under the original Mi'kmaw vision of the treaties: that the intention behind the treaties, and the governments who implement those treaties, are that they continue to be allies. Just as our ancestors had decided that peace and harmony and negotiation were key in the creation of the covenant chain of a treaty commonwealth with the king, today Joe B continues to advocate for our complementarity and interconnected treaty rights through peaceful means, based on education, negotiation and diplomacy.

Under our ancient constitutional rights, affirmed by the United Nations and by supreme law in Canada, Joe B states that Mi'kmaq are finding their way and becoming stronger. One of the ancestral Mi'kmaw powers that were retained in the treaties with the king was the right to control our language and pass on knowledge to our children. Joe B notes that this preserved treaty right was evaded in the treaty-denial era—especially in the era of the Indian residential schools—but he continues to stress the tremendous importance of our language and culture in education. As Elders have shared across Canada, our language and knowledge system are the window through which we see the world. Joe B teaches, "it is only through our language can we truly understand the teachings of our ancestors and retain the important wisdom and teachings within it about the treaties." He states that Mi'kmaw knowledge, law and culture are embedded in the language. Ultimately, it will be Mi'kmaq who have to fight to preserve our language and oral traditions and, in so doing, will come to understand what it means to be Mi'kmaq.

Among the other listed UNSI achievements, Joe B asserts that the creation of organizations has helped advance Mi'kmaw language, culture and education—such as Mi'kmaw Association of Cultural Studies and Mi'kmaw Kina'matnewey, which have supported major language initiatives and outcomes—and, more recently, a focus on treaty education.

Joe B says:

> All of the good things that have come from the judicial upholding of our treaties, the changes that have come about, it all leads to good things for the people. So many Mi'kmaq are becoming

skilled and educated. It's a snowball effect, and so now many, many Mi'kmaw people have better access to education, which means we have nurses and teachers, lawyers and Mi'kmaw people in business. There is more opportunity now to build lives.

He states that what Mi'kmaq most need in our community is to be strict with our children and make sure we push them to be educated. And we must remain strong in disciplining our children. Today we need it so bad. It will pay off in the future. They will have a good job and a good life.

Today, Joe B recalls that treaty implementation is part of the Mi'kmaw negotiation for Mi'kmaw and treaty rights. His decades of success in having the courts recognize the treaties have taught him the importance of perseverance and patience in implementing the treaties. Canada and the provinces depend on documentation from the Crown, but among Mi'kmaq, law depends on the oral tradition—speaking Mi'kmaw and listening to the Mi'kmaq—to understand reserved powers under the treaties. A master of humility in the Mi'kmaw oral tradition, Joe B would acknowledge that these accomplishments were "a group effort and there were a lot of people who worked hard to make sure Mi'kmaw rights and treaty rights were recognized and upheld over the years." He notes that trying to recall all the important people who were a part of the Mi'kmaw struggle for rights through the years is like asking a retired National Hockey League player to remember all of his teammates. Instead, and more importantly, he recognizes the collective efforts of so many people who played key roles.

As advocates for treaty rights through the past several years, the UNSI, the assembly, and chiefs and councils have suffered from many funding cuts that have minimized the efforts of UNSI to play a significant role as legal defender of Mi'kmaw rights, and there are always concerns about further funding cuts and how much unity and collaboration can be continued within the Mi'kmaw communities of Nova Scotia under such limitations. Joe B just smiles when looking at the struggles that lay before the organizations that he has worked with for more than forty years, through the many ups and the downs, and says: "The government stated from the very start that the UNSI was never funded to be a legal advocate and defender of Mi'kmaw rights. It is safe to say that in reflecting back that we are a little bit disobedient." Through the constitutional-rights agenda, he says, "Mi'kmaq are going forward in the best way, on our own terms, and in our own ways." It is important to restate: our rights do not come from the Crown, the treaties, or the court's decisions. They come from our Creator and ancestors and our law of *netukuli'mk* (environmental sustainability) that ensures we provide for our families, our communities and all our relations.

In his concluding remarks on treaty advocacy, and what he would like to pass down to future generations, Joe B states that it is important to let all Nova Scotians and Atlantic Canadians learn the history of the treaties of the Mi'kmaq and to learn about the full intent and our roles within those treaties. The written documents belonging to the treaty-making period recognize and affirm Mi'kmaw power and rights, but they did not create new rights. The treaties are the mutually agreed framework and procedures for our shared relationship with the Crown and all the people the Crown authorized under the treaties to live and trade with the Mi'kmaq.

Mi'kmaw knowledge and language are about Mi'kmaw family, relationship-building and continuity. The philosophy of the Mi'kmaq was and is about establishing and maintaining harmony or peace through our mutual relationships, respect and reverence for our agreements and the lands we share. Harmony with all of nature and with other humans is key, because we are in this together. Joe B states, "Harmony is the goal of the Mi'kmaw order. We must live so that we maintain a sustainable ecology in our environment and that having this in our curriculum in the schools moving forward is a great way to begin." To date, neither Canada nor the Atlantic provinces have come to grips with the constitutional imperatives of implementing treaty rights. This is the next aspirational goal for Joe B.

Harmony and friendship in Canada and the Atlantic provinces will emerge through education about the constitutional rights of the Mi'kmaq. He stresses that Mi'kmaq need to teach their children the importance of our depending on each other for our survival and our empowerment in the future; as the treaty imperative has illustrated, we still need each other. Sometimes, we think it's easier to pretend we are assimilated, but then Joe B concludes, eventually "you find you lose your ways and your way. We must never forget where we came from, what we endured when the rule of law failed to protect us, how our ancestors wanted us to live under the treaties, and where we are going."

References

Akins, T. 1869. *Selections from the Public Documents of the Province of Nova Scotia*. Trans. B. Currin. Halifax, NS: C. Annard.

English to Indians, Treaty. 1726. (U.K.), 12 Geo I., no. 3 enclosure to Duke of Newcastle, 5 September 1725, CO 217/38, Nos. 7, 7 (i, x-xvii).

Henderson, James Youngblood. 1985. The Doctrine of Aboriginal Rights in Western Legal Tradition. In *The Quest for Justice: Aboriginal Peoples and Aboriginal Rights*, ed. Menno Boldt and J. Anthony Long, 185-220. Toronto: University of Toronto Press.

Journals of the Legislative Assembly of the Province of Canada. 1847. June 2 to July 28, 1847. Appendix to the Sixth Volume: n.p.

Le Canada Francais. 1888. I at 17 and Report Canadian Archives, 1905, 2, App., 293.

Marshall, Joseph B. 1991. Hunting and Fishing Rights of Mi'kmaq. In *Paqtatek*, ed. Patrick Johnson, 35-39. Halifax: Garamond Press.

McNeil, K. 1982. *Native Rights and the Boundaries of Rupert's Land and the North-Western Territory*. Saskatoon, SK: Native Law Centre, 285-86.

McNutt, William Stewart. 1965. *The Atlantic Provinces: The Emergence of Colonial Society, 1712-1857*. Toronto: McClelland and Stewart.

Murdock, B. 1866. *A History of Nova-Scotia or Acadie*. Vol. 2. Halifax, NS: J. Barnes.

RG1, vol. 40a, and CO, Series 217/9, 117. NSARM (Nova Scotia Archives and Records Management).

RG1, vol. 40b, and CO, Series 217/9, 118. NSARM (Nova Scotia Archives and Records Management).

R. v. Denny. 1990. 9 W.C.B. (2d) 438, Nova Scotia Court of Appeal, March 5.

Royal Proclamation. 1763. 7 October 1763 (3 Geo III) R.S.C. 1970, app. 1, 123-29).

Schomberg à Maillard, 26 Octobre 1759, AN, AC C11A/105 at ff 59-59v.

Secular Ulnapskok, The: Human Rights and Nova Scotia Mi'kmaq. 1980. Membertou,NS: UNSI.

UK PRO (United Kingdom, Public Records Office). CO, 217 vol. 4, 82.

Natasha Simon

Beyond Cultural Differences: Interpreting a Treaty between the Mi'kmaq and British at Belcher's Farm, 1761[1]

The conversation with Leon, my aunt's partner, began in a normal, friendly kind of way. We were discussing my plans for the summer. I had just come to the reserve the day before and was looking for a job. I realize now, sitting there in my aunt's house and looking around at the pictures of my cousins, that I was trying to place myself somewhere. Anyway, I spoke up:

"I'm thinking about volunteering at the Restorative Justice Initiative—they said they might hire me, too. I'm hoping that I'll be able to do research on treaties. I'm going to present my proposal to the chief and council on Monday."

Leon, who is laying on the couch, trying to pretend that I didn't just interrupt his favourite TV show, scoffs, "Pfhh, they aren't going to want to hear anything about that."

While lifting an incredulous eyebrow, I ask, "Well why not?"

I say incredulous because the previous day I had just listened to my other uncle complain the about how the chief and council don't care at all about treaty rights. And then, only a few minutes later, he told me that he isn't concerned with changing anything, he just wanted to be able to live. He told me that this is what everyone on the reserve wants.

At the time, we were in the middle of a discussion/argument and I said that there wasn't much of a difference between his position and the position of the band council. He got mad at me and told me that I needed to be subtler about things. And I know he's right.

Leon, who had been lying down, sits up. "They sold us out. While we were working our butts off in the woods, they signed agreements with the government. When the RCMP came and told us this, we told them that this was Crown land and the band council's jurisdiction ends at the reserve line. Then we were arrested. Your cousin was involved in this too. (I knew this already, and I heard that his wife was ripping mad that he got himself arrested.) Now we're going through the courts to show that the Crown land was always reserved land: reserved for us. It's our right."

Getting more excited, he continues, "It's the same with fishing. They sign off our rights with agreements and now we can only catch snow crab for commercial sale."

I agree with him that all of that is completely preposterous. "Why would the band council do that? You guys seem to have the upper hand when it comes to fishing."

Looking down and then up again, he replies, "They [the government] flash lots of money in front of their faces."

I can feel this burning in the pit of my stomach and it all clouds in my head. "It's senseless," I say. Then I ask, "But, Leon, why do you think that you have this right?"

Looking at me like I have two heads, he answers, "the treaties."

My uncle Max's warning quickly flashes through my mind. But I go ahead with a very direct question: "So the terms in the treaties indicate that you have these rights?"

Leon answers: "We are a nation. That is what they indicate."

"I disagree with you."

Leon's back straightens. I know he is caught a bit off guard because he thought that we were in agreement about this. I continue.

"I don't think that our ancestors intended for the treaties to be about laying out the exact terms of our co-existence. I mean, the treaties are not about divvying up land in return for protection of their interests." I know at this point that there is a fine line between following those intentions and espousing some right-wing agenda about there being no such thing as a special right. So I feel a bit afraid about this, but, at the same time, I have this feeling of determination because

I've been thinking about this for so long and have been unable to write about it. Anyway, as you can well imagine, I could feel the life in me as well.

"What do you mean?" he replies. "My grandfather and his grandfather and your grandfather, too, they all knew that the treaties entitled us to fish."

"I know. My grandfather went to court over his treaty right to fish."

"Yeah. He lost that case." Leon continues, "I remember my grandfather telling me about how we had a right to fish and so we should fish no matter what. If they come to us and tell us we can't, ignore them. If they attempt to rock our boat or take our nets, push them away. And if they try to stop us by shooting at us, kill them."

Silence.

"Leon, I'm not trying to say that we don't have a right to fish. It's just that we have to start thinking about this in a different way. I think that treaties are about how we are going to share a common way of life."

"That's assimilation, we were always a nation. We didn't want a common anything. According to the wampum belt, the lines run parallel. They do not converge."

At this point, I feel unsure of myself again. What right do I have to think differently from him about this? Maybe I just don't understand. But instead of hiding behind this insecurity, which is necessarily a part of my relationship with my family. I falter for a moment, and then my voice raises a pitch. "I agree," my heart begins to race. "We have our own legal systems, we have our own way of being."

Now the words flow out of my mouth. "And if you really think about it, fundamentally, justice is about the relationship between the individual and the community. So if we are going to actually think through what treaties are about we shouldn't be looking at the terms of it. We should be looking at the type of relationship that should be established."

Leon is sitting up, ready to get into a good argument. I can see us discussing every part of this, testing each point of our arguments. Then my aunt walks in. We start discussing her job and my cousins.

I could tell Leon wasn't listening. He was in one of those distracted, trying-to-figure-things-out states. While my aunt and I were discussing what my cousins have been up to, Leon pops up, "Consistency? We are lacking consistency?"

Defining Treaties

When I first looked at the transcription of an agreement made at Lieutenant Governor Belcher's farm, in 1761, between the British and the Mi'kmaq, like Leon, I wanted to see that the Mi'kmaq had stood firm in their resolve to protect their nationhood. I thought that they would be clear about their interests: as a nation, they would have the right to land and all the resources therein, and in exchange for this assurance they would no longer be in warfare with the British. Also, I wanted to find in the agreement a clue to what they had perceived to be a just relationship. I thought that at least there would be no mention of submission and, most definitely, no mention of the Mi'kmaq as conquered.

Well, as I read what was transcribed by the British, my heart began to sink. In Lt. Gov. Belcher's opening statement, he stated, "I assure myself that you submit yourselves to [the king's] allegiance with hearts of duty and gratitude as to your merciful conqueror." And to make matters even worse, a Mi'kmaw chief, opening with "My Lord and Father," stated:

> certain it is that we would have wretchedly perished unless relieved by your humanity, for we were reduced to extremities more intolerable than Death itself. You are Master here: such has been the will of God, he has given you the Dominion of those vast countries, always crowning your Enterprises with success. (PRO CO 1761: 277r-283r)

So not only did Belcher state that the Mi'kmaq were a conquered people, but the Mi'kmaq seemed to affirm it. Of course, we have to take into account that this was transcribed by the British and translated from Mi'kmaw via a French priest. Nonetheless, as an indication of an agreement between the Mi'kmaq and British, there is enough supporting evidence to show that this was a treaty of surrender by an already dependant and conquered people. As you can imagine, I was forced to re-examine my premises and assumptions. While asking myself to what extent I could read this transcription literally, I figured out that I was on the wrong track. I had been reading the agreement with conquest or nationhood as the only possible alternatives.

The switch from thinking of treaty interpretation as an either/or problem began with my cousin sitting me down to tell me a story. He began by telling me about how his grandmother had sat him down one day, covered all of the crosses in the living room with sheets and then told him the Creation story. Kluskap was the first Mi'kmaq and he came from elements of the land. As a cultural hero with special gifts, Kluskap taught lessons to the Mi'kmaq through misdeeds and accidents. His lessons benefited them because they then would know what could happen, and in this way they learned. At the time, the story sounded strangely familiar to me. After thinking about it for awhile, I realized that without actually telling me this story, my mother had taught me to learn in a similar fashion. Then finally, as I was trying to write about treaties, I realized that the significance of the story did not lie in its authenticity, consistency or entirety. The pattern or guidance of the story reveals that our world view is constantly fluctuating. It is in constant motion, but a continuity is also evident; indeed, all of our relations are integral to the culture.

Understanding the Treaty

According to historian Stephen Patterson (1993), in 1761, the treaty at Belcher's farm, the Mi'kmaq surrendered to the British on British terms. Throughout the period leading up to this cession, the Mi'kmaq were autonomous peoples, "exercising choices which represented their best efforts to accommodate the European intruders and adjust to the challenges and opportunities they posed" (Patterson 1993: 23). He further argues that since cultural values are the equivalent of political decisions and self-interest is the equivalent of political conscience, the Mi'kmaq were not motivated by a collective sense of cultural identity. Instead, their choices were "driven by conscious political decisions rooted in people's often imperfect understanding of their own self-interest" (24). Cultural differences, therefore, were irrelevant to the process.

Following his argument that the Mi'kmaq were individually following their own interests, Patterson suggests that they miscalculated them when they had earlier allied with the French. After the

English defeat of the French at Louisbourg in 1758, Québec in 1759 and Montréal in 1760, Patterson argues that the Mi'kmaq, who were dependent on French supplies and ammunition, could no longer successfully conduct warfare with the British and were out of food. As a result, they were forced to eventually surrender to the British, as indicated by the 1761 treaty, in which a Mi'kmaw chief states that their intention in negotiating with the British was both "to yield [themselves] up to [the British] without requiring any Terms on [their] part" and also to submit themselves to the "laws of [the British] government, faithful and obedient to the Crown" (PRO CO 1761: 282r, 281r).

Patterson's argument obviously supports Crown sovereignty. But the way he makes his case is fairly surprising. Anyone would think that Patterson favours Aboriginal nations when he argues that they were autonomous peoples who were not victims of history. But things begin to shift when he argues that the implications of this self-sufficiency is that the Mi'kmaq made choices without concern to cultural values, or at least that the political decisions which represent self-interest are the extent to which cultural values can be taken into consideration. Patterson believes that, as reasonable beings, we make decisions according to local conditions and circumstances. And according to the tenets of liberal thought, we must all be reasonable beings in order to be rights-bearing individuals. If rights then serve to ensure that all are equal, then the rights here involve ensuring that we all have the equal right to make decisions.

Carrying this over to treaty interpretation, Patterson's argument favours looking at treaties as contractual agreements that set out absolute terms of a relationship. He finds, however, that since the Mi'kmaq were surrendering, they were not in a position to negotiate the most favourable of terms. As a result, the treaties merely assured the Mi'kmaq that, with their surrender, they would receive, like all other British subjects, the protection of the British Crown: they would be treated equally with other British subjects. The treaties, then, do not present any kind of special rights for the Mi'kmaq.

Like Patterson, Henderson et al. (2000) argue that the Mi'kmaq were independent peoples, but this argument differs on the issue of conquest. Henderson, Benson and Findlay argue that the treaties set out terms of peace and friendship with the British. As a result, the Mi'kmaq never ceded any land, they only agreed to shared jurisdiction of their territory. The premise of this argument is that the Mi'kmaq were distinctive peoples with their own language, institutions and legal codes. Upon entering treaties with the British, they did so on equal terms and as a sovereign people/nation. By exploring the treaty, of which the 1761 agreement at Belcher's farm was one part, Henderson, Benson and Findlay challenge Patterson's argument that the Mi'kmaq ceded their land. They find that the intent of prerogative treaties on both sides were to affirm terms of coexistence (Henderson, Benson and Findlay 2000: 436).

These terms of co-existence were not set in stone; instead, they were formed through relations between the Mi'kmaq and the colonists. In order to keep peace in Nova Scotia, the British made sure that the Mi'kmaq were happy by making numerous concessions. For example, when some of their property was violated by colonists, it was dealt with in a private way instead of hazarding "a decision in the courts, where the Verdicts if found against them for want of sufficient evidence of otherwise, might have discontented their Tribes, and have been of disagreeable consequences in the present situation of affairs" (PRO CO 1762: n.p.). This demonstrates that the terms of relations between the Mi'kmaq and British were not necessarily determined solely by colonial interests.

This requires, however, that the Mi'kmaq had some understanding of the meaning of the treaty. If I take as a given that the Mi'kmaq were not exchanging territory for protection, it seems that they are not addressing the terms laid out in either Belcher's comments above or the written treaty. The Mi'kmaw chief quoted above is vague in this regard, referring mostly to the generosity and good will of the British. And as demonstrated in the following excerpt from the ceremony, the only treaty term that he actually acknowledges is the one relating to religion:

> There is one thing that binds me more strongly and firmly to you than I can possibly express and that is your indulging me in the free exercise of the religion in which I have been instructed from my cradle. You confess and believe as well as I, in Jesus Christ, the eternal word of almighty God. I own I long doubted whether you was of this faith.... But at present I know you much better than I did formerly, I therefore renounce all the ill opinions

that have been insinuated to me and my brethren in times past against the subject of Great Britain. (PRO CO 1761: 282r)

Taking this into consideration, there seem to be two choices in interpreting the Mi'kmaw understanding of the treaty: either they did not understand it or they were concerned only with securing the more spiritual aspects of it.

In meetings that led up to the agreement, the Mi'kmaq had expressed their interests beyond religious freedom. These included interest in property, trade and liberty to fish and hunt. In 1762, the Indians made "great Complaints that settlements have been made and possessions taken, of lands, the Property of which they have by treaties reserved to themselves." Belcher then lists the areas that are not to be disturbed, which included a fair share of land in Nova Scotia. The Mi'kmaq also settled terms of trade with the British, which were "so much above what private dealers could have afforded" (PRO CO 1763: 160r). At a meeting between Chief Michel Augustine of the Richibucto, and Paul Laurent, chief of the tribe of LaHave, speaking on behalf of "several tribes of Mickmacks," they agreed to the terms of a peace and friendship treaty and that "truckhouses [trading posts] should be established for supplying [them] with what they should want" (PANS 1760: 135). During these meetings, religion was not mentioned by the chiefs, instead the truckhouses seemed to be the most urgent piece of business. In these discussions, Mi'kmaq were concerned with ensuring a general way of life.

The meetings that led up to the agreement at Belcher's farm seem to contradict the chief's statement in the treaty-signing ceremony that religion was of utmost importance. But what this is signifying is not that the Mi'kmaq were not at all concerned with the material aspects of life. Instead, the chief was indicating that in order to share the land, they were also going to have to share a common way of life. They would have to share an understanding that would let them both be. This perspective, then, does not at all conflict with the principles of the wampum belt. Religion, after all, is extremely important; it is a testament to how we should relate to one another, and it determines our conception of a good society. Before the peace treaty, as indicated in the transcription, the Mi'kmaq had been falsely led to believe that the British were not Christians. The French and the Acadians must have spread misinformation about the British and their Protestantism.

Nonetheless, this tells us something very important about the core issue of this treaty. The Mi'kmaq recognized that to secure peace and friendship, a relationship must be established based on a common understanding.

Rights as Relationships

Rights are generally construed as though they are limits on the power of the state in order to protect rights-bearing individuals. This suggests that rights are "trumps," which, according to philosopher of law Ronald Dworkin, "state a goal for the community as a whole" and overrule "some background justification for political decisions" (Dworkin 1984: 133). In the justification game, political decisions are "tricks." Rights claims are trumps that protect individuals from majority decisions and are based on the basic goals or values of the community. In this case, if a native treaty right stipulates a right to fish, then an official would have to allow them to do so, even if that official doesn't believe that the community as a whole would benefit from natives having that special right. But the right is not absolute. It is dependent on the justification for political decisions that it trumps. The goal of our community, according to Dworkin (1984: 133), is a form of utilitarianism that justifies "the fulfillment of as many of people's goals for their own lives as possible." If we agree with this, how then would rights that go against the interests of the majority be justified?

Dworkin finds that the purpose of utilitarianism is not consistent with majority rule. At the root of utilitarianism is egalitarianism: "people are treated as equals when the preferences of each, weighted only for intensity, are balanced on the same scales with no distinctions for persons or merit" (Dworkin 1984: 154). For the sake of consistency, the weight that tips the scales in favour of majority or minority interests must also be consistent with the goals of utilitarianism. A purely egalitarian goal may favour majority rule, as it would dictate that the preferences of a few should not outweigh the preferences of others. But if these preferences (slavery, for example) were inconsistent with the principles of justice that underlie utilitarianism, they would not be given the same weight. Justice, as a means of distributing goods and opportunities, serves utilitarianism by ensuring that everyone receives their fair share without regard to "who he is or is not, or that others think he should have less because of who he is or is not or that others care less for him than they do for other people" (158).

Jennifer Nedelsky disagrees with Dworkin's game rules. She does not think that rights as trumps is consistent with the way our society works in general. First of all, she argues that rights, like laws passed by the legislature, are collective choices. Rights represent the values of our society, which are embedded in the law and given effect by judges (Nedelsky 1993: 4). Therefore, the way that Dworkin has formulated the issue, as though there was a tension between individual rights and democracy, is not consistent with the role of rights in our society.[2]

Instead, she argues that rights are a "dialogue of democratic accountability" (Nedelsky 1993: 9). The game is not about tension and balancing, it is about interdependence and mutual recognition. According to Dworkin, tension is a necessary part of the rights discourse because, as individuals, we have our own goals, and the goal of the community is to allow us to realize those goals. This, Nedelsky argues, is not consistent with human nature and society. For example, the relationship between mother and child cannot function if it is perceived to be a matter of weighing the mother's interests against the interests of the child (Nedelsky 1993: 8). This also carries over into the way the Mi'kmaq seemed to perceive their relationship with the British. Despite that during negotiations leading up to the treaty in question they were concerned with hunting, fishing and trade, in the treaty ceremony itself they seemed unconcerned with their interests beyond religion. Likewise, the dialogue of which Nedelsky speaks would involve a consideration of the values of our society, and the best means of achieving desirable relationships.

Democracy, as an equal voice in determining the values that will be embedded in law, may not be easily separated from rights, but protection from democratic outcomes is a necessary function of rights (Nedelsky 1993: 4-5). Our autonomy, freedom of conscience and religion may need certain protections from majority decisions. Often this protection is perceived to be a matter of weighing interests against one another, according to some higher value. But this perception of rights is dependent on a definition of autonomy as independence. As this independence involves separation from others, rights therefore form a barrier of protection from others and from intrusion by others (8).

But if we think of autonomy as interdependence or the independence to form desirable relationships, the problem at hand is transformed from tension to dialogue.

Constructing a tension between democracy and rights, then, is not helpful because it is not consistent with the way people relate to one another. It is more useful, Nedelsky argues, to consider the source and content of the value against which we measure the democratic outcome. Once it is seen that individual rights are collective choices, and that judicial oversight of legislative and executive acts actually enhances democracy, we can begin to think of how rights as relationships can move us beyond the individual vs. collective-rights barrier—and also beyond the problem of the victorious vs. the defeated in treaty interpretation. Rights can be redefined as relationships instead of individualistic protections if, instead of focusing on the limits that they must enforce, we begin to ask, "what relations of power, responsibility and duty do we want rights to foster?" Further, following Nedelsky's argument for rights as democratic accountability instead of trumps, we would then ask whether the above relationship would "foster values that are integral to our culture."

Returning once again to the Kluskap story, how are all our relations, as integral to our culture, to be interpreted through rights? And how do we formulate a way of determining what relationships are of value in our society? The process of learning requires that we experience mistakes. A mistake is a fundamental blip in our order of things. When we experience it we have to stop, reflect and change. This is how my mother taught me to understand, and it is the foundation of a good society because it allows for our understanding and values to always change while the learning process itself remains the same. So, instead of there being an end goal of equality, we would be better discussing specific purposes, and the processes which are going to help us achieve our goals. At Belcher's farm, the Mi'kmaq understood that religion is a collective way of determining these goals, which is why they ensured that freedom of religion was included as a term in the treaty.

Their concept of rights was collective in nature. But not in a way that separated them from others. Freedom does not have to be about independence. Instead, our freedom and right to self-determination can be about establishing relationships of respect. As a result, treaty rights would no longer be about proving whether native peoples did or did not lose their nationhood as a result of being conquered.

Instead, the descendants of the British—non-indigenous citizens of Canada—would respect the guarantee in the treaties that there would be freedom of religion in the manner the Mi'kmaq understood it.

While discussing the importance of religion, my grandmother succinctly told me that religion was good. I asked her why. She gave me this look. At the time, I thought that I had offended her, but now I think that it was more of an exasperated look. I was asking too much of her. But trying to answer it anyway, she said that she had been baptized, confirmed and always attended church. Then she stopped, and told me that church and prayer are two different things. Her parents had taught her to pray. Of course, I now begin to realize that all of our relations are integral to the culture.

Notes

1. An earlier version of this chapter was published as: Powers (Natasha) 2005. Beyond Cultural Differences: Interpreting a Treaty Between the Mi'kmaq and British at Belcher's Farm, 1761. *Atlantis: Critical Studies in Gender, Culture and Social Justice* 29 (2): 47-54. Reprinted with permission.

2. This is also evident in the debate over judicial review. See, e.g., Morton and Knopf, *The Charter Revolution and the Court Party* (Toronto: Broadview Press, 2000).

References

Dworkin, Ronald. 1984. Rights as Trumps. In *Theories of Rights,* ed. Jeremy Waldron, 153-67. Oxford, UK: Oxford University Press.

Henderson, James (Sa'kej) Youngblood, Marjorie Benson and Isobel Findlay. 2000. *Aboriginal Tenure in the Constitution of Canada.* Scarborough, ON: Carswell Press.

Nedelsky, Jennifer. 1993. Reconceiving Rights as Relationships. *Review of Constitutional Studies* 1:4-26.

PANS (Public Archives of Nova Scotia). 1760. Nova Scotia Executive Council Minutes, February 29. RG-1, v.188, 135.

Patterson, Stephen. 1993. Indian-White Relations in Nova Scotia, 1749-61: A Study in Political Interaction. *Acadiensis* 23 (1): 23-59.

PRO CO (Public Records Office [UK]–Colonial Office). 1761. Governor's Farm Ceremony, June 25. 215, v.18, 277r-283r.

———. 1762. Belcher to Board of Trade, June 02. 216, v. 19.

———. 1763. Remarks on the Indian Commerce carried on by the Government of Nova Scotia, April 05. 217, v.20, 160r.

Daniel N. Paul

Racism and Treaty Denied

When I was young, I often heard the Elders, who we called aunts and uncles, talk about how the white man wasn't honouring the treaties that their ancestors had entered into with ours, which included the right to hunt and fish and to harvest natural materials to produce arts and crafts. Also, I heard them talk about wildlife bounties, such as when the provincial government would place bounties on certain wildlife, such as porcupine. The Elders would state that the animal was suffering the same fate as the Mi'kmaq, who several times in the past had bounties placed on their heads by the colonial British. I will discuss both items further, after I give a little background.

I was born a status Indian in 1938, on the Shubenacadie Indian Reserve (now called Indian Brook), Nova Scotia. At that time, the *British North America Act, 1867,* classified us as wards of the Crown, a classification that gave us the same legal rights and status as drunks and asylum patients. Because of this we had few avenues for redress which emboldened Indian agents to act as if they were God almighty—our food, clothing and shelter were dependent on staying on the good side of the agents. Our Elders had to call them "sir" or "mister" when dealing with them, and they more often than not addressed our people by their first names only, showing little respect. To put it mildly, we were a poverty-stricken people who constantly suffered overt racial discrimination. I'll relate several of the personal experiences I've had with racism.

My place of birth was preordained by an act of racism. Here's the gist of that story:

Until the fall of 1935 my father worked on the Saint John, New Brunswick, waterfront as a stevedore, thus he was a taxpayer. That year, because of Depression-era work shortages, he and many others were laid off. Unemployed, with a growing family to support, he had to apply for municipal welfare to assure the family's survival, which was duly granted. A white resident of the city, viewing this as an affront to his sense of fairness, went to the city's fathers and complained bitterly that they were feeding a bunch of Indians. The city fathers agreed with his complaint and reacted with the proper indignation of the day. Thus, in late November of 1935, my parents and their five small children were rounded up and deported by the city council from Saint John to the Shubenacadie reserve, a place they had never been and in another province. Upon arrival, with little more than the clothes on their backs, and with cold weather setting in, the local Indian agent gave them a roll of tar paper and told them to build a shack, which they did, living in it more than two years before moving to the tiny log cabin where I was born.

When I was very young, four years old, I had my first encounter with a human failing previously unknown to me: racism, which, I thought for several years after, was just normal treatment for Indians. This was the way we were naturally treated. But, even at that young age, I resented it greatly.

It happened this way. My father had found work with a sawmill that was forty-eight kilometres from our home on the reserve. We did not own a car; in fact, there was only one Mi'kmaq on the reserve who owned a car at that time, and it was an old clunker that was not working half the time. Therefore, he had to walk to work on Sunday afternoons and walk home Saturday afternoons—that was the plan.

We ran out of food on Friday of the first week he was away and, as fate would have it, Dad couldn't make it home that Saturday. Early Monday morning, very hungry from going two days without food, I set out with my mother to walk about five kilometres through the woods to the state-run Indian agency farm, located on the other side of the reserve. We arrived shortly after the agency opened for the day, at 8:30 a.m., and were sent into the Indian agent's office to meet with him. Mom explained the situation and, without any consideration, the agent refused a ration because he knew that my father had found a job and was working. How he knew, I cannot tell you. She started crying and begged him to have pity on her eight hungry children, and told him she wouldn't be there if her husband could have made it home. He finally relented and told her that he would reconsider his decision.

At 11:45 a.m., shortly before the well-fed Indian agent went for lunch, he called Mom back into his office and gave her a small food ration. I can remember all this as if it happened yesterday. My reaction, as I looked at the mean agent, was "when I grow up, no bastard like you is ever going to do to me what you've done to my mother!"

Attending the Indian Day School

Two of my older brothers were enrolled in the Shubenacadie Indian Residential School when our family first arrived because the small on-reserve Indian day school had no room for them. They spent two years there. The horror tales they told us in later years about that place were scary to us, to say the least. Children were being forced to eat their own vomit, boys being whipped, boys and girls not being taught but used as forced labour to keep the school functioning—the boys having to work as farm labourers, and so on. When we were misbehaving, Mom used to say, "if you don't behave I'll put you into the residential school," which brought us quickly into line!

I was eight years old when I first attended school at the new day school that opened in 1947 on our reserve. The parish priest was principal and nuns from the Sisters of Charity Mother House were our teachers. The stereotypical image of the bloodthirsty Indian savage having been instilled in the minds of Caucasians was proven to me when one of the nuns sent to teach us was so frightened by being among Indians that she had to be sent back to the Halifax congregation, and a replacement sent out.

My sister Violet had taught me how to read and write. Therefore, the morning of my first day of school I was put in grade primary, in the afternoon I was moved to grade one, and the next morning placed in grade two. The only difference between the Indian residential schools and day schools was that we could go home at night. No Mi'kmaw was to be spoken on the grounds and there was no Mi'kmaw history in the curriculum except for one small paragraph, which stated that we were good at making baskets, axe handles and other arts and craft items. The rest of the curriculum was Eurocentric, especially as concerned the wonders of the British Empire, and the prideful fact that the sun never set on it. The Roman Catholic religion and its teachings were a top priority, along with drumming into us that we had descended from an inferior, savage culture; therefore, we were told that if we wanted to succeed in life we had to pursue the white way, which was the right way. This was a case of teachers having absolutely no knowledge of something they were degrading, instead basing their teaching on commonly held stereotypes.

The belief that we were descendants of an inferior, barbarous culture was reinforced by the movies of the day, which depicted bloodthirsty savage Indians attacking, killing and torturing saintly God-fearing white settlers. It wasn't unusual to go to the movies on a Saturday afternoon and see a group of Indian children cheering on the good guys (the settlers and cowboys). Of course, there was never any mention that these saintly folks were in the process of stealing an entire continent from its indigenous occupants; books, magazines and other media promoted similar degrading racist material.

My grade-school education ended in the first quarter of grade nine, in the fall of 1952. This came about when we had a math exam and I finished mine in about twenty minutes of the hour allotted. The sister corrected it and called me up and told me that I had scored one hundred; however, because there was quite a bit of time left she ordered me to do it over, which I refused. She then sent for the priest and he, in his capacity as principal, escorted me off the school grounds, with no consultation with my parents. Dad did ask the Indian agent if he could arrange for me to attend the Mill Village school, which was about five kilometres for me to walk, one way, from the reserve. The agent's response was, "it would be too upsetting for the ratepayers of the area to have an Indian attend their school." All this, and much more, began to build in me a significant inferiority complex.

Life on the Reserve

When I was young, homes on our reserve had no electricity, no water system, no central heating and had outhouses for toilets; most of the homes were not much more than shacks. After snowstorms, the one road leading into the reserve would not be plowed for up to two or three weeks; in the spring, the road was not passable for several weeks due to seasonal frost, thaw and flooding. The Department of Indian Affairs (now Indigenous and Northern Affairs Canada) food rations meted out to us by the Indian agents were meagre, covering just the absolute necessities. All services to us, including medical, were provided to us by political appointees not necessarily by qualified persons. The store owners who filled our food rations were also politically beholden, labouring under the dictate that they could not, under pain of losing their appointment, deviate from the rations listed.

William and Sarah Paul and two of their fourteen children. Taken at Brown Hill, Shubenacadie. Date and photographer unknown. Courtesy Daniel N. Paul.

In May 1940, the department's superintendent of welfare and training, in Ottawa, ordered a reduction of the 1940 welfare rates; food rations being provided to First Nations peoples at that time were near malnutrition levels. Also during this time, the government decided to implement its centralization policy, whereby all Maritime band members were relocated to four locations, two in New Brunswick and two in Nova Scotia (Eskasoni and Indian Brook). These racist policies are very complex, and a full review of them is available in many writings, including my book, *We Were Not the Savages* (Paul 2006).

Entering the Workforce

Following my schooling, I applied for a clerk job at the agency's co-op store, and was hired at $8 per week—working six days and one night. I stayed there until the early fall of 1953, at which time I ran away from home and went to Maine, to pick potatoes, and then on to Boston. In order to work at fourteen years of age, I had to have a work permit, which I managed to arrange. As a registered Indian, I didn't need to worry about immigration because we were covered by the Jay Treaty, which permits us to live and work in the United States. That treaty, signed in 1794, recognized the rights of First Nations people to unrestricted passage over the artificial boundaries created by Canada and the United States. While Canada and the British would later not honour the treaty provisions, saying that the War of 1812 negated them, the United States continues to uphold and recognize the treaty.

At sixteen, I contacted my parents and told them I was living and working in Boston. During the summer of my seventeenth year I went home to visit and had an experience with an Indian agent that I still chuckle about. I was sitting on the steps of the co-op store when he pulled up in front of the Indian agency, which was adjacent to the store and opened the trunk of his car, which was full of unopened paint cans. He glanced my way, snapped his fingers, and said, "hey boy, bring the cans into the agency!" Then he started up the steps to enter the building. I stopped him in his tracks by telling him to go do something that was anatomically impossible.

Sometimes, being discriminated against has its rewarding moments. Probably around 1958, two of my Marshall cousins from Millbrook, my aunt from Chelsea, Massachusetts, and her granddaughter and I decided we would go to New York City to participate in the city's New Year's Eve Times Square celebration. Our plans were to lodge at the YMCA and YWCA. When we arrived in the city, we decided to park our car in a parking garage for the duration of our visit and get a cab to our lodgings.

Upon acquiring a cab, because none of us had stayed at a YMCA or YWCA before, we asked the cab driver if anyone could stay at the hostel. His response, in a heavy Brooklyn accent, was "Sure, anyone can, except dogs and Indians!" My aunt replied, "Well, five Indians will be staying there tonight." The poor man was so humiliated and apologetic for his racist statement that he never charged us anything for the ride and the following day, as further apology, picked us up and gave us a free tour of the city's prime tourist spots!

When I was nineteen, I was employed in a hat factory in Boston, one of many low-paying jobs I had since I left home, and was befriended by a middle-aged black woman from Mississippi. She told me many tales about the humiliation of living under the segregation laws of the southern United States, and I told her about my experiences. One day she told me she wanted us to have lunch together because she wanted to have a serious talk with me.

The lady opened the conversation with this truism: "Boy, you walk around here with your head down and I know by that you have been convinced by the white man that you are inferior to them. Well, I want tell you something. You are just as good as all of them and in many cases probably much better." She then asked about what I knew of the true history of my people. My response was that I had heard of treaties, scalp proclamations and derogatory comments, such as we were cowardly, dirty, uncivilized and so on. But in reality, I knew practically nothing. She strongly suggested that I make every effort to learn about our history and that, when I finished, I would probably wind up being extremely proud of it. With the knowledge I've since acquired, indeed I am! I began to reassess my prospects that day, and over the next few years eventually concluded that my lack of education held no good prospects for my future. Therefore, at the age of twenty-one, I decided to return home and continue my education.

Acting on My Decision to Pursue Higher Education

During the summer of 1960, I filled out an application to attend Success Business College, in Truro, Nova Scotia. In the follow-up interview, the principal, Mrs. Wright, accepted my application but informed me, because I had only grade eight, that I would probably not be able to keep up with the rest of the student body, who were mostly high-school graduates. With acceptance in hand, I went home and asked the Indian agent for financial assistance to attend the college. He responded by advising me to forget about it and to get myself a pick and shovel and do what I was most suited for. Fortunately for me, my aunt Rebecca knew Cyril Kennedy, then the member of Parliament for the riding, from a previous employment. She called him up and told him about my situation, and his positive attention to the matter resulted in the Indian agent reluctantly funding me to attend college. I shall be forever grateful for this.

The school had a policy that permitted students to proceed at their own pace over the ten-month term. To the principal's surprise, I completed the school's introductory bookkeeping, general and advanced bookkeeping courses in less than four months, a record that stood until the school closed many years later. I only mention this achievement of mine as an admonishment: never judge a book by its cover! After Christmas break, I took cost accounting.

One of the courses that we were required to take was business law. It was during a lecture by a court judge that I learned about the legal standing of registered Indians—having the same capacity as drunks and insane persons when making contracts. When this item came up, most eyes in the class turned in my direction.

Re-entering the Workforce

In 1961, I landed my first job after business college as an office clerk with the Indian Affairs agency office in Shubenacadie. It was there that I learned, once again, that Indian Affairs employed quite a few bigots. It unravelled in this way. Two of us from the college had applied for two vacancies and both of us were hired. The Caucasian applicant, who had proceeded through business college at a much slower pace than I and who had struggled with the courses, was hired full time, without training. As for me, I was told that I would have to be trained for six months. By the end of the first day, I told them to shove it and left.

The following week I travelled to Halifax and acquired a job as assistant accountant with the now defunct Nova Scotia Abattoir. From there, I went on to a few more jobs, and was eventually working as chief bookkeeper at Stadacona's Non-Public Funds in 1970. It was then that I received a call from Rod Brown, Indian Affairs regional director at the regional office in Amherst. After exchanging a few pleasantries, he asked me to consider working for the department at the new district office they were establishing in Halifax.

Before I go any further, I want to mention a meeting I had, in 1967, at the Ponderosa Tavern, in Bible Hill, with an old friend, the late Noel Doucette, a member of the Chapel Island First Nation, who later served as chief and was a founder of the Union of Nova Scotia

Indians. Noel asked me to join in the effort to establish that organization. I mulled it over for a few days but eventually declined, with the explanation that I didn't think I had the knowledge sufficient for such an activity at that time.

After getting two more calls from Brown at Indian Affairs, I decided, after recalling my meeting with Noel, that perhaps this would be a golden opportunity to acquire an in-depth knowledge of the workings of the department and to do research. Thus, I accepted the offer in June 1971 and began working at the Halifax district office.

From the outset it was an eye-opening experience—and often humiliating. I'll just relate that I went from a senior position at Stadacona to an inconsequential position at Indian Affairs. I soon realized that I had been employed along with two other status Indians to fulfill a requirement that the department start to "Indianize" itself. I sat around doing nothing for almost a month to see how long it would last before some real work was sent my way. Tiring of it, I finally went into the district manager's office and asked him what the hell he had hired me for? They then made me construction clerk. What I saw over the next fourteen-and-a-half years of employment with Indian Affairs often prompted one non-racist Caucasian employee to tell me, "Someday you are going to write a book about this."

Until the Lion has his Historian, the Hunter will Always be the Hero.

The aforementioned is only an overview of the racism that I've encountered during my travels; to relate it all would take a book of considerable proportions. In December 1985, I left the department and agreed to become the founding executive director of the Confederacy of Mainland Mi'kmaq. From that point onward, I worked openly to advance the causes of First Nations and other excluded peoples.

It was at this was the time that I decided—with the knowledge garnered from talking to Elders, and working with the knowledgeable research assistance of Donald Julien and doing my own research—to take up the challenge and write the lion's side of the story that my fellow Indian Affairs employee predicted I would. My book, *We Were Not the Savages*, was on the way. This was no easy task. In addition to carrying out the work to establish a complex organization, I was writing weekly newspaper columns for the Halifax *Chronicle Herald*, establishing a Mi'kmaw newspaper, sitting on several provincial boards, including the Nova Scotia Court Restructuring Task Force, and involved with several other public organizations.

Perhaps the book's title, *We Were Not the Savages*, sums it up—perhaps it doesn't. But the conclusion I reached as a result of my research is that when Europeans invaded the Americas, morphing from explorers to settlers to colonizers, the justification used to subdue indigenous populations was a Christian duty to civilize the uncivilized. Yet the reverse was true—advanced European warmaking technologies, a thousand years of international hostilities and a history of genocide is most assuredly uncivilized. Here is a quick refresher:

First Nations History
WE WERE NOT THE SAVAGES
Daniel N. Paul
THIRD EDITION

Collision between European and Native American Civilizations

European Society	Mi'kmaw Society
War-making	Peace-loving
Brutal aristocracy	Benevolent chiefs who were mindful of the fact that the people could replace them
Mass starvation	Food was plentiful and shared
Greed	Honour and sharing
Slavery	
Prisons and asylums	

One is left wondering how, in spite of claimed Mi'kmaw ruthlessness and beastliness, and such able and ruthless enemies, the poor, "peaceful" European colonists managed to steal two continents. The Mi'kmaq had to be demonized in order to do their first level of business. Imaginative tales created by the Europeans have attributed to our ancestors the commission of inhuman crimes capable of chilling the stoutest spine. During colonial days, these lies and half-truths were used as justification by authorities to issue proclamations for Mi'kmaw scalps. For instance, in response to the 1744 request of the British governor of Nova Scotia, Jean-Paul Mascarene, for military assistance, William Shirley, the British governor of Massachusetts, declared war on the Mi'kmaq and offered a bounty for the scalps of Mi'kmaw men, women and children (Paul 2006: 107). In 1749, Nova Scotia Governor Edward Cornwallis also offered a bounty for Mi'kmaw scalps, women and children included (115). Consider that newborns, helpless infants, were included in the bounty.

But perhaps we sell those newborns short; they may have collectively presented a stupendous fighting force that had to be extinguished because of the danger they posed for European settlers. Such could be the only viable justification that an apologist could use to excuse the undertaking of something so barbarously cruel by "civilized" English colonial officials.

There is no doubt in my mind that, at that time, the Mi'kmaw chiefs, being intelligent men, were well aware of the brutality that was visited upon First Nations people of what is today the New England states by the British. Treaties made by area nations with the British Crown—after British officialdom had concluded that the said tribes had been suitably pacified and reduced to a poverty-stricken status—were not honoured by the British colonialists. Thus, Mi'kmaw chiefs probably had little expectation of being treated honourably and with respect afterward, which proved to be the case.

As I cover extensively in my book, I hold that the 18-century peace and friendship treaties between the Mi'kmaq and the British were viewed by the latter as pacifications, not of peace or friendship. The British had no intention of honouring those treaties. Cornwallis, for instance, requested from his superiors in London, in 1749, leave for grievous actions already initiated—a proclamation offering a bounty for scalps. This excerpt from his memo is insightful for its treachery.

> When I first arrived, I made known to these Micmac His gracious Majesty's intentions of cultivating Amity and Friendship with them, exhorting them to assemble their Tribes, that I would treat with them, and deliver the presents the King my Master had sent them....

The Saint John's Indians I made peace with, and am glad to find by your Lordship's letter of the first of August, it is agreeable to your way of thinking their making submission to the King before I would treat with them, as the Articles are word for word the same as the Treaty you sent me, made at Casco Bay, 1725, and confirmed at Annapolis, 1726. I intend if possible to keep up a good correspondence with the Saint John's Indians, a warlike people, *tho' Treaties with Indians are nothing, nothing but force will prevail.* (Qtd. in Paul 2006: 119; emphasis added)

A hundred years later, Joseph Howe described the enmity between the British and the Mi'kmaq:

The Indians who scalped (fought) your forefathers were open enemies, and had good reason for what they did. They were fighting for their country, which they loved, as we have loved it in these latter years. It was a wilderness. There was perhaps not a square mile of cultivation, or a road or a bridge anywhere. But it was their home, and what God in His bounty had given them they defended like brave and true men. They fought the old pioneers of our civilization for a hundred and thirty years, and during all that time they were true to each other and to their country, wilderness though it was. (Qtd. in Paul 2006: 9)

In an earlier report, in 1842, Howe, as Nova Scotia Indian Commissioner, submitted the following to the colonial governor of the day. Howe was trying to have the colonial government make an effort to end the starvation-level existence suffered by remaining Mi'kmaq.

I trust, however, that should your Excellency not be satisfied with the results of these first experiments, the blame may be laid upon the Commissioner, rather than be charged upon the capacity, or urged against the claims of a people, for whose many good qualities a more extended intercourse has only increased my respect, and who have, *if not by Treaty*, at least by all the ties of humanity, a claim upon the Government of the Country, which nothing but their entire extinction, or their elevation to a more permanent, and happy position in the scale of Society, can ever entirely discharge. (Qtd. in Paul 2006: 10; emphasis added)

In an era when attitudes toward the Mi'kmaq in Nova Scotia were not unlike those toward blacks in the American South, Howe's comments were profoundly progressive. His appeal to a new era of ethics fell on deaf ears, of course—you probably won't find his comments reprinted anywhere else than in my book. I reprint them here because, to me, they illustrate that influential people knew the difference—and failed, or refused, to act. Peace and friendship treaties were not differently interpreted by the parties, they were ignored by one side. Intentionally ignored.

Indian Act—Legal Rights

Insincerity and even treachery did not and does not invalidate the treaties—no matter how much time has passed. Section 88 of the *Indian Act* confirms that the terms of the treaty of 1752 state:

> Subject to the terms of any treaty and any other *Act* of Parliament, all laws of general application from time to time in force in any province are applicable to and in respect of Indians in the province, except to the extent that those laws are inconsistent with this *Act* or any order, rule, regulation or by-law made thereunder, and except to the extent that those laws make provision for any matter for which provision is made by or under this *Act*.

Armed with s. 88, the Union of Nova Scotia Indians went to the Supreme Court of Canada to appeal a lower-court decision that convicted a Shubenacadie Band member for hunting out of season. In *R v. Simon* (1986), the Supreme Court ruled in favour of the appeal—registered Mi'kmaq do not need a provincially issued licence to hunt, or to fish.

First, let's look at the lower-court decision, which dates, in fact, to *R v. Syliboy* (1928) tried before Judge Patterson. It was a telling and heartbreaking example of the prevailing racism of the time. Patterson's position reflects the bias against indigenous people interacting with the justice system. In his decision, Patterson wrote:

> Two considerations are involved. First, did the Indians of Nova Scotia have status to enter into a treaty? And second, did Governor Hopson have authority to enter into one with them? Both questions must, I think, be answered in the negative.
>
> (1) "Treaties are unconstrained *Acts* of independent powers." But the Indians were never regarded as an independent power. A

civilized nation first discovering a country of uncivilized people or savages held such country as its own until such time as by treaty it was transferred to some other civilized nation.

The savage's rights of sovereignty, even of ownership, were never recognized. Nova Scotia had passed to Great Britain, not by gift or purchase from or even by conquest of the Indians, but by treaty with France, which had acquired it by priority of discovery and ancient possession; and the Indians passed with it.

Indeed the very fact that certain Indians sought from the Governor the privilege or right to hunt in Nova Scotia as usual shows that they did not claim to be an independent nation owning or possessing their lands. If they were, why go to another nation asking this privilege or right and giving promise of good behaviour that they might obtain it?

In my judgment, the Treaty of 1752 is not a treaty at all and is not to be treated as such; it is at best a mere agreement made by the Governor and Council with a handful of Indians, giving them in return for good behaviour, food, presents, and the right to hunt and fish as usual—an agreement that, as we have seen, was very shortly after broken.

(2) Did Governor Hopson have authority to make a treaty? I think not. "Treaties can be made only by the constituted authorities of nations, or by persons specially deputed by them for that purpose." Clearly our treaty was not made with the constituted authorities of Great Britain.

But was Governor Hopson specially deputed by them? Cornwallis's Commission is the manual not only for himself, but for his successors, and you will search it in vain for any power to sign treaties.

Judge Patterson's disparaging comments are offensive in the extreme, declaring that the values of the colonizers are civilized, and that those of the Mi'kmaq are uncivilized. Not surprisingly, he makes no comment about the civility of Cornwallis's scalping proclamation or the other barbarous actions of colonial officialdom.

As quoted in *We Were Not the Savages* (Paul 2006: 272), the Supreme Court decision reads, in part:

[The] Appellant, a Registered Micmac Indian, was convicted under Section 150(1) of *Nova Scotia's Lands and Forest Act*....

Although appellant admitted all essential elements of the charges, it was argued that the right to hunt set out in the Treaty of 1752, in combination with Section 88 of the *Indian Act*, offered him immunity from prosecution under the Provincial *Act*.

Article 4 of that Treaty stated that the Micmac have "free liberty of hunting and fishing as usual" and Section 88 provided that provincial laws of general application applied to Indians, subject to the terms of any Treaty.

The Court of Appeal upheld the trial judge's ruling that the Treaty of 1752 did not exempt appellant from the provisions of the provincial *Lands and Forests Act*. At issue here was whether or not appellant enjoys hunting rights, pursuant to the Treaty of 1752 and Section 88 of the *Indian Act*, which preclude his prosecution for certain offenses under the *Lands and Forests Act*.

Held: The appeal should be allowed.

Both Governor Hopson and the Micmac had the capacity to enter into the Treaty of 1752 and did so with the intention of creating mutually binding obligations. The Treaty constitutes a positive source of protection against infringements on hunting rights and the fact that these rights existed before the Treaty as part of the general Aboriginal title did not negate or minimize the significance of the rights protected by the Treaty.

[...]

The Treaty of 1752 continues to be in force and effect. The principles of international Treaty Law relating to Treaty termination were not determinative because an Indian Treaty is unique and *sui generis*. Furthermore, nothing in the British conduct subsequent to the conclusion of the Treaty, or in the hostilities of 1753, indicated that the Crown considered the terms of the Treaty terminated. Nor was it demonstrated that the hunting rights protected by the Treaty have been extinguished. The court expressed no view whether, as a matter of Law, Treaty rights can be extinguished.

[...]

The Treaty of 1752 is an enforceable obligation between the Indians and the Crown and is therefore within the meaning of Section 88 of the *Indian Act*. Section 88 operates to include all agreements concluded by the Crown with the Indians that would be otherwise enforceable Treaties, whether or not land was ceded.

[...]

It was not necessary to consider Section 35 of the *Constitution Act, 1982* since Section 88 of the *Indian Act* covered the present situation and provided the necessary protection for the appellant.

This case demonstrates how vitally important Indian Registration is when affirming entitlement to aboriginal rights. If Jimmy Simon had not been registered as an Indian, he would not have won his case, because it would have been impossible for him to prove his ancestry otherwise.

When considering *Simon*, the Supreme Court of Canada reviewed Judge Patterson's 1928 racist decision in *Syliboy*, which had considered the question of the capacity of the parties to enter into the Treaty of 1752. In finding that the Treaty of 1752 was a valid treaty, the Court stated: "With regard to the substance of Judge Patterson's words, leaving aside for the moment the question of whether treaties are international-type documents, his conclusions on capacity are not convincing." The decision continued:

> The Treaty was entered into for the benefit of both the British Crown and the Micmac People, to maintain peace and order, as well as to recognize and confirm the existing hunting and fishing rights of the Micmac. In my opinion, both the Governor and the Micmac entered into the Treaty with the intention of creating mutually binding obligations which would be solemnly respected.
>
> It also provided a mechanism for dispute resolution. The Micmac Chief, and the three other Micmac signatories, as delegates of the Micmac people, would have possessed full capacity to enter into a binding treaty on behalf of the Micmac. Governor Hopson was the delegate and legal representative of His Majesty the King.
>
> It is fair to assume that the Micmac would have believed that Governor Hopson, acting on behalf of His Majesty the King, had the necessary authority to enter into a valid treaty with them. I would hold that the Treaty of 1752 was validly created by competent Parties. (Paul 2006: 272-74)

Despite the ruling of the Supreme Court in *Simon*, both the federal and provincial governments have refused to act since in good faith. To date, the only matters they have shown a willingness to negotiate are those beneficial to their own interests. And, as exemplified in the highly publicized Donald Marshall Jr. wrongful conviction case (1983), the racist attitudes expressed by Judge Patterson in 1928 prevailed in the Nova Scotia justice system into the late 20th century. Section 88 of the *Indian Act* has been the subject of litigation in many other situations, and no doubt will be prominently mentioned in others for years to come.

Peace and Friendship Treaties

The insincerity of the British Crown, and later the Canadian government, in fulfilling the obligations that their ancestors undertook by signing these documents with our ancestors is a complete disregard of the law.

As I stated at the outset, I was aware of the treaties made by our ancestors with the British when I was very young. However, I never actually read one until 1971. From that reading, I gathered that we had the right to hunt, fish and gather as usual but, most importantly, that there had been no cessation of Mi'kmaq land. Curiosity caused me to locate and read about the Burying of the Hatchet Ceremony and treaty signing, held at Nova Scotia Lieutenant Governor Jonathan Belcher's farm, on June 25, 1761, between Mi'kmaw district chiefs and the colonial governor. The ceremony officially ended approximately 130 years of warfare between our ancestors and the British.

From reading that document, and reading about the historic, acrimonious relationship between the two parties, I concluded that the main reason the British were burying the hatchet and signing treaties was to pacify the Mi'kmaq, who, although in a very impoverished state at the time, and without the aid of their French allies, they still had great fear of. Even in the late 1780s, during the French Revolution on the Continent, the paranoia persisted. Lieutenant Governor John Wentworth thought it essential to pacify the Mi'kmaq in Nova Scotia with gifts of food and clothing so "that the peace of our scattered Inhabitants may not be disturbed by them" should they take up arms and join with the French. Keep in mind that the Mi'kmaq were now living in a state of near starvation and abject poverty. On the other hand, I've concluded from research, and the consequent mistreatment of our ancestors, that the chiefs buried the hatchet and signed treaties with the British in the hope of survival in what would henceforth be a very hostile social environment.

—

During my employment with Indian Affairs, I would occasionally receive calls from Nova Scotians inquiring about the Mi'kmaw treaty right to hunt, fish and gather as usual. My response was "yes"; however, I never relayed that the Canadian Crown was resisting acknowledging and respecting that. Related to the fact that the Mi'kmaq never ceded our land, I was once asked, during a 1980s discovery hearing,—I don't remember the exact date or the exact case—where I lived. I responded that I lived on Mi'kmaw land. The Crown attorney, in an "I gotcha" moment, stated "but you have listed here an address in Halifax." I countered with "who said Halifax was not Mi'kmaw land, you cannot show me a document where my ancestors ceded any land to the British or Canadian governments." The attorney was about to carry on with his rant when the adjudicator intervened with this: "unless you can prove otherwise, we will have to accept Mr. Paul's declaration."

During my term as a founder and executive director of the Confederacy of Mainland Mi'kmaq, from 1986 to 1993, chiefs offered to arrange meetings with both the federal and provincial governments, to negotiate, instead of litigating, settlement agreements that in the long term would be beneficial to all—and far less expensive than litigation. The response from both levels of government was that the courts would have to provide the answers to our questions, to our contentions. The bureaucrats believed they would prevail in court. That hasn't worked out too well for them. The Mi'kmaq have won almost all the Aboriginal-rights court decisions we were forced to undertake.

In the legal sense, it seems, justice prevailed in recognition of rights. Now what is needed is a civilized approach by all levels of government to overcome and dispel the centuries of systemic racism and demonizing propaganda, a burden that we have all carried for far too long.

Reference

Paul, Daniel N. 2006. *We Were Not the Savages*. 3rd ed. Halifax, NS: Fernwood Publishing.

Douglas E. Brown

Litigating Section 35 of the *Constitution Act, 1982*: Aboriginal and Treaty Rights in Nova Scotia

Perspective

I am Doug Brown. I am the son of Katlin ("Soda") Sorbey and Douglas Brown. My sisters are Donna Brown-Paul (Membertou) and Madonna Johnson (Eskasoni). Both my mother and her brother, the late Alex Denny, were activists for the human and treaty rights of the Mi'kmaq. My mother was the president of what is now known as the Native Council of Nova Scotia, although when she was president in the 1970s it was known as the Metis and Non-Status Indian Association of Nova Scotia. Uncle Alex was a grand captain of the Mi'kmaw Grand Council, the traditional governing structure of the Mi'kmaq nation. Although I had heard of their activism from an early age, I did not come to appreciate what it really meant until my mid-twenties. It was then that I started to engage with the documentary materials and various human resources that provided me with the larger context of the long struggle for Mi'kmaw self-determination in the context of ongoing oppression.

My high-school education in Canton, Massachusetts, taught me nothing about this struggle. Similarly, my time in the U.S. military taught me nothing of this struggle. (In 1983, I joined the U.S. Army infantry for four years; I spent two years in West Germany and two years at Ft. Benning, Georgia.) Once I completed my military service, I began university studies at the University of Massachusetts Boston, where I became the president of the American Indian Student Association, an organization that shared office space with another university organization, Students for Educational Access, composed of a group of students with a decidedly Marxist approach to social-justice issues. It was my short but intense exposure to this group and their insightful discussions that stirred me to look with more depth at the activism of my mother and my uncle, and at the injustices surrounding my own people, the Mi'kmaq.

From UMass Boston I moved to Membertou, Nova Scotia, in 1988, and continued my education at Cape Breton University (CBU), Sydney. I completed a four-year degree with an area major (Mi'kmaq Studies, History and Political Science) in 1992. It was during this time that I learned in depth about Mi'kmaw nationhood and the chain of pre-confederation treaties of peace and friendship between the Mi'kmaq and the British monarchy. I also learned of the Canadian state's subsequent efforts to systematically conceal and deny this history and reality. In this way, I learned about the larger context of my mothers' eight years of Indian residential schooling and my uncle's efforts concerning Aboriginal rights to call for the assistance of the International Commission on Human Rights against the Government of Canada. I became aware of the significance of the historical research and legal work performed by the Union of Nova Scotia Indians (UNSI).

After CBU, I attended St. Mary's University (SMU) in Halifax in the masters program for Atlantic Canada Studies—continuing with my focus on Mi'kmaw history. After completing one year of course work at SMU, but not my thesis, I began Dalhousie Law School in 1993 and graduated in 1996. For the next year I was an articled clerk at the Nova Scotia Department of Justice in Halifax, and was called to the Nova Scotia bar in October 1997.

The Union of Nova Scotia Indians

In May of 1998, I began working as junior legal counsel for the UNSI, where I was mentored by Bruce Wildsmith, Queen's Counsel, a brilliant and well-published constitutional-law lawyer and university professor at Dalhousie. I assisted him with an assortment of Aboriginal and treaty-rights cases and learned a lot about the practice of Aboriginal law, the law of evidence and the adversarial system. I also became aware of the existence of the Nova Scotia Public Prosecution Service, which, ironically, originated out of the recommendations made by the 1989 royal commission into the prosecution of Donald Marshall Jr., a Mi'kmaq from Membertou, which found, among other things, Marshall to be wrongfully convicted of murder and the Nova Scotia justice system to be riddled with racism.

About five or six months after being with the UNSI, I began working on what I thought would be a relatively simple case, with respect to section 35 of the *Constitution Act, 1982*, involving food-hunting rights of the Mi'kmaq. Nova Scotia had charged Eskasoni First Nation member Allison Bernard Jr. with violating s. 68 of the provincial wildlife act, which prohibits "hunting with the assistance of a light or flambeau." The UNSI agreed that this was an issue they would support and thus agreed to provide legal representation. Going into this issue in 1998, I thought I would simply argue that provincial sport-hunting regulations are not enforceable against Mi'kmaw hunting for food. That is, in fact, the law.

As it turns out, a simple legal issue can quickly become complicated or made complex by those wielding power. The special-prosecutions unit of the Nova Scotia Public Prosecution Service appears to be one such power base. It is within their discretion to decide to prosecute s.

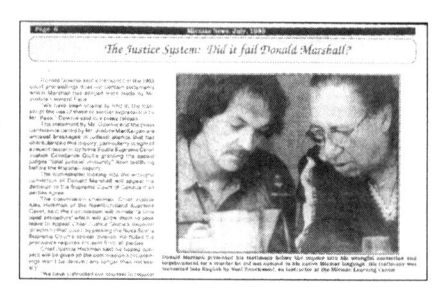

Caption reads: *Donald Marshall presented his testimony before the inquiry into his wrongful conviction and imprisonment for a murder he did not commit, in his native Micmac language. His testimony was translated into English by Noel Knockwood, an instructor at the Micmac Learning Centre. MicMac News, 1988, vol. 18(7): 6. http://beatoninstitute.com/micmac-news-1988.*

68 charges against Aboriginal food hunters. By choosing to prosecute, the unit has decided that protecting the Aboriginal right to exemption from s. 68 is inconsistent with, as they cite, the "public interest." It is as if the "public" had no interest in maintaining the constitutional rights of the Aboriginal people of Nova Scotia. What could motivate such a position? A greater entity, perhaps; such a power is the Nova Scotia legal system.

The following is the story of how an unpopular method of exercising the Aboriginal right to hunt for food unfolded judicially (and otherwise) since 1998. This drama continues at the time of this writing, there will be no hard and fast conclusion to the issue in Nova Scotia, as the *Francis and Paul* case, which will be discussed later, is ongoing as of this writing. There will, however, be lessons and implications that can be extracted already.

Jacklighting for Food

Jacklighting is the decidedly unsporting practice of shining a bright light into the eyes of a deer or moose, or some other nocturnal species, which causes the animal to stop in its tracks, making it an easier shot for a hunter. It is also a practice that is widely outlawed in most North American jurisdictions.

The reason this method is considered unsporting is because it is such an efficient means of killing of moose or deer—thus depriving the hunt of the element of sport. Generally speaking, however, Aboriginal hunters do not hunt for sport, they hunt for food, and in Canada they have a constitutional right to do so. In court, if an Aboriginal accused were hunting for sport (rather than food), they would *not* be entitled to rely upon a s. 35 Aboriginal-rights defence.

Much of the commentary that follows can also be applied to the food-hunting activities of any food hunter in Nova Scotia, whether Aboriginal or not. Non-Aboriginal food hunters represent a segment of the poor who are largely the forgotten victims of outdated and elitist regulations. The difference between Aboriginal and non-Aboriginal food hunting is the legal mechanism that is available as recourse to prosecution. For the non-Aboriginal, hunting is a highly regulated privilege bestowed by provincial statute (the *Nova Scotia Wildlife Act*) rather than a constitutional right. As such, the non-Aboriginal food hunter, who is by law coerced into hunting in a "sporting" manner, has no recourse to the courts, which must apply the law as written. Instead, the non-native food hunter must seek recourse through lobbying the provincial government for legislative change. However, the strongest lobby effort thus far on provincial hunting practices is that of the Nova Scotia Federation of Anglers and Hunters, a group that strongly advocates against the practice of jacklighting. For Aboriginal peoples, the Constitution of Canada (s. 35) recognizes their right to hunt for food. Thus, Aboriginal food hunters are able to raise a court challenge against any legislation that unjustifiably infringes upon that right.

The Supreme Court of Canada has previously recognized the practice of jacklighting as a permissible method of food hunting for Aboriginal peoples. The subject is not ambiguous in any way, as the court has endorsed the practice on numerous occasions. However, provincial courts, including courts of appeal, across Canada have not been consistent with the Supreme Court on this matter. Nova Scotia is one such province.

Historical Origins of Section 68 of the *Nova Scotia Wildlife Act*

The prohibition or ban on using a light to assist the hunt does not originate from public-safety concerns, as it is often cited as the case, but rather originates from concerns to keep the sport in the hunt. I say this not as part of a persuasive argument, but as a simple matter of historical fact.

The concept of hunting for sport originated in, and then was imported from, England, from as far back as the 1830s, popularized in the writings of Henry William Herbert. In North America, sportsmen's organizations such as the Boone and Crockett Club soon began to form themselves around the newly imported concept. These early organizations were made up primarily of the wealthy and elite—notably including judges, lawyers, doctors and politicians. They devoted themselves to the protection and preservation of game.

These groups promoted hunting ethics and codes of conduct that were designed to ensure that the hunt was a real test of a sportsman's mettle and truly a challenge. These rules allowed game a fair chance at eluding capture and at ensuring the game population remained healthy. For example, according to the ethics of a sportsman, it was forbidden to chase deer or moose into deep rivers or lakes before shooting them. This was not a "fair chase" to the animal. In other words, it was the *act* of hunting that became the motive for hunting, rather than the game that was killed as a result.

Because these sportsman associations were primarily made up of the wealthy and elite, they were very influential in terms of lobbying for game laws, framing certain legislation; sometimes their members were actually part of the law-making class. This was the case in New York in 1897, where, the State Assembly passed the Adirondack Deer Law, which outlawed the "jacking of deer" (hunting with the assistance of a light), not on the basis of safety or conservation but on the basis that the practice was "unsportsmanlike." Members of the assembly who sponsored the bill were also members of the sportsmen club that endorsed those very same ethics and codes—not the least of which was an absolute disdain for the unsportsmanlike technique of jacklighting.

Jacklighting, to those groups, was seen as cowardly and made the hunt far too easy for a true sportsman. Over time, laws and hunting ethics were expanded (as technology advanced) to include more prohibitions on methods such as hunting with poisons, hunting with explosives, or hunting with or from vehicles (boats, trucks, helicopters, etc.). Other laws to the same end included a prohibition on hunting game with dogs. All of these laws had one thing in common—to make the hunt for game a truly challenging and sporting endeavour. They were also put into place to make room in a quickly diminishing forest for a small group of wealthy elite that wanted exclusive access to nature and the hunt for themselves—never mind that many poor people, as well as Aboriginal people, hunted not for the sport, not for the leisure and not to test their mettle—but to simply put food on their plates.

Crown Approach to Section 68 in Nova Scotia: Safety of the Public

On the subject of Aboriginal hunting rights generally, the Supreme Court of Canada has already defined some parameters of these rights. What the court has said is that the exercise of Aboriginal hunting rights extend only as far as "public safety" and that "conservation of the species" is not compromised by the exercise of those rights. In other words, Aboriginal hunters can hunt for food as long as their hunting does not endanger the lives of others, and/or as long as the practice does not put any species of animal or fish at risk of extinction. Provincial laws that do not sufficiently relate to either of these issues (such as s. 68 of the NS *Wildlife Act*) are not enforceable against Aboriginal food-hunting activity.

According to constitutional law, then, the safety of the public is considered a justifiable reason for the province to regulate aspects of the Aboriginal food hunt. In other words, Aboriginal food hunters must obey provincial laws of general application that ensure the "safety of the public."

Well aware that this is the state of the law on Aboriginal rights, the Crown in Nova Scotia has prosecuted Mi'kmaw hunters under s. 68 of the *Wildlife Act* on the bald assertion that public safety is compromised by the practice of hunting with the assistance of a light. The legal approach of the Crown's special-prosecutions office is that a sport regulation (s. 68) is also a public-safety regulation, and is thus applicable to the Aboriginal food hunter. This approach, however, ignores that (1) s. 68 is not aimed or even rationally connected to ensuring public safety, (2) the Supreme Court of Canada has already pronounced the practice of jacklighting to be a permissible method of Aboriginal food hunting, and (3) there are several public-safety regulations within the *Nova Scotia Wildlife Act*, and in provincial regulations, whereby Aboriginal hunters who *do* pose a risk to public safety during night-time food hunting can be charged. Section 68 is not one of them.

Public Safety: A Concern More Apparent than Real

When thinking about the issue of jacklighting, one of the most forgotten realities is this: virtually all hunting, whether during the day or night is "inherently dangerous"—after all, it usually involves the firing of a high-powered rifle of some sort. That's why the province has established hunter-safety courses and created those public-safety laws mentioned above. But hunting, overall, is like driving a car: it might be inherently dangerous, but it is still considered by both Aboriginal and non-Aboriginal society to be a risk worth taking—even for nothing more than sport or recreation in the majority case.

The irony of the issue is this: hunting by day is simply more dangerous than hunting with a light at night. Consider the following: daytime sport hunters are not prohibited from hunting in foggy, snowy or rainy conditions when visibility is severely diminished. Daytime sport hunters are generally more susceptible to fatigue (due to trekking and tracking game animals) and are therefore potentially more susceptible to overeagerness (are trigger-happy) than the generally more laid-back night hunters who usually do their trekking and tracking from a vehicle. No matter how clear a day it might be, daytime sport hunters still cannot see through a bush, a tree or tall grass—no matter how far behind and beside the target they might visually check. Daytime sport hunters are also more likely than jacklighters to take aim at a moving target since the animal is not immobilized by the glare of a spotlight. And, lastly, during the daytime there are simply more people (hunters, hikers, anglers) present in the woods.

Despite these inherent dangers, daytime sport hunting is not only permitted, it is purposely made more "challenging" or "sporting" by certain provisions of the *Nova Scotia Wildlife Act*. And let us not forget the most telling of statistical facts: the vast majority of hunting fatalities and accidents occur during daylight hours—most involving some sort of mistaken identity. Despite these permissible daytime-hunting safety concerns, sport hunters are merely expected to deal with them with nothing more than the exercise of sound judgement and due care.

What about the safety advantages of hunting with a jacklight? After all, a light is simply a tool used to increase a person's visual capacity during the hours of darkness. A jacklight used prudently can be just as effective for scouting the area behind and to each side of an animal as a daytime hunter's vision. A jacklight would be a much better early-warning device to others that might happen to be in the vicinity of a targeted animal. (I know if I saw a bright shining light in the woods, I'd be quick to make my presence known or at least be quick to take cover.) Furthermore, a jacklight has the effect of freezing a moose or deer in their tracks (which is why it is said to be unsportsmanlike), generally giving the hunter an immobile target at which to aim—and thereby creating even less chance of an errant shot. Is the exercise of sound judgement and due care exclusive to the daytime sport hunter?

R. v. Bernard: My First Aboriginal-Rights Case

My very first court case as UNSI legal counsel involved the assertion of an Aboriginal-rights defence to the charge of "hunting with the assistance of a light," contrary to s. 68 of the *Wildlife Act*. The trial was held in Eskasoni in the basement of the NADACA (Native Alcohol and Drug Abuse Counselling Association) centre where I was defending Allison Bernard Jr. The facts of the case were that Bernard was observed shining a spotlight out of his pickup truck window in Northside East Bay into a farmers field while in possession of a rifle. No shots were fired. Court was held before Judge David Ryan, and began in 1998.

It should be stated again that at the outset of the trial my thinking on this case was that it would be somewhat easy and somewhat obvious, as the legal point in question, to my mind, was simply whether Mi'kmaw food-hunting activities were exempt from sport-hunting regulations such as s. 68. The answer is easy and the law emanating from the Supreme Court of Canada on the subject was unambiguous. In Nova Scotia, however, being legally correct does not necessarily equate with legal victory. What follows are the highlights of that case, which are illustrative of the point.

Trial Level: First Attempt

At the beginning of the *Bernard* trial, held in the First Nation community of Eskasoni, the Crown prosecutor from the special-prosecutions unit introduced into evidence an expired one-year hunting agreement (from 1991) signed between the thirteen Mi'kmaw chiefs of Nova Scotia and the Nova Scotia minister of natural resources. The agreement was introduced by the Crown for the purpose of demonstrating to the court that night hunting with the assistance of a light was agreed to be not practised by Mi'kmaw food hunters for the term of the agreement. The broader significance of the agreement was that it was made (unbeknownst to me at the time) "without prejudice to the Aboriginal and treaty rights" of the Mi'kmaq. In other words, neither the agreement nor any of its contents had any place being introduced as evidence in a court of law adjudicating on the treaty rights of the Mi'kmaq.

At the time it was proffered as evidence in the trial, I did not object to it on the basis that I thought it was nevertheless irrelevant as it had long since expired and was not renewed. I later conferred with Bruce Wildsmith about this. He informed me that he knew that it was made "without prejudice" to the Aboriginal and treaty rights of the Mi'kmaq and, thus, should not have been introduced or received as evidence in the trial. Before the trial could advance further, we successfully motioned for a mistrial. Judge Ryan agreed with our motion and he ordered a new trial (see *R. v. Bernard* 1999).

Trial Level: The Second Attempt

The retrial of Bernard was scheduled to be heard before Judge A. Peter Ross. At the retrial, the provincial Crown, despite the outcome of the initial trial before Judge Ryan, attempted to read into the court record the terms of the "without prejudice" Mi'kmaw hunting agreement mentioned above. I objected to the Crown's attempt on the basis that the terms of the agreement were irrelevant, and were the very subject of the mistrial declared by Judge Ryan, to which Judge Ross agreed.

Despite the evidentiary ruling of Judge Ross, the Crown responded that if it could not introduce the agreement itself, nor could its contents be read into the record, than it therefore intended to issue subpoenas to each of the signatory Mi'kmaw chiefs in order to force them to testify as to the contents of the "without prejudice" agreement.

These subpoenas were indeed issued by the Crown. I was then forced to make formal application to the Court to quash the subpoenas. However, I could not do this until I was again before Judge Ross on the date of the continued trial itself—all of which meant that some (or all) of the chiefs who were subpoenaed could prospectively be there too, in answer. Fortunately, not one single chief bothered to show up to testify. At least they had an understanding of the term "without prejudice." I proceeded and successfully argued for the quashing of the subpoenas on the same basis that the expired "without prejudice" hunting agreement was not permitted in the first two instances.

Again, the conduct of the special-prosecutions unit in attempting, on three separate occasions, to introduce the terms of the "without prejudice" agreement into evidence only adds to the irony mentioned above—that the Nova Scotia Public Prosecution Service had its origins in the recommendations made by the royal commission into the Marshall persecution.

Evidentiary Issues Arising

Once the subpoenas were quashed, the trial continued. Defence witnesses in the trial included Allison Bernard Jr., the accused; John Prosper, then director of the Mi'kmaw Fish and Wildlife Commission; Officer Bruce Nunn of the Department of Natural Resources (DNR); and Mi'kmaw hunter Fred Sylliboy. Crown witnesses included the three arresting DNR officers, and John Mombourquette, director of enforcement at the DNR.

Essentially, all of the Crown's witnesses were testifying how, in their opinion, hunting at night with the assistance of a light was a "dangerous" and "risky" practice that should and could not be allowed for reasons of "public safety."

At this point, it should be stated clearly that it is a well-known juridical fact that it is the role of the *judge* to interpret and apply the law. Part of that role sometimes involves the determination of a law's purpose and effect—such as the purpose and effect of s. 68 of the *Act*. The judge in this case is not supposed to permit the opinions offered by the DNR officers to usurp his role and, in effect, replace or even influence his own independent legal analysis of a law's purpose. In other words, opinion-based testimony of the DNR officers ought to have been excluded as evidence or else given little or no weight by the presiding judge. Yet Judge Ross did give weight to their opinions. It appeared that he fully accepted their testimony as evidence of the "public safety" purpose of s. 68, with no independent judicial analysis thereof (particularly the "sport" purpose and effect of s. 68). This is evident in the decision, wherein Judge Ross ruled that s. 68 was a "preventive safety measure" and that, as such, did not *prima facie* infringe the Mi'kmaq right to hunt for food.

Expert Historical Evidence Not Necessary

It should be noted that the entire Bernard trial proceeded without any "pre-European contact" historical evidence of Mi'kmaw nighthunting practices. The position was that such evidence was not necessary for the determination of the case on the basis that the Mi'kmaw right to hunt and fish for food had already been well established in law in Nova Scotia (see *R. v. Denny, Paul and Sylliboy 1990*). The existence of the Mi'kmaw right to hunt and fish for food was recognized and, in fact, acted as a *presumption* in Canadian law. It was this right that was being exercised by Bernard and was infringed by the application of s. 68. After some back and forth on the issue of the necessity of this type of evidence, Judge Ross ruled that no such evidence was necessary. The Nova Scotia Court of Appeal later agreed with this evidentiary aspect of the lower-court ruling.

Supreme Court of Canada Authority

At trial, Bernard argued that if public safety was the major concern driving this prosecution, then he ought to have been charged with a public-safety violation, such as "hunting too close to a dwelling" or "hunting unsafely." This would have been the proper way to proceed rather than charging him with violating s. 68, clearly a sport-hunting prohibition that Aboriginal peoples are exempt from when exercising their right to hunt for food.

This line of reasoning was already laid out by previous Supreme Court of Canada decisions that predated the inclusion of s. 35 in the *Constitution Act, 1982*. In *Myran v. R.* (1976), the Supreme Court made the distinction between permissible methods for Aboriginal hunting for food and safety provisions, where they state:

> ...it is clear from *Prince and Myron* [v. the Queen] that an Indian of the Province is free to hunt or trap game in such numbers, at such times of the year, **by such means or methods and with such contrivances, as he may wish, provided he is doing so in order to obtain food for his own use** and on unoccupied Crown lands or other lands to which he may have a right of access. But that is not to say that he has the right to hunt dangerously and without regard for the safety of other persons in the vicinity. *Prince and Myron* deals with "method." Neither that case nor those which preceded it dealt with protection of human life. (*Myran v. R.* 1976: 6, emphasis added)

More specifically, *Prince and Myron v. The Queen*, a 1964 Supreme Court decision, deals with the "method" of the use of a spotlight to assist Aboriginal night hunting for food. In other words, the Supreme Court does not see the ban of jacklights arising out of a concern for public safety.

In *R. v. Prince 1964*, the Supreme Court cited with approval *Rex v. Wesley* (1932), which clearly makes the distinction between hunting for food and hunting for sport. A justice in *Wesley* wrote:

> I think the intention was that in hunting for sport or for commerce the Indian like the white man should be subject to laws which make for the preservation of game but, in hunting wild animals for the food necessary to his life, the Indian should be placed in a very different position from the white man who, generally speaking does not hunt for food and was by the proviso to sec. 12 reassured of the continued enjoyment of a right which he has enjoyed from time immemorial.

In a post-section-35 case, *R. v. Horseman* (1990), the Supreme Court discusses permissible "methods" of Aboriginal food hunting and states clearly that:

> Further, the means employed by [Indian people] in hunting for their food was placed beyond the reach of provincial governments. For example, **they may hunt deer with night lights** and with dogs, methods which are or may be prohibited for others. Nor are the Indians subject to seasonal limitations as are all other hunters. That is to say, they can hunt ducks and geese in the spring as well as the fall, just as they may hunt deer at any time of the year. Indians are not limited with regard to the type of game they may kill. That is to say, while others may be restricted as to the species or sex of the game they may kill, the Indians may kill for food both does and bucks; cock pheasants and hen pheasants; drakes and hen ducks. It can be seen that the *quid pro quo* was substantial. Both the area of hunting and the way in which the hunting could be conducted was extended and removed from the jurisdiction of provincial governments. (*R. v. Horseman* 1990: par. 60; emphasis added)

There is no lack of clarity or any ambiguity in the reasoning of the Supreme Court in this regard. Yet despite the legal precedent set by the top court, Judge Ross ruled that s. 68 of the *Nova Scotia Wildlife Act* was a "preventive safety based provision," and, as such, was not an infringement of the Mi'kmaw right to hunt for food, and, further, that if it did infringe the right, that it was nevertheless justified by reason of public safety (see *R. v. Bernard 2000*).

First Appeal: Summary Conviction Appeal Court

The UNSI agreed to appeal *Bernard* to the summary convictions appeal court held before Associate Chief Justice Michael MacDonald. *Bernard* argued that s. 68 of the *Wildlife Act* is not aimed at ensuring public safety but rather is based on "preserving the sportsman ethic of giving game a fair chance at eluding capture"—in other words, s. 68 is a sport-hunting prohibition and was not enforceable against Aboriginal food hunters. Justice MacDonald agreed that the purpose of s. 68 was at best unclear, and as such, there *was* a prima facie infringement of the Mi'kmaw right to hunt for food with *no* clear justification. He therefore entered an acquittal for Bernard on the charge (see *R. v. Bernard 2001*).

Media Bias

It turned out that Justice MacDonald's 2001 ruling in Bernard's favour made for front-page news in major Nova Scotia newspapers at the time. Who would have thought? Instead of giving accolades to Justice MacDonald for upholding the constitutional rights of the Mi'kmaq, the papers focused on vocal critics of the decision—of which there were many. The media coverage of the ruling was immediate, immense and virtually all negative. It elicited public opinion for weeks in op-ed pages and made for lively commentary on talk radio. One politician, Brooke Taylor, publicly characterized the ruling as "incompetent."

Virtually none of the media coverage pointed out that s. 68 was a sport-hunting prohibition wrongly applied to an Aboriginal food hunter; nor did the coverage point out the ease by which public safety could have been ensured by other authentic public-safety sections of the *Nova Scotia Wildlife Act*; nor did the media reference any previous Supreme Court of Canada rulings on the subject. Aside from one op-ed article, none of the media coverage even drew a distinction between Aboriginal food hunting and non-Aboriginal sport hunting. Instead, the mass media blindly followed and favoured the Crown's simplistic assertion that public safety was the driving purpose of s. 68 and the prosecution of Allison Bernard Jr.

Second Appeal: Nova Scotia Court of Appeal

Shortly after the outcry in the media, the Crown filed a notice of appeal of the decision of Justice MacDonald. The appeal would be heard by the Nova Scotia Court of Appeal—a panel which no doubt had been privy to the overload of the negative and sensationalized media surrounding Bernard's acquittal. In the disappointingly predictable end, the Nova Scotia Court of Appeal overturned Justice MacDonald's findings and agreed with Judge Ross that the purpose of s. 68 is indeed public safety and, therefore, is not a prima facie infringement of the Mi'kmaw right to hunt for food. And further, they stated if it was a prima facie infringement, it was nevertheless justified for reasons of public safety. The Court of Appeal therefore struck Bernard's acquittal and reinstituted the guilty verdict (see *R. v. Bernard 2002a*).

Third Appeal: Supreme Court of Canada

The UNSI agreed to launch an application for leave to appeal the decision of the Nova Scotia Court of Appeal to the Supreme Court of Canada. The application was accompanied by a media statement made by the Assembly of Nova Scotia Mi'kmaq Chiefs and a supporting affidavit. On September 26, 2002, the Supreme Court dismissed the application "without reasons" (see *R. v. Bernard 2002b*).

It should be noted here that the Supreme Court is not obligated to give reasons for a denial of leave to appeal. A denial of a leave to appeal "without reasons" does not necessarily mean that the Supreme Court agreed with the decision of the Nova Scotia Court of Appeal in this case—it just means that at that moment, it had more pressing matters to attend to. And herein lies the chasm that forms the very basis of the de facto federal-provincial judicial division of powers in Canada. This division is not often taught in law schools, nor does it appear very often in law textbooks.

The result has been that, in Nova Scotia, the Court of Appeal decision in *R. v. Bernard* has been the last word on the subject of Mi'kmaw night hunting in Nova Scotia since its ruling of January 5, 2002. The Department of Natural Resources has treated it as such in any event, as they continued to prosecute Mi'kmaw food hunters with violating s. 68 of the *Nova Scotia Wildlife Act*, as we will see.

R. v. Paul 2013: The Saga Continues

On September 5, 2006, two Mi'kmaw hunters from Eskasoni, Charles Francis and Aaron Paul, shot a moose decoy deployed by the DNR while they were food hunting during the hours of darkness in the Cheticamp Lake area of the Cape Breton Highlands. The headlights of their vehicle were used to illuminate the target decoy, which was remotely operated by a DNR officer. Like Allison Bernard Jr., Francis and Paul were apprehended and charged with "hunting with the assistance of a light," contrary to s. 68 of the *Nova Scotia Wildlife Act* (their legal case is known as *R. v. Paul*).

When Paul and Francis first approached the UNSI, their main concern was the return of the two high-powered rifles that had been seized during the arrest. I informed them of the *Bernard* 2002 decision and how it was treated by the DNR as if it were legitimate legal precedent within Nova Scotia, and that getting their rifles returned, for one, was thus going to be tricky. I also informed them that, in my opinion, the *Bernard* case was decided incorrectly and went directly against Supreme Court legal precedent. I assured them that I would have counsel with the UNSI board of directors and discuss their request for legal assistance. The UNSI board eventually approved the legal representation of Francis and Paul. The approval was not only based on my advice that the Nova Scotia Court of Appeal was incorrect in law in *Bernard*, but also based upon the then recent news (December 22, 2006) that the Supreme Court of Canada, in *R. v. Morris* (2006), had again approved night hunting for food for the Tsartlip First Nation in a case where the facts were almost identical to the facts of their own case.

R. v. Morris: Apparent Redemption

In *R. v. Morris*, two aboriginal food hunters from British Columbia shot an officer-deployed deer decoy at night and were charged with two separate violations: "hunting at night" and "hunting with the assistance of a light," contrary to the *British Columbia Wildlife Act*. In the Nova Scotia case, the hunters were only charged with "hunting with the assistance of a light." It is worthy to note, however, that in *Morris* the Supreme Court of Canada treated the "hunting with the assistance of a light" charge as being *subsumed* by the "hunting at night" charge; in effect, the Supreme Court dropped the "hunting with the assistance of a light" charge on the basis that you don't really hunt at night unless you do so with the assistance of a light.

In *Morris*, the Supreme Court stated as follows:

> 39 Nor can it be said that such a blanket exclusion should now be implied as a matter of law. If a night hunt is dangerous in particular circumstances, it can (and should) be prosecuted under s. 29....

It should be noted that with "and should" the Supreme Court of Canada was providing clear direction on what the Crown should do if a particular night hunt was a legitimate safety hazard. Appropriately, the referred-to s. 29 prohibits hunting "without due consideration for the lives, safety and property of other persons."

The Supreme Court went on, stating:

> Protected methods of hunting cannot, without more, be wholly prohibited simply because in some circumstances they could be dangerous. All hunting, regardless of the time of day, has the potential to be dangerous.

In *Paul*, the two hunters were not charged with an analogous safety provision to section 29 above, even though one exists in the *Nova Scotia Wildlife Act* (s. 87 prohibits "careless hunting").

Nevertheless, Francis and Paul were charged solely with "hunting with the assistance of a light." As one can plainly see, the judicial reasoning of the Supreme Court in the *Morris* case was very similar to the arguments that were made in *Bernard* 2002a (as well as previous Supreme Court decisions noted above)—and simply ignored by the Nova Scotia Provincial Court and the Nova Scotia Court of Appeal.

Pre-trial Matters

The plea date was set for January 22, 2007, at Baddeck. The prosecutor on the file was Sydney Crown attorney Darcy MacPherson. Prior to entering a plea, I proposed to the Crown attorney delaying the trial pending his reading and review of the law as stated in *Morris* and another similar case (*R. v. Polches*) that was before the New Brunswick Court of Appeal. In that case, Aboriginal hunters were also charged with hunting with assistance of a light. We jointly agreed to adjourn the plea matter until February 26, 2007.

It was during this adjournment that the Crown was to determine, based on a reading of both *Morris* and *Polches*, whether to dismiss or withdraw the s. 68 charge. It was also during this time period that the Halifax-based special-prosecutions office, with Crown attorney James Clarke, became involved. The Crown chose to proceed with the charge. In other words, the Crown would attempt to maintain the clearly erroneous 2002 Nova Scotia Court of Appeal ruling in the *Bernard* case.

One must remember that the Public Prosecution Service, a representative of the "public interest," chose to represent that interest contrary to Mi'kmaw hunting rights, as well as the law as enunciated by the Supreme Court of Canada. What does this mean? What could motivate the office to oppose clearly stated superior law? Is this what makes the special-prosecutions office so "special"?

Francis and Paul thus formally entered not-guilty pleas before Judge A. Peter Ross presiding. Judge Ross, as you will recall, convicted Bernard at the trial level five years earlier. He initiated a discussion of whether I (or my clients) wished to have him recused from the trial because of his previous ruling. I replied that I had not considered it. However, in the end, without going into detail, he was in fact recused and a new provincial-court judge was appointed to the case. The new judge was Judge David Ryan—the first judge in the *Bernard* matter that declared a mistrial in 1999 based on the "misreception of evidence" (the "without prejudice" 1991 hunting agreement). So, to sum up, the Bernard case shifted from Judge Ryan in 1998 to Judge Ross in 1999, then, in the Francis and Paul case, from Judge Ross in 2006 to Judge Ryan in 2007.

The *Polches* Case of New Brunswick

This is what happened in the *R. v. Polches* case in New Brunswick. After the Aboriginal hunters lost their appeal at the New Brunswick Court of Appeal, they filed an application for leave to appeal to the Supreme Court of Canada. The Supreme Court did not grant the leave requested; instead, the Supreme Court remitted the matter back to the New Brunswick Court of Appeal, with instructions to amend its first ruling to be consistent with the ruling in *Morris*.

At this point, in *Paul*, the Crown and defence thought it would be prudent to yet again adjourn the trial until the New Brunswick Court of Appeal revealed its *second* ruling in the *Polches* case. The second ruling was not released until January of 2008. In this ruling the Court of Appeal stated:

> 8 On January 25, 2007, the Supreme Court of Canada remanded the present case to this Court pursuant to s. 43(1.1) of the Supreme Court Act, R.S.C. 1985, c. S-26. The remand order directs this Court to deal with the case "in accordance with" *Morris*. (*R. v. Polches* 2008)

The New Brunswick Court of Appeal went on to state unambiguously the following:

> 50 I unhesitatingly accept the proposition that the views expressed at paragraph 31 of our first decision regarding the inherent dangerousness of hunting at night with firearms do not accurately reflect the current state of the law. Those *obiter* views, although apparently in synch with the minority judgment in *Morris*, are no longer authoritative, if they ever were, in light of the majority decision in *Morris*.

The words above, despite their succinctness and clarity, are probably less important than the fact that the Supreme Court sent the case back to the province for reconsideration. It should be noted that in remanding the *Polches* case back to the New Brunswick Court of Appeal, the Supreme Court was expressing an implicit but clear intention that its pronouncements in *Morris*, despite involving Aboriginals from British Columbia with their own treaty, were to be applied uniformly to *all* holders of s. 35(1) Aboriginal and treaty hunting rights.

It bears repeating that despite the absolute clarity of both *Morris* and *Polches*, the special-prosecutions unit in Halifax used its discretion to proceed with the s. 68 prosecution of Francis and Paul, purportedly on the basis that, in its view, the *Morris* case was "fact specific" and "treaty specific" and thus did not apply to Nova Scotia or the Mi'kmaq. So, finally, after multiple delays waiting on the *Polches* case, the trial of Francis and Paul began with the reception of evidence.

Evidentiary Burden

Generally speaking, in Aboriginal-rights cases the evidentiary burden of proving a prima facie infringement rests with the Aboriginal claimants, in this case Francis and Paul. Despite the awareness that historical evidence was not viewed as necessary in the

Bernard case, I enlisted the services of William Wicken, a historian who agreed that he could produce a written report and give evidence in the Francis and Paul defence. Specifically, he was tasked with two research items. The first was researching the historical record as to the "pre-European contact" night-hunting practices of the Mi'kmaq. The second was to research the legislative and social history of s. 68 of the *Nova Scotia Wildlife Act*. My aim was to provide evidence of a prima facie infringement by proving that the Mi'kmaq historically hunted for food at night; and that the historical origins of s. 68 proves it to be, without doubt, a sport-hunting regulation rather than a public-safety regulation. This would more than sufficiently satisfy the prima facie evidentiary burden upon Francis and Paul.

We additionally argued, with ample legal authority, that the general right to hunt for food subsumes the "timing and method" of exercising such a hunt. In other words, if there was a right to hunt for food then that right automatically encompassed reasonably incidental activities, such as hunting at night and hunting with the assistance of a light. (The right would also cover other such "methods," such as hunting with dogs, or killing a moose while it is swimming—methods not permissible to sport hunters of Nova Scotia.)

In response to the introduction of our expert witness, the Crown took the position that they would utilize their own two experts, namely Stephen Patterson, a historian, and Alexander von Gernet, an archaeologist. These witnesses were purported to rebut Wicken's testimony.

However, instead of being focused on rebutting Wicken's report and expected testimony, both Crown witnesses entered reports that specifically dealt with the question of whether the historical evidence they had dug up satisfied the "integral to culture" test. The integral-to-culture test is the analytical tool set out by the Supreme Court of Canada in *R. v. Van der Peet*, which a court is to use when assessing the existence and extent of a new and as of yet unproven aboriginal right.

Proving such a new and distinct right was *not* our evidentiary burden—that burden had already been dispensed with many years prior, in 1990, in *R. v. Denny, Paul and Sylliboy*. That case was the uncontested ruling of the Nova Scotia Court of Appeal that found decisively that the Mi'kmaq of Nova Scotia have a s. 35(1) Aboriginal right to fish (and hunt) for food in Nova Scotia. Since our position was that the right to hunt for food already existed and is recognized as a presumption in law in Nova Scotia, there was no reason for the Crown to direct its two experts to focus on the integral-to-culture test.

It became quickly clear that the Crown wanted the provincial-court judge to determine, by an examination of historical, "pre-European contact" evidence, whether Francis and Paul possessed an Aboriginal right to "hunt big game at night with the assistance of a light in the Cheticamp Lake area of the Cape Breton Highlands," which is how the Crown repeatedly phrased it throughout the course of the trial. The Crown was attempting to persuade the judge that the historical evidence in its entirety had failed to establish that the Mi'kmaq had an Aboriginal right to "hunt big game at night with the assistance of a light, etc." This is at a completely different purpose than a rebuttal to Wicken's report and testimony addressing the issue of prima facie infringement. It specifically addressed an evidentiary burden that we did not have. I strongly felt, and expressed so in writing, that this ploy of tailoring the Crown-expert reports and testimony to reflect the integral-to-culture test was nothing short of a dishonourable attempt to bamboozle the court.

In other words, the Crown was planting an evidentiary red herring for the judge. I knew the judge had little experience adjudicating s. 35(1) Aboriginal-rights cases so, as somewhat of a response to the Crown's ploy, I filed a dual application requesting that (1) Judge Ryan summarily dismiss the case based on the authority of the *Morris* and *Polches* cases, and (2) Judge Ryan declare all the expert historical evidence as inadmissible, including that of our own expert, for being unnecessary, irrelevant and a waste of the courts' time. This second aspect of the application was based on what the Court of Appeal said in *Bernard 1999* to the effect that such historical evidence was not necessary to properly address the issue.

In response to the early dual application, Judge Ryan ruled that he would neither summarily dismiss the case nor declare the expert evidence inadmissible. He reserved his reasoning for the end of the trial.

The trial of Francis and Paul resumed sporadically from 2008 to 2010, hearing from (aside from the *actus reas* evidence of the arresting DNR officers) eleven Crown witnesses and three defence witnesses. The Crown's evidence (aside from the expert evidence referred to above) was to the effect that:

1) night hunting with the assistance of a light is unsafe,

2) there are many various users of the Cape Breton Highlands who could potentially be harmed by night-hunting activity,

3) beef cattle had previously been shot in the Cape Breton Highlands, likely at night, and likely for being mistaken for moose,

4) moose are plentiful and easy to catch in the daytime.

Defence evidence was to the effect that:

1) Mi'kmaq night hunting for food predates European contact,

2) Mi'kmaq use of a light to assist night-time food-hunting activity occurred prior to European contact,

3) the legislative origins of s. 68 prove its purpose is sport, not public safety,

4) Francis and Paul were hunting for food when they were arrested.

The Decision of Judge Ryan

The final arguments by the Crown and defence were concluded on June 25, 2010. In August of 2013, Judge Ryan rendered his 188-page decision, convicting Francis and Paul and reaffirming the continued authority of *Bernard* 2002 in Nova Scotia. On September 12, 2013, the UNSI as well as Francis and Paul were briefed and, after deliberations, approved appealing Judge Ryan's ruling.

The sentencing of Francis and Paul occurred on September 25, 2013. Judge Ryan, referring to the provincial *Remissions of Penalty Act*, fined each of the accused $250 (instead of the normal $2,500 fine as prescribed by the *Wildlife Act*) and ordered the return of the rifles and gear that were seized from the two hunters in September of 2006. In handing out such relatively low fines, Ryan opined that the Francis and Paul case was a test case. The Crown, however, still thought *Bernard* was the test case of the Mi'kmaw night-hunting issue. Ryan clarified that he disagreed with the Crown on that point as he, in *R. v. Paul* (Francis and Paul), found that no such right existed from the outset (referring to the historical evidence of the experts)—while the *Bernard* decision made no such finding. (Remember, the *Bernard* proceedings did not utilize any historical evidence.)

In other words, just as I had feared, Judge Ryan was indeed bamboozled by the Crown-tailored expert historical evidence in the reports and later testimony of von Gernet and Patterson—which was *strenuously* objected to by the defence in writing, and in great detail. Nevertheless, Judge Ryan had misapprehended the evidentiary burden upon Francis and Paul and instead wrongly applied the integral-to-culture test laid out in *Van der Peet* to the entirety of the expert historical evidence. As noted, the so-called test was meant only for cases which are establishing an Aboriginal right for the first time. Francis and Paul were only required to demonstrate a prima facie infringement of their right to hunt for food, not establish the existence of a new Aboriginal right.

A reading of the long-awaited decision revealed several fundamental errors of law, which eventually formed the grounds of appeal upon which Francis and Paul would make their appeal. The appeal was scheduled to be heard in September, 2014, at Sydney in the summary conviction appeal court before Justice Robin Gogan, newly appointed to the Supreme Court of Nova Scotia. As it turned out, a new judge was appointed to the case, Justice Patrick Duncan. The appeal was scheduled to be heard in July of 2015.[1]

Grounds of Appeal

The grounds of appeal are meant to identify the errors that are alleged to have been committed by a lower court, in this case the ruling of Judge Ryan of the Nova Scotia Provincial Court. In the *R. v. Paul* appeal, the grounds are stated as follows:

1. THAT the provincial court judge erred in law by his finding of admissibility of evidence that was otherwise unnecessary and irrelevant.

2. THAT the provincial court judge erred in law by misapprehending the evidentiary burden necessary to establish a prima facie infringement of an existing Aboriginal right.

3. THAT the provincial court judge erred in law in finding that the Supreme Court judgment in *R. v. Morris* [2006] S.C.J. No. 59 had no precedential value to the case at bar.

4. THAT the provincial court judge erred in law and fact that the appellants had not established a prima facie infringement of their existing Aboriginal right.

5. THAT the provincial court judge erred in law and fact that had a prima facie infringement been found to exist, that its infringement was nevertheless justified.

It remains to be seen how the Court of Appeal will deal with these issues (see note 1).

Conclusion

In November of 2014, before Justice Duncan, I attempted to add a further ground of appeal to the five listed above. That ground states:

> [6] THAT the Crown and trial judge failed to adhere to the Supreme Court of Canada mandated principles of the "Honour of the Crown" and/or "Fiduciary Duty" in carrying out their discretionary decisions leading up to, and then into the trial process, all of which cumulatively resulted in a miscarriage of justice and wrongful conviction of Aaron Paul and Charles Francis, aboriginal persons to whom s. 35(1) of the *Constitution Act*, 1982 applies.

In arguing for the addition of ground six, I make reference to the findings and recommendations of the Marshall inquiry as well as the Public Prosecutions Service policy on Aboriginal-rights cases. I argue that the standards articulated in those findings and that policy are not being complied with by the Crown's prosecution of the Francis and Paul case. I also argue that five of the six provincial-court judges (the exception being Associate Chief Justice Michael MacDonald) exhibit a consistent pattern of error and indifference with regard to Mi'kmaw hunting rights despite the wide-ranging critique of the Nova Scotia justice system made by the Marshall inquiry twenty-five years earlier. In short, I am arguing that both the *Bernard* and the *Paul* cases have been and continue to be an exercise of prosecutorial misconduct and an abuse of the (somewhat complicit) provincial judicial process.

These two cases demonstrate with an unparalleled clarity the reality of the context of litigating s. 35 Aboriginal and treaty-rights cases in Nova Scotia. The simplicity and clarity of the night-hunting issue as expressed by the Supreme Court of Canada is the element of these cases that forces the veil of justice in Nova Scotia to be momentarily lifted in a way that exposes that not much has substantively changed in Nova Scotia since the Marshall inquiry.

At this point, I await the decision of Justice Duncan on the addition of ground six as outlined above and I also await the appeal hearing itself. I intend to continue writing about the remainder of this case and intend to publish an comprehensive account. I should also clarify that, as of April of 2014, I am no longer legal counsel for the UNSI, as a budget no longer exists for such a position. I have since been representing both Francis and Paul on a pro bono basis and will continue doing so until the case's completion.

Note

1. Just as this book was going to print, on April 13, 2016, Judge Duncan released the NS Supreme Court rulling against the appeal, the *Chronicle Herald* reported. "The court ruled that notwithstanding aboriginal rights to hunt for food and ceremonial purposes, the government is justified in limiting aboriginal hunting at night because it isn't safe."

"The Nova Scotia Supreme Court ruled trial Judge Ryan hadn't erred in his conclusions, citing Ryan's quote of Chief Justice Antonio Lamer that

> 'aboriginal rights are not general and universal; their scope and content must be determined on a case-by-case basis. The fact that one group of aboriginal people has an aboriginal right to do a particular thing will not be, without something more, sufficient to demonstrate that another aboriginal community has the same aboriginal right. The existence of the right will be specific to each aboriginal community.' (Government justified 2016)

> A decision on an appeal is pending.

References

Government justified in limiting aboriginal hunting rights at night: N.S. Supreme Court. 2016. *Chronicle Herald*, April 17. http://thechronicleherald.ca/novascotia/1357577-government-justified-in-limiting-aboriginal-hunting-rights-at-night-n.s.-supreme-

Myran v. R. 1976. 2 S.C.R. 137.

R. v. Bernard. 1999. N.S.J. 149.

R. v. Bernard. 2000. N.S.J. No. 58.

R. v. Bernard. 2001. N.S.J. No. 48.

R. v. Bernard. 2002a. N.S.J. No. 15.

R. v. Bernard. 2002b. S.C.C.A. No. 123.

R. v. Morris. 2006. S.C.J. No. 59.

Myron v. The Queen 1964

R. v. Paul 2013

R. v. Polches. 2008a. N.B.J. No. 4.

R. v. Polches. 2008b. N.B.J. No. 412.

R. v. Prince. 1964. S.C.R. 81.

Kerry Prosper

Born to Fish

I was born in Paq'tnkek, in northeastern Nova Scotia, in 1955 with my twin sister, Karen Ann Prosper. There were thirteen of us altogether: six boys and seven girls. My father was Wilfred Prosper, the son of John Prosper and Caroline Kennedy. My mother's parents were Frank Martin and Julia Kane. We lived on the Paq'tnkek reserve in an old house where my father's parents had lived before us. It was a two-story house heated by an old wood-burning stove. The winters were long and cold. There was a square hole in the upstairs floor with a steel grate positioned just over the stove. This was the best place to be on cold evenings. We would lie on the floor enjoying the rising heat and eavesdrop on any visitors that dropped by. As the evening went on, we would be scolded for staying up late—and for being nosey.

We children mostly slept in one big bed, though the older ones had their own beds. On colder nights we would cover up with a large wool overcoat from the army-surplus store. To this day, I sleep most comfortably in the cold with a heavy blanket covering me. We slept with mice, rats and squirrels, hearing them fight during the night. The mice kept to certain areas and scurried around scavenging for any food that was left uncovered and not hidden away. We hauled water from a well. The water at the top of the well would eventually freeze, and when the hole we kept open grew smaller, we replaced the bucket with a lard can on the end a rope. The can had to be pushed under the ice into the water, so it would take a little longer to fill. Any water left indoors after a long cold night would be frozen by morning

We went to a one-room school just up the hill from our house: the Afton Day School. Jenny Forbes taught all the classes up to grade nine. The youngest children were seated in the first rows, and so on, the grade niners in the back. We learned all the subjects at our own grade level and a little bit from all the other grades as well. We went home for lunch and played outside during recess. We played hide-and-seek and tag and war in the yard and in the woods nearby.

The best day of the year was the day a certain truck pulled into the schoolyard and the driver carried some large black boxes into the school. He set up a machine with two big wheels on it, like bicycle wheels with no tires. He wound a long flat tape on one of the wheels, then he put a large white blanket up on the wall and covered the windows with thick black cloth. This frightened me a little bit; I was not sure what was going to happen when all the lights were shut off. We were told to sit down and be quiet. A clicking noise would start as the wheels turned, and a light shone on the white blanket. The image was black and white with numbers counting down, from four to zero, then a large picture in beautiful colour would appear.

One time we watched a film about frogs in a swamp. They were making the same noises we heard near swamps in Paq'tnkek. I finally saw how frogs make these sounds, their lower jaw filling with air and then emitting a loud croak. The pictures were so real, and the animals and trees and water were so beautiful in colour.

I remember the days when the *National Geographic* man came to our school just like it was yesterday; they left a lasting impression.

Early Memories of Fishing

I remember the very first trout I caught. I used to fish in a small creek near our old house. The creek also flowed by the general store. An old man called Pops Coutts owned the store. His daughter Helen and her husband, Wally, helped him. We grew up with their children: Steven, who was my age, Angus, who was younger, and Debby, who was the baby girl. We would go to the store and buy a small fishing kit that had a small bundle of green fishing line with a single hook and a sinker. It cost ten cents. We would dig worms close to my grandmother Caroline Prosper's home, where a path led to the river.

The best spot for worms was under one particular medium-sized apple tree, and it was used by many fishermen in the community. Someone always got there before me, and my grandmother would complain about missing shovels and garden tools. I knew where to find them for her. I got my worms, and off to the creek I went. Early spring rain showers, the sound of water flowing in the ditches and the smell of grass fires would bring the excitement of fishing. I remember playing along the flooded ditches with a fishing stick just pretending to be fishing. We also made small boats and played a game of whose boat would float the furthest down the ditch. Pussy-willow buds and the sound of frogs singing were my signs that the fishing season had begun. According to Francis Johnson, trout begin to bite when the alders begin to make pollen.

Along the shoreline, I would sneak up to the spots that would likely be hiding a trout. I had a hard time hooking trout in the beginning. When I think of it today, I don't think I was setting the hook right or pulling it from the water at the right moment. I did not let the trout get a good enough bite on the bait. There was a bend in the creek and one day I spotted a trout lying just under the bank. I got close to the bank and put the line in the water. The trout took the bait, I hauled the line and lost the trout. The trout was more careful after that. He would take small nibbles on the worm and rip it apart, avoiding the sharpened hook. He did this a few times and I was getting frustrated. I eventually had to leave the trout alone so he would forget about my attempt to catch him. I would come back to the spot awhile later and tempt him with the worm again. I eventually caught him. This experience taught me a lot about fishing, and it helps me to this day.

The younger fishers in Paq'tnkek could not understand the purpose of a provincial fishing licence. As we got older, we teased the younger ones about fishing without a licence and having to be wary of the provincial fish warden. In my mind the warden was a big, mean-looking individual who would check on you to see if you were fishing with a licence and, if not, you could be sent to jail. We were never bothered along the creek and we knew that we were too young to need a licence, but as we got older we became wary of licences and official seasons. Our fishers fished when the ice was gone. Some went earlier and would fish in Heatherton on the Pomquet River, fishing through the ice for salmon.

Things changed. We heard the older boys talking about seasons, licences and the fishery warden, especially if they were venturing down along the coastal area in Bayfield. We also began to hear about a regulated season for fishing. We thought it was spring; to us, that was when the ice thawed. I always heard that Indians did not need a licence; in any event, we were always afraid of confronting the warden. As we got older and ventured further away from our own community, we began to experience different things. Non-natives confronted us. They did not want us fishing salmon near them. I think we were disturbing their attempts to poach salmon. A warden would show up in the area not long after these altercations, and we were always on the lookout for them.

Food Hunting at an Early Age

There were always guns around the house. There were .22-caliber rifles stored above the door on a rack made from two maple branches cut off with the trunk attached. The trunk was split and nailed to the wall. We were taught that these guns were very powerful and that playing with them could hurt someone very badly or even kill them. The consequences of playing with a gun were severe, like a good switching. The boys in our family got BB guns when they about ten years old. We were taught to very careful with them.

Hunting food began early in our lives. As with fishing, a young hunter had to be accompanied by an older hunter when travelling to the shore for hunting. The boys would follow an older brother in the woods, the younger one carrying the BB gun and the older carrying the .22 rifle. Every day after school I would accompany my older brother John on a rabbit hunt. We would hunt on an old trail called Gakpesawtek, meaning "the road to the smelts." This trail followed the Afton River and wound in and out from the river's bank. The trail led all the way to the shore of St. Georges Bay, to a place called Bayfield, a small estuary at the mouth of Afton River. This trail was used by the Paq'tnkek Mi'kmaq for years and years. The halfway point for us was an old steel culvert placed by someone logging the area in the past. There was a spot where there was a tall oak tree, and in its branches near the top bald eagles built a nest. I often heard about this large nest from the older boys who tried (and failed) to climb up to the nest. Someone had a fall but was not seriously hurt. I think someone did eventually reach the nest and discovered the enormity of the material, like large branches and the many grasses that lined it.

One spot that still remains on the trail today is a large hemlock tree, a tree that has a large carving on it. A man by the name of Jimmy Simon carved a man-sized figure of a devil on this tree, with carved horns, head and a body. We called it the devil tree. The younger boys that were travelling the trail with us would have to listen to horror stories conjured up by the older boys. Every time I pass this tree, I think of Jimmy Simon and some of the stories that were made up for our younger hunters and fishers as we passed by this spot.

Seasonal Harvests

Travelling in groups, we would walk down to fish smelts in the spring. Everyone made a fishing rod fashioned from their favourite tree for such. I was fond of pin-cherry trees because they are so straight and long. We would make treble hooks from three single hooks wrapped with rabbit wire, and use them to jig smelts. Schools of smelts turned the bottom of the river black. Boys and girls would jig a few dozen smelts. If you were lucky, you could also jig a good-sized trout every so often. Trout followed the smelts into the river and fed on the smaller ones.

My older sisters were always happy to go fishing smelts and these times were always fun for us. Fathers and mothers would go fishing with their sons and daughters, making this a time of passing knowledge on to their children, just as older siblings taught their younger siblings how to fish and hunt.

In the full moon of June we would fish eels and lobsters. The whole family would walk to the rocky shore at Bayfield along a point called Davies Rocks. The family would pack a lunch and the fishing gear—rods, spears and forks. The elders set up along the shore, preferably on a low tide. The summer solstice brings very high and very low tides. The low tide exposed a large amount of the rocky bottom along Davies Rocks. The older men would wade along the rocks looking under the kelp and Irish moss for eels and lobsters. They carried spears made from pieces of strapping of about three feet long.[1] At the end of the spear there were four sharpened nails. The moment a fisher exposed an eel or lobster hiding under the kelp or moss, he would spear it.

Children were not out fishing with the older men were digging clams and gathering anything else useful that they could find: snails, driftwood for the fire, and things that washed up on the shore during the winter storms. Sometimes we found old homemade wooden fishing buoys painted in bright colours. We cooked clams and lobsters on the shore, and the tea always tasted the best when steeped on an open fire. This communal fishery continued for a few weeks, until the daily fluctuation of the tides weakened and the eels had moved on.

The bridge that made that beach accessible used to wash away during big spring storms and eventually it was not replaced. The other access to the beach was through private property, and that became unwelcoming. Today we hardly ever go down to fish along the shore, not the way we did back then.

In late summer we would often swim at a small stream pool just below my grandmother's home. The water level would be lower then, and we would build a dam from the largest rocks we could move. This deepened the pool a little. One day while swimming I saw the Johnson boys fishing for eels in the river. There was Abraham ("Boy"), Richard ("Boody"), John ("Sewdoll") and Francis ("Blacky"); they all had nicknames. The brothers were carrying sharpened table forks and they were slowly turning over large flat stones. They turned over each stone very slowly with one hand and checked to see if an eel was hiding under it. If an eel was there, they speared it quickly with the fork in the other hand. I was very surprised at this simple technique of fishing eels. Just knowing that eels were hiding under those big flat stones amazed me. My grandmother did not like eating eels caught in fresh water, but the Johnsons did not mind, and they ate them.

Adapting Technology: Mi'kmaw Intuition

Edward Lafford came to our community when I was about thirteen years old and became a friend of mine. He would come from Maine with his parents, Mary and Noel Lafford. He had been named after his father, but he went by Edward. Edward loved fishing and we fished a lot together, experimenting with different fishing techniques. The trout in the late summer did not feed very aggressively so we began using jigs to catch them, which was not easy. We would tie on a jig, cast out the line, wait for the trout to pass over the spot where the jig lay on the bottom, and pull. It was hit-or-miss. During the summer, large trout pool up in the deeper areas and we worked on better ways of hooking them. We finally were able to cast out the jig and reel it in just above the bottom, at the same depth the trout were hovering. We would reel in the jig to the side of the trout's cheek and hook it by the gills or jaw. This was sure to hook the fish firmly and we would land it. We did not like hooking trout on the body because the fish could get off the hook and leave injured.

We were always thinking about new ways of fishing with new gear. This came naturally; the ideas came from the opportunities the gear presented to us. I think this is true of all Mi'kmaq; we adapt to new technology as readily as any other peoples. The ability to see something new, and imagine its full potential is a characteristic of all humans. We learned from other indigenous nations on Turtle Island (or North America), and they contributed to our culture. We will always continue to develop in this manner.

Edward and I began using wire to catch trout after we heard of some older men fishing salmon with snares. We took a single strand of rabbit wire and tied small snares on the end of sticks. In the late summer and early fall trout were easily snared with these small hoops. This became our best technique for catching larger fish, such as the salmon and brown trout that came upstream in the fall.

We could snare a trout that was hiding under the stream bank. When it saw us approaching, a trout would swim to the opposite bank and hide under the bank. I would reach across the creek and extend the snare in the water beneath the bank, just a little way upriver from where the trout went under. I would move the snare until I felt the bank, pull back a bit, move the snare down a bit, and then pull. If I did not catch the trout I would lower the snare again, a bit further, and pull again. I would repeat this until I snared the fish—usually on the second or third try. We were determined to catch fish for food and we were not playing around with them. We ate what we caught.

As we got older we began to fish in places that were not as close to home, and this increased the likelihood of running into a warden. I remember my brother John talking about fishing in Bayfield. He had hooked some nice trout that tasted very good. I wondered where he caught them. John would go down to Bayfield on the Gakpesawtek

River and stand under the bridge. No one would see him fishing before the provincial fishing season opened; he was the only one down there.

We felt righteous when we fished, and considered it an imposition whenever we were questioned about a licence. I always heard that Indians did not need licensing, but the thought of getting into trouble and paying a fine was always in the back of our minds. We always tried to avoid any confrontation with the authorities. Some wardens did not bother us. It seemed that they knew something about us that they did not want to admit, and just left us alone.

The Afton River flows through the community of Paq'tnkek and has been a good source of trout, smelts, gaspereaux, salmon and eels for as long as I can remember. The Afton River is where I snared my first salmon. Boys my age, mid-teens, were becoming more independent, travelling to different places to fish and hunt, and developing a sense of competition. We were all trying to be the first to catch a salmon or shoot a rabbit. We would ask each other about such, but most often we couldn't really believe one another's claims. So when asked, usually I did not answer.

One time, I was talking to my friend Gerard Julien (the son of Ethel and Charlie Lewis) about fishing salmon, and he was telling me about catching salmon with a snare. In our region, salmon run in the fall when the river is flowing well, and in deeper water, and our parents did not like us fishing salmon alone without older men with us. The younger guys were fishing salmon at night with a light. Salmon moving at night can be seen in shallower water than during the day. Gerard and I went out fishing one fall night on the Afton River; we each had a snare that was made from about six strands of rabbit wire and was easily carried in a back pocket. We had a six-volt box light that was very bright. As we walked down the river we checked the deep pools and shallow fast glides. Finally I spotted a salmon. I let Gerard snare it since he had snared one before and I could learn from him. I held the light to help him get a good view of the fish. He worked the snare around the salmon, just past its gills without touching the fish with the wire; then, I said "pull!" and he hauled the fish out of the water and threw it on the bank.

What happened next told the story. The fish bounced on the bank and wiggled off the snare. Gerard pounced on the salmon and began to subdue the fish so that it would not get back into the water. He was acting as if it was his first fish and he sure did not want it to get away. He finally subdued the fish by punching it until it lay still, and he looked up at me with gleam of excitement in his eyes, and it was written all over his face: I said, "like hell you caught a salmon before!" I knew then and there that this had been his first salmon and we laughed about it. These are the memories were share with our friends and community while securing food for our families. (I would finally catch a salmon myself when I was alone on the river.)

The Cooperative Nature of the Fall Salmon Fishery

The fall salmon fishery was a very exciting and fun time. The local store was selling a lot of rabbit wire. The younger men fished the Afton River, and the older guys who had access to a vehicle or were willing to walk a long way went to Nektowek or Heatherton to fish in the Pomquet River. We also went to Barney's River and the French River near New Glasgow. At each place there would be a number of fishers and we would all work together and split the catch. We would check all the deeper pools where there might be a small school of eight to ten salmon, and we would devise a strategy to snare them. Many times the pool was wide and deep, so we hoped for a sunny day and good visibility. We had to cooperate. One person would climb a tree close to the pool and one or two would each take a snare on a long pole. Two guys threw stones to scare the salmon back if they got nervous and began swimming farther up or downstream. We had one guy on the lookout for wardens.

The spotter in the tree would let the snare men know if salmon were within reach of the snare poles. The snare men would extend their poles out to the middle of the river where the salmon were laying and far enough upstream as directed by the spotter. Then the spotter would guide them down to the waiting salmon. The snare man should feel the snare on the rocky bottom as he moves the snare toward the salmon. The salmon would at times move to the side or further down, and the spotter would give instructions, such as "down further," "out more," "you're just in front of him," "a little further," and when the snare slipped around the salmon past its gills, "pull!" and out came the salmon.

There were times when there were a few of us in the same tree looking for salmon in a pool. One time I was standing out on a branch overlooking a deep pool. The sun was partly covered by clouds and a little wind picked up, making it hard to keep the salmon in sight. Gerard Julien climbed up to the same branch and ventured out a little farther, past me. I was a bit taller than Gerard and I was standing like he was, with one hand on the branch above us. We would lean out over the branch beneath our feet while holding the upper branch. Suddenly a salmon was spotted. Gerard ventured farther to get a better view. So did I. I took a step, still holding on to the branch above. Adding my weight to the branch beneath bent it, creating distance with the upper branch. Looking down into the water, Gerard switched hands just as I ventured another step further. Unwittingly, he reached for the branch above, but it was no longer there; it was now out of his reach. He looked back at me with wide eyes and fell downward into the deep, cold pool. To this day he does not believe me that it was bad timing and not intentional. We all had a good laugh at his expense, but knew that someone else's turn would come.

There was an Elder who was the best salmon spotter. Tom Sylliboy was his name. I was fishing with a group one time when the water was deep and flowing fast; everything was a blur and I could not see any fish. Tom walked up alongside the river and when he reached the bank, he said, "There's one." I said, "Where?" He repeated to me, "Right there!" and I said no, I could see nothing. He said, "I will show you." He had a pole with him and tied his snare to it. He stuck the pole into the current and hauled out a three-foot salmon, just like that. Developing the eye to see salmon in such conditions takes time and practice. Tom had lots of skill through practice.

Gerard told me a story of the agility of this Elder. Tom Sylliboy accompanied a group of fishers that included Gerard, Francis Johnson and his brother John Johnson ("Sewdoll"). They were fishing salmon, and there was a pool that always held salmon just across a pasture. The boys climbed over the fence and then waited for the Elder. Tom was wearing hip boots that slowed him down, and everyone was in a hurry to get to that pool; it gets like that when anticipating a salmon catch.

Tom got over the fence, and the boys started across the pasture for the pool. Then someone shouted, "Run!" and they heard the sound of heavy hooves pounding the ground and coming their way from some nearby alders. All the younger guys were running past Tom back to the fence, and when Tom spotted huge work horses stampeding toward him, he turned and ran, too, flying past those young men and clearing the fence with one jump, like an Olympic hurdler. You never know what energy you have stored within you when you really need it. I wish I had been there to witness this amazing feat of strength, or fear, whatever it was.

—

These activities were fun. We felt that we were exercising our rights, although we did not really understand the nature or source of our rights. We continued to hunt and fish without realizing that, under provincial law, we were committing offences. We felt indigenous when we were hunting and fishing, but there was a system set up to block our way, and we got used to sneaking around and playing cat-and-mouse with the authorities.

Exercising the Mi'kmaw Treaty Right to Fish

In 1928, Mi'kmaw Grand Chief Gabriel Sylliboy was charged with unlawful possession of wild game (muskrat skins) while not on a reserve. He contested the charge. During the court proceeding, Sylliboy argued that he had a treaty right to hunt. He stated:

> I am a Micmac and was chief for six years. Became chief in 1909. Heard that according to treaty we had right to hunt & fish at any time. I cannot read. Heard it from our grandfathers. Heard that King of England made treaty with Micmac, with the whole tribe. [Objected to] Remember hearing that goods were given—blankets—under treaty. [Objected to] About 65 years ago. In the fall before Christmas. Big coats and old fashion guns & and powder horns also. And some hides to make moccasins. And some food. In the spring potatoes & [?] some for seed. Tobacco too. And some spears for spearing eels. Where people had little farms they got oats. These goods distributed every six months. Where people hunting they were supplied with powder & shot & a guns. (Whitehead 1991: 327-28)

The court did not recognize the validity of treaties between the British Crown and the Mi'kmaq. The right to hunt was limited to reserves, and all hunting activities off reservation remained criminalized unless licensed. Sylliboy was found guilty. I think this was the first legal case dealing with Mi'kmaq hunting rights. The Supreme Court of Canada ruled otherwise nearly sixty years later, in *R. v. Simon*

(1985), affirming Mi'kmaw treaty rights, constitutionally recognized in 1982 with that year's *Constitution Act*. Grand Chief Sylliboy was right when he recalled his ancestors' memories of the treaty talks with the Crown.

—

Tom Sylliboy was fishing in Nektowek or Heatherton at what was called "salmon hole." This spot is a deep pool where the salmon gather. It is also on reserve land. Tom was fishing and had just caught a salmon when he noticed an individual in a green uniform approaching on the opposite side of the river. The officer told him he was breaking the law, and Tom stated that he was an Indian and was not breaking the law. The officer told him to stay right there while he went up river to cross. The officer found a place to cross and came downriver to where Tom was standing in the water. As the officer got close, Tom waded deeper into the pool and the officer told him to stop. Tom replied, "No, come and get me!" as he waded up to his chest through the river until he stood on the opposite shore, and wrung out his socks. The officer was red-faced mad and ordered Tom to stay right where he was. The officer went back upriver to cross. When the officer crossed back and returned to the spot where Tom was told to wait, Tom was now standing on the opposite shore. Tom said, "Good-bye, see you later," and disappeared into the woods as he made his way home.

Some time later we were all fishing in the same pool when we spotted two fishery wardens in green uniforms coming up river, so we grabbed our salmon and disappeared into the woods and walked home. Tom was getting tired of having the wardens bothering him while he was trying to gather food from the river. I remember him stating that he was not going to run anymore. He said, "They can charge me if they want, but I'm not running." This was the first time I heard anyone in our community talk of resistance to authorities.

A few years later, after I was elected a member of the Paq'tnkek Band Council (formerly the Afton Band), Tom was fishing below a bridge on the Trans-Canada Highway that went through our reserve. Tom was charged with fishing salmon without a license. A representative of the Union of Nova Scotia Indians approached me as a council member and asked if they should fight Tom's case, and I agreed that it would be a good idea. Tom Sylliboy's case went to the Nova Scotia

Supreme Court, where his rights were upheld (see *R. v. Paul, Denny and Sylliboy 1990*).

I am grateful for the perseverance of Grand Chief Gabriel Sylliboy and Tom Sylliboy, two individuals that acted on what they had heard and believed about the treaties, passed down through oral tradition. They knew, and challenged the authorities when they were confronted for exercising their rights. We continue to enjoy the Mi'kmaw treaty rights that they defended.

Today, my grandsons Chuck Augustine (Tom Sylliboy's great grandson) and Kadien Nevins (David Nevins's grandson) fish eels and trout with me. Chuck is the son of Virginia Sylliboy, the daughter of Ann Sylliboy, Tom's daughter. Kadien is the son of my daughter April Rose Prosper and of Jimmy Nevins. We hunt and fish together with their friends. These young Mi'kmaq can exercise their rights without fear of the authorities. They do not have to sneak around the woods or along the river banks and coastal shores. The new teachings are the customs and values that come with their exercise of treaty rights; they will shape the responsibilities they have to all the resources they have access to. These hunters are born into the newly recognized rights, and the stories of our game of cat-and-mouse with officials are the adventurous realities and hardships we and their ancestors went through to affirm their grandchildren's future of a better life.

Note

1. Strapping are long strips of narrow, thin, milled lumber.

References

R. v. Denny, Paul and Sylliboy. 1990. CanLII 2412 (NS CA). http://canlii.ca/t/1msnj.

R. v. Isaac. 1975. 13 N.S.R. (2d) 460.

R. v. Simon. 1985.

Whitehead, Ruth Holmes. 1991. *The Old Man Told Us; Excerpts from Micmac History, 1500-1950*. Halifax, NS: Nimbus Publishing.

Victor Carter-Julian

Tables, Talks and Treaties

When I was a child, I spent much of my time on Pictou Landing First Nation in Nova Scotia. My aunt's home there has always been sort of a nest for our family. Throughout her home, she has many dream catchers, drums and other pieces of indigenous art, each of which has its own story. Of all the rooms in the house, the most decorated is the dining room, perhaps because it is most used. This makes sense considering that it is around the table that the most important family time is spent. The dining room, and its circular table at the centre, brought the family together, whether it was for a simple quiet breakfast or an extravagant holiday dinner. It was at this table that I had my first experience with treaties.

As a child I enjoyed reading. Books at home were sufficient, but I was always looking for more. One day while sitting at the dining-room table I realized that my aunt had laid two new posters underneath the clear plastic tablecloth. One showed a map depicting where each of the Mi'kmaw reserves was located in the Maritimes. The other had renditions of multiple treaties printed on it. These posters were created as part of an initiative to educate, and they were doing just that. At the time, I found the language of the treaties to be quite confusing, but one thing that was clear was that Indians were a party to treaties that had passed rights and obligations onto their descendants. That meant me.

Throughout my education, I encountered treaties in various forms. In grade eleven I took a class in American history. American history cannot be taught without mentioning indigenous people, so I waited for this lecture to come, and I was very excited to learn more about how our people helped to shape North America. Remarkably, our teacher summed up the entire impact Native Americans made in the early stages of building America in just one class. The focus was on the forced relocation along the Trail of Tears in the south, and the only mention of treaty had to do with the controversial "sale" of Manhattan Island to early settlers. After class, I spoke with my teacher and informed her that our people, the Mi'kmaq, were still very much on the eastern coast of North America, in Canada, where we even have a land base. Her suggestion was that this may have only occurred because treaties had protected indigenous people in Canada differently than in the United States. This motivated me to learn more about the topic.

At some point the treaty posters at my aunt's moved from the dining-room table to various doors in the house. I remember reading them intently one day as my older cousin passed by. "Why are you over there staring at a door?" he asked. I laughed and told him I was reading the treaties and trying to understand what they meant. As a teen I could comprehend the words but not quite understand the language. Not only was it legal jargon, but some of the language was archaic, dating from as far back as the early 1700s. Some treaty clauses were much easier to grasp than others, even expressed in terms commonly used today. Others were complicated and did not immediately reveal their meaning to me.

After high school I attended university in Antigonish, Nova Scotia. It was a learning experience both inside and outside the classroom. It was the first time I spent any significant time living off-reserve. It was the first time talk of treaty and Aboriginal rights did not surround me, were not a part of everyday discussion. It was also the first time I realized that most non-Aboriginal Canadians did not possess what little information I had, and that they were largely content with this lack of knowledge. After (ironically enough) being called a "government thief" by my university-dorm moderator, I decided the topic of treaty implementation might not be best discussed with my university peers.

The only time treaties were a topic of discussion in an academic setting was in a class on "Sociology of Deviance." That class generally focused on deviant behaviours in individuals and in groups of people. During one particular class we examined the events leading up to, and following, the controversy over what is now referred to as the "Marshall decision." In August 1993, Donald Marshall Jr., a Mi'kmaw man from the Membertou First Nation in Sydney, was arrested for fishing eels without a provincial license, for using an illegal net and for selling the eels. In 1999, Marshall was fully acquitted of the charges when the Supreme Court of Canada ruled that Mi'kmaw treaties of 1760-1761 preserved his right to fish and sell fish in the manner he was practicing, and that this Aboriginal right was constitutionally protected.

I found it interesting that one man could spark so much discontent in the country over exercising a treaty right. National attention, and consternation, was cast on a man simply looking to catch and sell some eels. Treaties became relevant because, in this instance, they were the driving force for groups of Mi'kmaq to rebel against rights repression. After the decision was rendered, other Mi'kmaw fishermen expressed their solidarity by continuing to exercise rights upheld by courts but negated by governmental policy. These unsung heroes faced much animosity from people outside the community, and especially from governmental agencies. They continued to fish in manners they believed were within their recognized treaty rights. Small conflicts emerged on wharfs throughout the Maritimes between non-natives and native fishermen looking to exercise the newly affirmed treaty right. Perhaps the most well-known dispute occurred between the federal Department of Fisheries and Oceans (DFO) and Mi'kmaw fishermen of Burnt Church First Nation, New Brunswick. Video footage from the conflict, deeply embedded in my mind, shows a small boat with a few Mi'kmaw fishermen aboard being twice run over by a large DFO boat, forcing the fishers into the open water, where they were set upon by police.

By the end of the class, we learned that Marshall was successful in his case and that, eventually, government agencies developed policies that accommodated the Mi'kmaw treaty right to hunt and fish, among others rights, while maintaining regulation of native fisheries. What I took away from the class was that the government had not been proactively acknowledging treaty rights, even where the Supreme

Court had affirmed these rights. At times, Crown agencies engaged in opposition to the expression of treaty rights until courts ruled otherwise, and others continued to resist until political authority—in the form of legislation, regulation or whatever else—obligated reasonable cooperation. This has stirred Aboriginal individuals and groups to function as perceived deviant members of society in exercising their treaty rights. These rebels may appear as troublemakers or criminals at a certain point in time, only to be recognized as heroes and leaders once the dust settles.

A few years later, I graduated from university and decided I would attend law school in Halifax. Over those three years in law, my understanding of what treaties were and how they function was significantly refined, and frustrated. Being around future legislators who knew very little on the topic made me realize that things may continue as they have if people are not "deviant" and do not take the steps necessary to educate others outside the classroom. Laws will not change on their own, and often change seems to come more readily when people are willing to accept it or demand it en masse. The Idle No More movement is one example of such en masse action to educate and to raise the consciousness of people through their protests and educational campaigns.

Studying law made some issues regarding treaties clearer. I began to think more along the lines of nation-to-nation relationships, considering that only a sovereign can make treaty with another nation. I also began focusing more on history and how North American laws developed alongside treaty obligations.

During my third year, I was fortunate enough to attend the Indigenous Bar Association's annual fall conference in Rama, Ontario, on the Chippewas of Rama First Nation. On our first night, we received the honour of having specific wampum belts presented and interpreted by Allen Cobiere, an Anishinaabe academic from M'Chigeeng First Nation. I learned a great deal in that one evening from a man who was not a legal scholar but who received an education nonetheless, and one just as important, if not more. I remember how I was shocked to observe the beauty and size of these wampum belts. The images depicted on them were simple yet conveyed important messages.

The first couple of belts were examples of treaties formed prior to European contact. Indigenous nations would depict stories and messages within the belt with mutual intention, as any contract would be formed. In order for the belt to take true effect, both sides would recite the treaty to each other to ensure a "meeting of the minds." On specified occasions the nations would come together to recite and renew the mutual promises. Once a mutual understanding was agreed upon, the two would continue in their way of life. It was incredible to hear Cobiere read off the important message the gorgeous array of beads conveyed.

I remember that one belt was very simple in appearance. It was white with a purple circular image in the center. The ideogram represented "a dish with one spoon"—a tool not used as a weapon and a dish both parties could eat from. This belt was displayed by travellers in foreign territories and signified the end of a long conflict between indigenous nations in Ontario. It was described as being equivalent to a modern-day passport for the holders.

Another belt displayed a fish and the pattern of the beads told a story. When Cobiere was done interpreting the images, he showed us something incredible. He used words to express how these agreements were intended to be lasting—to further express this visually he held the belt end-to-end, creating a loop. The new image that emerged displayed the fish travelling in a circular motion, flawlessly depicting the intended continuity of the shared promises.

Another image that sticks in my mind is the scene depicted on the Covenant Chain Wampum of 1764. On one side are twenty-four indigenous folk holding hands. The individuals were to represent different indigenous nations functioning in North America at the time and being party to treaty. The first person is on a rock and is holding hands with others to form a chain, extending to the bow of a ship. This image seemed straightforward in comparison with the others, but its interpretation was just as important. At the end of the presentation, I lined up with many others to thank this man for his words shared and the overall expansion of my concept of treaties and their meanings.

When I think of treaties, two teachings I have received are often repeated. The first is that our Mi'kmaw ancestors were thinking of us, then and now, when they entered into these agreements so many years ago. I believe this to be true, especially when considering what foresight and intelligence it must have taken for people who could not read or write European languages to create documents that are still effective in protecting many treaty rights hundreds of years post drafting.

The other teaching relates to the lack of enforcement for certain treaty rights. Someone once said that you would have to believe our ancestors did not care for us if you accept the proposition that the treaties are currently being implemented properly. You would have to believe they did not love their descendants and, therefore, were quite willing to hand over power, land and rights to other irreplaceable resources.

Over the years I have read more articles, books and cases relating to treaties, but I still turn back to the original texts. I've learned much—from my time at the dining-room table to the present—and I am always learning more. When assessing the current political landscape, it is hard at times to envision a nation-to-nation relationship between Canada and various indigenous nations. Aboriginal rights have been eroded or altogether ignored. The power imbalance, which exists today between Canada and its various treaty partners, is growing more prevalent, yet the treaties of the past continue to symbolize a previous relationship indigenous nations should strive to revive. When Europeans arrived, the monarchs of the European nations respected the political systems of the Indian nations and entered into alliances and into sacred and inviolate treaties with them. These treaties became part of the supreme law of the European and indigenous nations, and now constitutes the constitutional law of Canada. Today, many nations are fighting to regain power that has been lost. The treaties shine as beacon of what once was, and what may be possible to attain if the march toward progress continues.

Additional Resources

Burnt Church crisis—http://www.theguardian.com/world/2000/sep/03/sandrajordan.theobserver.

Burnt Church/DFO confrontation—https://youtu.be/HsvG4KpFHOA.

"Marshall 2" decision—http://ojen.ca/sites/ojen.ca/files/sites/default/files/resources/Marshall%20English.pdf.

Covenant chain treaty—http://www.wampumbear.com/W_Annual%20Present%2024%20Nations%20Treaty%20Belt%201764.html.

A dish with a single spoon treaty—http://www.wampumbear.com/W_Dish%20With%20One%20Spoon%20Belt.html.

Naiomi Metallic

Becoming a Language Warrior

My name is Naiomi Metallic. I'm a Mi'gmaw lawyer. I live and work in Halifax, Nova Scotia, advising First Nations on various legal issues and also appearing in court from time to time. I'm now seven years into my law practice. I didn't start my career with the intention of making Aboriginal language rights a major focus of my work, but my path seems to be going in that direction. That might not surprise anyone who knows me, given the important place that the Mi'gmaq language holds in my family.

Nnuìsi basêk ichkàjij basna mè bem ginàmasi. That means: "I only speak Mi'gmaq a little bit, but I am still learning." That I am not yet fluent may surprise you, as I am the daughter of a famous Mi'gmaw linguist, Emmanuel Nagugwes Metallic, who is known throughout Mi'gmagi but especially in Gespe'gewa'gi, the seventh district, where I am from.[1] I recently completed a major project, writing a chapter in the third edition of the leading language-rights textbook *Language Rights in Canada / Les droits linguistiques au Canada*, examining the legal protections that exist for Aboriginal languages under Canadian law. From these two facts, you would expect that I would be fluent. I am not. Not yet. But I am determined I will be able to carry on a full conversation in Mi'gmaq by the time I'm forty (I'm currently thirty-three).

I grew up in the Mi'gmaq community of Listuguj First Nation located in Gespe'gewa'gi. Listuguj is across the Restigouche River from Campbellton, New Brunswick. That is where my father met my mother in 1967; she was a French Canadian nurse from La Redemption, Québec, who could barely speak a word of English. They were married in 1969 and first moved around, living in Saint John, New Brunswick, and Carlton Place, Ontario, among other places. In the summer of 1973, my father got a job at the Listuguj Band office, helping a linguist translate various sections of the Bible into Mi'gmaw. This is when he realized that he wanted to work with the Mi'gmaw language. The following year, he furthered his education by taking courses in linguistics in North Dakota. That summer, he accepted a position working with the Mi'gmaw language at Manitou Community College, in Québec, and in 1976 he co-authored a textbook, *Mi'gmaq Teaching Grammar.*

In the late 1970s, my parents moved back to Listuguj, where my father continued to be active in the language. One of his major accomplishments was devising his own writing system for Mi'gmaq, the "Mi'gmaq Fully Representational Writing System." This was the first orthography created entirely by a Mi'gmaw linguist, a revolutionary system that was truly phonetic in nature. Another major accomplishment was compiling and editing the 11,000-word *Metallic Mi'gmaq English Reference Dictionary*, published by Laval University Press in 2005. My father worked on this project for ten years, consulting with various elders from our community on the meaning of Mi'gmaw words, including his parents, Noel and Jean Metallic, and his long-time friend and mentor David Basque.

My parents had three daughters. I am the youngest. We mainly spoke English at home when we were together (my mother had learned English by this time). However, when my mother was alone with us, she spoke to us in French, in which I am fluent. Given the importance of the Mi'gmaw language to my father, it is surprising that he did not speak to us more often in Mi'gmaw when we were growing up. As an adult I questioned him about this. He said that there was already French and English in the household, so he thought adding Mi'gmaq might confuse us. I realize now that there was more to it. Many of my generation at Listuguj had parents who knew Mi'gmaq but didn't speak it to their children. Like my father, they had attended the federal day school on the reserve, where they were punished for speaking their language and taught that it had no value. I heard a story that, in the 1950s, the priest and the chief went visiting the different households in our community and told parents not to teach Mi'gmaw to their children. They said the children would go further in life without it. In my time, there were no schools on the reserve and they bused us to an English-language provincial school in Campbellton, so we got very little exposure to Mi'gmaw during our childhood.

Colonialist efforts to assimilate the Mi'gmaq are part of my personal history and explain why I didn't grow up speaking Mi'gmaw. Sometimes I feel ashamed that I am not yet a fluent speaker, but I know it's not my fault, or my father's fault, or the fault of the people in my community. At the same time, as a *Nnu*,[2] I feel a personal responsibility to learn it to the best of my ability.

I draw a lot of inspiration from my older sister, Jessica Metallic. Like me, she did not grow up speaking Mi'gmaw. But she taught herself in her twenties and thirties to speak the language by learning from our father, grandmother, uncle and other Elders in the community. She is now a very good speaker and, in fact, teaches Mi'gmaw, drawing on our father's work. Our father passed away in 2008, and my sister's goal is to continue his life's work, even to publish some of his unfinished writings on our language. My sister's perseverance has been truly inspiring.

Jessica Metallic and Emmanuel Metallic. Photo courtesy Naiomi Metallic.

Although at first I did not share my father's passion for the language in the same way as my sister, I was influenced by his interest in history, pre-contact as well as more recent colonial history. I remember him coming to speak to one of my grade six classes about native issues, and I was so proud. When I was at university, I began reading about Canada's mistreatment of First Nations, such as at Indian residential schools and the 1969 federal white paper on Aboriginal policy, building on my father's knowledge and the stories he told me. I got fired up about these issues, supported by some wonderful Mi'gmaw people on my path, including Professor Patricia Doyle-Bedwell, who encouraged me to consider a career in law. I applied to Dalhousie Law School and was accepted.

I did well at law school and when I completed my studies, I applied successfully to clerk for Justice Michel Bastarache at the Supreme Court of Canada. He is an Acadian from New Brunswick and one of his passions is the protection of minority language rights. It was a wonderful experience to work for him at the Supreme Court, and he later invited me to write a chapter on Aboriginal languages for the third edition of his treatise, *Language Rights in Canada / Les droits linguistiques au Canada* (2013). Nothing like this had been done before. In addition to the difficulty of collecting information about Aboriginal languages across Canada, I had to write the chapter in French. It was certainly a challenge at times, but I thought about my father, my grandparents, and my sister and her current work, and I am really glad that I did it.

A Crisis Facing Aboriginal Languages

The threats to Aboriginal languages in Canada are serious. There are at least fifty different First Nations languages in Canada, belonging to eleven distinct language families. Mi'gmaw belongs to the Algonquin-language family. Add to this Inuktitut and Michif, which are the languages of the Inuit and Métis peoples, respectively. A 1991 study found that in 70 per cent of First Nations communities, Aboriginal languages were either declining or "critically endangered" (i.e., where there are fewer than ten speakers). Aboriginal languages were considered stable in 18 per cent of communities, and flourishing in only 12 per cent of communities. The only flourishing Aboriginal languages were Cree, with 80,000 speakers, Ojibwe (45,000 speakers) and Inuktitut (25,000 speakers), although the use of Cree and Ojibwe was declining. Mi'gmaw was classified as stable (7,000 to 15,000 speakers).

The decline of Aboriginal languages was largely caused by assimilation policies pursued by the Canadian government since Confederation, including, most notably, Aboriginal residential and day schools that sought to "take the Indian out of the child" and forbade children from speaking their Aboriginal languages. There are terrible stories of children being beaten, forced to eat soap, even having needles shoved into their tongues for speaking Aboriginal languages at these schools.

The importance of language to indigenous peoples has been stressed in the reports of the Royal Commission on Aboriginal Peoples (RCAP 1996) and the Task Force on Aboriginal Languages and Cultures (TFALC 2005). Aboriginal languages are directly linked to indigenous peoples' traditional knowledge, traditional territories, collective identities, cultures, customs and traditions, personal identity and spiritual well-being.

Gaining National Attention for Language Loss

The Assembly of First Nations (AFN) has tried to make the loss of Aboriginal languages a national issue since the 1970s. When Canada was considering amendments to the *Constitution Act, 1982*, First Nations leaders advocated amending section 35 to expressly recognize the right of First Nations to preserve and develop their languages and cultures, but they did not succeed. A federal Ministerial Task Force on Aboriginal Languages and Cultures was established in 2002 to make policy recommendations, but following the defeat of the federal Liberal government in 2006, the report was not implemented.

In 2007, Senator Serge Joyal introduced a bill in the Senate, a proposed act for the advancement of Aboriginal languages of Canada, to recognize and respect Aboriginal language rights (Bill S-237 2009). The proposed law would have recognized the right of Aboriginal peoples of Canada to use, preserve, revitalize and promote their languages, all with the support of the Government of Canada. It would have directed the responsible minister to increase opportunities for Aboriginal persons to learn and become more proficient in their languages, to increase the number of circumstances in which Aboriginal languages are used, and to foster a positive attitude among all Canadians toward Aboriginal languages. Unfortunately, the bill went no further than a second reading.

Authority to Make Laws on Aboriginal Languages

In my chapter in *Language Rights in Canada / Les droits linguistiques au Canada*, I examined the question of who has authority to enact laws regarding Aboriginal languages. I conclude that both the federal and provincial governments have power to enact laws to promote and protect Aboriginal languages. I think this is a good thing, because I believe that both federal and provincial legislation a role to play on this issue.

There is a further question of the authority of First Nations and other Aboriginal (Inuit, Métis) groups to enact laws to protect their languages. There is nothing in the *Indian Act* or other federal laws expressly recognizing this power, but that is not the end of the matter. First Nations possess the inherent right to self-government described in the United Nations Declaration on the Rights of Indigenous Peoples (UN 2007). In 1995, Canada adopted an "inherent right to self-government" policy that lists subjects over which Aboriginal peoples have the right to enact their own laws, including their languages, cultures and religions. However, it was the Government of Canada's intention to implement this policy through the negotiation of modern-day treaty agreements with individual First Nations. The negotiation of modern-day treaties has been slow, and only a handful of such agreements have been completed thus far in the country.

There is an argument that First Nations should just "do it," exercise their inherent right to self-government without federal agreements or legislation—for example, with respect to their languages. The Migmawei Mawiomi Secretariat, representing the three Mi'gmaw communities in Québec (including my home community of Listuguj) recently issued a declaration that Mi'gmaw is the official language of Gespe'gewa'gi. This is an important symbolic gesture. The problem is that concrete steps to save and protect endangered languages require funding. This can be seen in areas of the country where there are minority French-language communities. Governments have invested in programs to help the French language flourish in those communities. So while First Nations can enact laws to recognize their languages, they also require funding for programs to save these languages, which most First Nations lack.

Existing Protections for Aboriginal Languages

In *Language Rights in Canada / Les droits linguistiques au Canada*, I also reviewed what the federal and provincial governments are doing to protect Aboriginal languages in Canada. With regard to the federal government, the answer is: not very much. Despite that the AFN, the royal commission and the task force all recommended that Ottawa take greater action to protect Aboriginal languages. There is no specific reference to Aboriginal languages in the ammended *Indian Act* (1985), the *Official Languages Act* (1985), or the *Canadian Multiculturalism Act* (1985). The task force's report, for one, noted that the federal government has done little to encourage Aboriginal language instruction. Some funding for Aboriginal language immersion programs is available as part of federal funding for schools on reserves, but is as a matter of policy rather than law, and competition for dollars is tight. Overall, funding for education on reserves is so inadequate that it is the subject of a complaint before the Canadian Human Rights Tribunal. The Aboriginal Language Initiatives Program under the federal Department of Heritage Canada also funds some community-based language projects, but again, resources are limited.

Some of the stronger efforts to protect and promote Aboriginal languages are undertaken by the northern territories, where there is a high concentration of Aboriginal peoples. Although the Yukon's *Languages Act* adopts only English and French as official languages, it "recognizes the significance of Aboriginal languages in the Yukon," and commits the territorial government "to take appropriate measures to preserve, develop, and enhance those languages" (*Languages Act* 2002). It grants status to Aboriginal languages in the legislative assembly, and it authorizes the provision of territorial services in one or more of the Aboriginal languages of the Yukon. Similarly, the Yukon's *Education Act* (2002) directs the responsible minister to include courses on the linguistic and cultural heritage and history of Yukon's Aboriginal peoples in schools. On request, the minister can approve the teaching of courses in Aboriginal languages. Several First Nations in the Yukon have self-government agreements that permit them to enact their own laws concerning languages and education.

The Northwest Territories' *Official Languages Act* (1988) recognizes eleven official languages, including nine Aboriginal. Local and regional government offices must provide their services in the official Aboriginal languages of the area, and all the official languages have status in the legislative assembly and court. The *Education Act* (1995) provides that school boards may provide instruction in any of the official languages, given certain demand. The Northwest Territories has an official language commissioner, with a duty to investigate language issues and complaints.

Nunavut has the strongest laws for protecting Aboriginal language, specifically Inuktitut. Its *Official Languages Act* (2008) establishes Inuktitut, French and English as the official languages of the territory. There is also an Inuit *Language Protection Act* (2008), which promotes fluency in written and oral Inuktitut. Public institutions must post all signage in the three official languages, and government offices (territorial and municipal) as well as private businesses must be able to provide services and communicate with the public in all three official languages. People have the right to speak Inuktitut in the legislative assembly as well as in the courts. While laws do not have to be published in Inuktitut, bills placed before the legislative assembly must include a version in Inuktitut, and the government can publish an Inuktitut version of a law at its discretion. Also, parents have the right to have their children instructed in Inuktitut, and Nunavut's *Education Act* (2008) requires bilingual education for all children, consisting of Inuktitut and either French or English. An official language commissioner has the power to investigate any violations of language rights, and Nunavut has established a fund for Aboriginal language intiatives.

Outside the territories, two provinces have been most receptive to Aboriginal languages: British Columbia and Manitoba. In 1996, the Government of British Columbia adopted the *First Peoples Heritage, Language and Culture Act* (1996) with a view to protect, revitalize and enhance First Nations heritage, language, culture and arts. The *Act* creates a First Peoples Heritage, Language and Culture Council to finance projects that promote Aboriginal languages and culture. Under a trilateral agreement (provincial, federal, First Nations), British Columbia also adopted the *First Nations Education Act* (2007), giving First Nations in the province greater control of education on their reserves including standards for language of instruction within the classroom.

In 2010, Manitoba adopted the *Aboriginal Languages Recognition Act* (2010), which recognizes seven Aboriginal languages spoken in Manitoba, and affirms in its preamble that the provincial government has "a role to play in recognizing and promoting the preservation and use of Aboriginal languages." The minister of education is developing a program for the instruction of Aboriginal languages from kindergarten to grade twelve within provincial schools.

In Saskatchewan, Alberta, Ontario, New Brunswick and Newfoundland and Labrador, the only action taken to promote Aboriginal languages has been a policy of supporting some level of Aboriginal language instruction for Aboriginal children in public schools. Prince Edward Island lacks even this level of minimal commitment to Aboriginal languages, even though there are two Mi'gmaw communities within the province.

The Québec government has a policy of recognizing the Aboriginal languages of Québec and sets out measures to protect, develop, maintain and support them. The Québec Charter of the French Language exempts French-language requirements for First Nations on reserves. The exemption also applies to Cree under the James Bay agreement, which requires that certain services be provided to Cree and Naskapi in their own language. In Québec, a unilingual First Nations or Inuit speaker can serve on a jury.

Nova Scotia signed a tripartite agreement with the federal government and the Mi'gmaq of Nova Scotia, resulting in the *Mi'kmaq Education Act* (1998). This gives Mi'gmaq greater control over education on reserves, including control over the language of education. The province also has a policy of teaching Mi'gmaw language and culture within public schools, and, in 2008, Nova Scotia launched a pilot project to hire Mi'gmaw-speaking victim-services workers.

Legal Grounds for Greater Protection

No Canadian court has ruled on whether the federal, provincial or territorial governments have an obligation to provide greater funding or services for Aboriginal languages. The Canadian Charter of Rights and Freedoms (part 1 of the *Constitution Act, 1982*) does not mention Aboriginal languages, although equality rights as proscribed in section 15(1) would appear to prevent discrimination thereof. Sections 15(2) and 25 of the Charter would protect Aboriginal groups from claims of "reverse discrimination" by non-Aboriginal people in the case of government programs to support and protect Aboriginal languages.

The protection of Aboriginal and treaty rights in section 35 of the *Constitution Act, 1982*, does not specifically mention Aboriginal languages, either, but many scholars have argued that the right to speak an Aboriginal language is clearly an Aboriginal right protected by s. 35. Academics have also argued that instruction in Aboriginal languages may be a treaty right—at least in the numbered treaties that specifically include promises of education. I have yet to see an argument for Aboriginal languages based upon our Mi'gmaw peace and friendship treaties. Dating from 1725 to 1779, these treaties made with the British Crown do not specifically refer to language or education. This is understandable. I can only think that our ancestors expected their descendants to continue speaking Mi'gmaw forever without hindrance. I am not sure whether this gives rise to a specific treaty right arising from our peace and friendship treaties with the Crown, at least based on the current judicial test for treaty rights, but I think it is an important consideration in building a case.

Even if Aboriginal languages are protected as Aboriginal and treaty rights, it is uncertain how far Canadian courts would go in requiring governments to provide services and programs to protect those rights. Some academics argue that Canada's governments—in particular the federal—have obligations to promote Aboriginal languages. They argue that Canada largely caused the contemporary crisis facing Aboriginal languages, thus it has an obligation to fix the problem, informed by Canada's international undertakings, including the U.N. Declaration on the Rights of Indigenous People (UNDRIP 2007). Article 13 of UNDRIP recognizes the right of indigenous peoples to "revitalize, use, develop and transmit to future generations their histories, languages [and] oral traditions," and the responsibility of states to "take effective measures to ensure that this right is protected." Article 14 recognizes that indigenous peoples have the right to establish and control their own education systems, including providing education in their own languages, with the assistance of the states in which they live.

I believe we are fast approaching the time when some group of Aboriginal people will advance a legal claim based on s. 35 of the Charter, and international law, to require Canada to do more to protect Aboriginal languages. With my research background, as well as my experience in court, I hope to be one of the people advising that group. I have spoken with other lawyers about raising First Nations' awareness of the possibility of making this type of claim. I feel that this would be something I would do to honour the legacy of my father and our Mi'gmaw ancestors.

Along the way, I will honour my pledge to become a fluent speaker.

Notes

1. This district includes the Gaspé Peninsula (Québec), which derives its French name from its Mi'kmaw name.

2. Nnu or l'nu, a human being in the Mi'gmaw language.

References

Aboriginal Languages Recognition Act. 2010. CCSM c A1.5.

Bastarache, Michel. 2013. *Language Rights in Canada / Les droits linguistiques au Canada.* 3ième ed. Montréal: Éditions Yvon Blais.

Bill S-237. 2009. *Act for the Advancement of Aboriginal Languages of Canada,* 2nd Session, 40th Parliament, 57-58 Elizabeth II.

Canadian Multiculturalism Act. 1985. RSC 1985, c 24 (4th Supp).

Constitution Act, 1982. Schedule B to the Canada Act 1982 (UK), 1982, c 11.

Education Act. 2002. RSY 2002, c 61.

Education Act. 2008. SNu 2008, c 15.

Education Act. 1995. SNWT 1995, c 28.

First Nations Education Act. 2007. SBC 2007, c 40.

First Peoples Heritage, Language and Culture Act. 1996. RSBC 1996, c 147.

Indian Act. 1985. RSC 1985, c I-5.

Inuit Language Protection Act. 2008. SNu 2008, c 17.

Languages Act. 2002. RSY 2002, c 133.

Metallic, Emmanuel N., Danielle E. Cyr and Alexandre Sévigny. 2005. *The Metallic Migmaq-English Reference Dictionary.* First Edition. Saint-Nicholas, QC: Les Presses de l'Université Laval.

Mi'kmaq Education Act. 1998. SNS 1998, c 17.

Official Languages Act. 1985. RSC 1985, c 31 (4th Supp).

Official Languages Act. 1988. RSNWT 1988, c O-1.

Official Languages Act. 2008. SNu 2008, c 10.

RCAP (Royal Commission on Aboriginal Peoples). 1996. Report of the Royal Commission. Ottawa: Canada Communication Group Publishing.

TFALC (Task Force on Aboriginal Languages and Cultures). 2005. Towards a New Beginning: A Foundational Report for a Strategy to Revitalize First Nation, Inuit and Metis. Report to the Minister of Canadian Heritage. http://www.afn.ca/uploads/files/education2/towardanewbeginning.pdf.

United Nations. 2007. United Nations Declaration on the Rights of Indigenous Peoples. UN.org. http://www.un.org/esa/socdev/unpfii/documents/DRIPS_en.pdf.

Eleanor Tu'ti Bernard

Kina'matnewey Education:
How Our Ancestors Imagined Our Success

The Mi'kmaq of Nova Scotia have gone through so many changes in the education of their children: through oral traditions and storytelling; teaching by example; federal day and residential (boarding) schools; schools controlled by Indian and Northern Affairs Canada (now Indigenous Affairs and Northern Development Canada); band-operated and jurisdiction schools; and finally, via a self-government agreement. There have been so many policies and programs for educating the Mi'kmaw child in the past that the Government of Canada's new programs and policies are suspect. The legacy of the Aboriginal residential and day schools have proven to the Mi'kmaq that federal policy-making does not often lead to success in educating Mi'kmaw children, nor in ensuring their well-being.

I am speaking from my experiences, and from those of my parents and ancestors. I am director of the Mi'kmaw Kina'matnewey (MK), a regional education management organization in Nova Scotia. Having been educated by provincial schools for most of my life, I have witnessed the need for the decolonization of education within the public school system. There have been some changes in the provincial assessment results, what with the hiring of race-relations coordinators by the school boards; however, this makes for just a small contribution—the current statistics show very little improvement in assessment results.

MK is a regional management organization with legislated jurisdiction over education. In 1999, Nova Scotia passed similar legislation recognizing the jurisdiction of education for Mi'kmaw communities. Presently, twelve of the thirteen First Nations communities in Nova Scotia are part of MK. Many changes in education have occurred, the largest being the improved graduation rates in the schools. At the present time, MK communities are working collaboratively to improve literacy and numeracy rates as well as second-level services in the schools. When communities cannot afford to pay, for example, a speech-language pathologist, they work together by pooling their resources so that each community will share at least one specialist. There are so many benefits when the communities work together; so much more can be achieved for the best interests of students.

Race-relations coordinators are staff of Mi'kmaw ancestry who that work for the various public school boards in Nova Scotia. The race-relations coordinator provides sensitivity training as well as Mi'kmaw cultural-awareness training to teachers and other staff in the school boards. I am not being critical of the public schools because there is still much work to be done in the Mi'kmaw communities and Mi'kmaw schools as well. Mi'kmaw students on-reserve are not doing as well as we would want. The statistics have drastically improved with respect to graduation rates, but improving the quality of graduates requires more skills development in literacy and numeracy. As reported in the MK annual report for 2014-2015, Mi'kmaw students score significantly lower in the provincial schools. The L'nu Sipu Kina'matnuo'ko'm (LSK) in Sipekne'katik (Indian Brook First Nation) in Nova Scotia is a great example of success, as the literacy rates of the students in this school have improved greatly (see MK 2014). Through the efforts of MK, by providing resources to the LSK and through the professional development of teachers, there has been much improvement. MK has also facilitated changes in the classrooms, such as "Learning through Play," a program that focuses on literacy improvement. The mentoring of teachers for numeracy and literacy has also created positive change. The facilitation of change and the exercise of jurisdiction of education in Mi'kmaw First Nations has been the best benefit for the MK communities.

—

Understanding how Mi'kmaq have been displaced as educators in the home requires a brief overview of that life. Before the arrival of European settlers to Mi'kma'ki, parents, relatives and communities educated their children through oral tradition and hands-on learning. Boys were taught to hunt and fish by the men, and the girls were taught by the women to cook, clean game, prepare the skins for clothing and care for the younger children. Families had traditionally assigned areas of Mi'kma'ki where they hunted game and fished. They would move with the seasons, living in the cover of the woods in the winter months and moving to the shores during warmer months. In the winter, their wikuo'ml (homes) were insulated from the cold winds by snow piled up on the outside. The summer wikuo'm did not need as much covering, just a sheet of birchbark and spruce boughs for cover from the wind and rain. The children were always learning from their elders. In the evenings, as the families gathered around the fire, they shared stories of how things were done traditionally as well as the events of the day.

With the arrival of the Europeans, things began to change and the Mi'kmaq were forced to live on reserved lands. Next, the Mi'kmaw children were to attend settler schools, and while in school they were taught to forget about the ways of living as Mi'kmaq. They were taught and educated to become tradesmen. Christian churches and the federal government then cooperated to open Aboriginal residential schools. Mi'kmaw children who went to these schools were taught to forget *everything* about being Mi'kmaq—their language and culture were suppressed—and to learn a skilled trade. Many of the Mi'kmaw children in the residential schools were abused and beaten by staff members. The Government of Canada has since apologized for the assimilationist policy and school system, and many of the former students have received money in compensation for the abuse they endured while in the residential schools. To this day, many communities face the intergenerational effects of the abuse that the survivors suffered while in these schools: a legacy of abuse, indifference to the education system and, of course, alcohol and drug abuse in coping with the physical and emotional trauma.

Mi'kmaw children who did not attend residential schools lived at home and attended the Indian day schools that were run by the federal government on their reserves through Indian Affairs. But the basic premise of the Indian day schools were similar to that of residential schools, in that Mi'kmaw children were expected to become skilled workers in the trades and to forget their culture. The girls were expected to become secretaries or cleaning ladies. The federal government did not expect students to amount to anything significant within Canadian society. The Indian day schools on reserves in Nova Scotia, for example, were only offered until grade six, and if students wanted to further their education they would have to leave home and attend a boarding school. It was always the same outcome for Mi'kmaw students: they would never be anything more than prospective labourers. This same mentality was evident throughout the education system under the control of Indian Affairs.

As a Mi'kmaw student attending the provincial school system, I witnessed comparable expectations as those of my parents, who had attended residential school and the Indian day schools. In high school, I was never expected to attend university, or to become a teacher. When I started grade ten in a provincial school in Sydney, there were 167 students on the school buses making the trip from Eskasoni First Nation. By October, less than half were making the trip. After Christmas break, only one bus was required. In May of that year, only a handful of us were left and the bus driver decided to use his van to drive us to school, as he was embarrassed to take the near-empty bus. In my second year of high school it was the same story. At the end of my grade twelve, only five Mi'kmaw students were in the graduating class.

There are many reasons Mi'kmaw students drop out of school. The first, most definitely, is racism, although other reasons included the distance of off-reserve schools, low self esteem of Mi'kmaw students, and of course, feeling out of place in schools that did not recognize Mi'kmaw identity. I can recall many times the awkward feeling of our being singled out as a group to go to the office, or when the "Eskasoni students" were summoned to our bus, while the non-Mi'kmaw students were on numbered buses. There were many other situations that were most uncomfortable for me and for other Mi'kmaw students. During breaks, we would hang out on the second floor of the business building, which became referred to as the "reserve," while the other students went to the cafeteria.

In the 1980s, Mi'kmaw First Nations took control of their education from the federal government, and this is when significant changes began to take place. Indian teacher-education programs were being set up across Canada by virtue of the *Indian Control of Indian Education* paper released by the National Indian Brotherhood/Assembly of First Nations, which the federal government accepted in 1973. One cohort of such teacher candidates was established at the University of New Brunswick, with the first graduates in 1984.

By the 1990s, it became evident that the community of Eskasoni needed to build a high school. When a riot broke out among students (Mi'kmaw students had to be escorted off the school grounds by police) Mi'kmaw students felt they could no longer safely attend the provincial high school. The community decided to build a high school in Eskasoni. Since 1998, when the high school opened, there have been, on average, approximately forty to forty-five students graduating each year, a graduation rate of 87 per cent for the Eskasoni students under MK jurisdiction.

Undated photo of a recent graduating class at the high school in Eskasoni. Photo courtesy Jaime Battiste.

In conclusion, I have witnessed many changes as a Mi'kmaw student, teacher and administrative executive in Mi'kmaw education. My education in an on-reserve school for my early elementary years and, after grade two, mostly in the provincial public schools, was delivered in English. I missed out of all of the services and teachings of the Mi'kmaw language and culture that are now available to Mi'kmaw youth in our MK schools. However, my parents', grandparents' and relatives' teachings, delivered to me in Mi'kmaw, will remain etched in my mind and heart forever. My children have now had the advantages of being educated by Mi'kmaw teachers and professors, and I must say they have done very well in education, filled with confidence and pride. They have been able to move on to provincial schools and higher education with confidence in their Mi'kmaw knowledge and skills. Their success is matched in many other Mi'kmaw communities as well. This was in the minds and hearts of our ancestors when they signed the treaties.

References

MK (Mi'kmaw Kina'matnewey). 2014. Annual Report, 2014-2105. http://kinu.ca/sites/default/files/doc/2014/Feb/mk_annual_report_2015_oct._8-2.pdf.

Marie Battiste

Resilience and Resolution: Mi'kmaw Education and the Treaty Implementation

As a Mi'kmaw educator from Potlotek First Nation in Nova Scotia, and a professor in the College of Education at the University of Saskatchewan, I have been deeply honoured to have been educated not just to empower my own capacity to learn but also to nourish and empower the learning spirit of indigenous people to their own educational goals and achievements. Though most of my own education was one that did not include Mi'kmaw or indigenous curricula, I was privileged to have learned from my parents and communities about the value of the Mi'kmaw assets of language and culture, as well as to have attended some of the best Eurocentric universities to build the necessary skills and knowledge to unpack that education and to help rebuild our histories and knowledge in our schools. From my parents and, later, from Mi'kmaw Grand Captain Alex Denny, I have learned to use my education to empower Mi'kmaw education and to urge the provincial and federal government to comply with the treaty and Aboriginal-rights obligations of the Canadian Constitution.

It has taken us since 1973—and the then policy proposed in *Indian Control of Indian Education*, a paper released by the National Indian Brotherhood (a precursor to the Assembly of First Nations)—to work toward reversing the effects of assimilative federal Aboriginal day schools, Aboriginal residential schools, and provincial public schooling of Mi'kmaq to enable them to once again be successful learners of their own language, building on their own community heritage and cultures. Provincial education curricula have now embraced Mi'kmaw education and histories, and teacher education is pursuing antiracist education and Mi'kmaw holistic learning. These have given rise to Mi'kmaw Kina'matnewey, an education authority that has demonstrated significant effect in regenerating success among Mi'kmaq.

Personal Location

I am the daughter of the late John and Annie (Lewis) Battiste; both were born and raised in Potlotek, the capital of the Mi'kmaq nation since 1850. They spoke Mi'kmaw as their first language and, gradually, both learned English during our years living in Maine, USA. I have had the wonderful privilege of hearing, writing and publishing my mother's life story (Battiste 1993), she telling me in Mi'kmaw and me writing in English. My mother was born in 1911, my father in 1916; she died in 1997, he in 1990; both had little education, but both were witness to many changes in Mi'kmaw education. My mother was pulled out of school when her White settler teacher shot a sharpened pencil at her in anger, which hit her in the head, upsetting her parents, my grandparents. She did not return to school. Her father reasoned that she only needed to know how to read the word "poison," because schooling at that time held little promise for anyone who was Mi'kmaq. But she was a committed lifelong learner in the Mi'kmaw tradition, and deeply knowledgeable of her language, the land, territory and its resources, and what it provided toward their family's sustenance and well-being.

John and Annie Battiste. N.d. Photo by Roin Caplan, Cape Breton's Magazine, *1993, vol. 64: 29. Courtesy,* Cape Breton's Magazine.

My mother was a great storyteller with a great sense of humour that everyone loved. Her stories were most often about her relatives and their trying to make a living through making and selling baskets throughout the Maritime provinces. My father did not have much formal education either, having been also pulled out of school by his father because he was getting little out of it—it was discovered that his only activity there was feeding the school stove and chopping wood. With his few years of schooling, he learned to read and was a lifelong learner, equally equipped with deep family knowledge of the land, artistry and the common knowledge of men his age, including playing the fiddle and knowing how to make baskets. Together, my parents set out to create a family life that eventually took them from the reserve in Nova Scotia in 1947 to the potato harvests in Maine, where they resided off-reserve for more than twenty-five years. Protected by a Mi'kmaw treaty with the United States, the Jay Treaty (1794), Mi'kmaq can travel and work unhindered between the two countries. Their main focus was on their livelihood and raising their family, which kept them away from their reserve and their extended families while they survived on low wages, living in low-income housing in Houlton. What kept them in Maine was not the life, but the education that their children were receiving and what they perceived as opportunities they could not get by living on their reserve in Nova Scotia.

Living for most years in the border town of Houlton, ME, we all attended Maine schools. I was very young when I heard my father say, which he repeated often, that my educational opportunities would be greater for going to Maine schools. Their wishes inspired me with the additional motivation to do well for my parents and try to make their aspirations for us come true. My parents made their life living as most poor folk did, through sacrifices and challenges; my father worked as a manual labourer and my mother worked as a domestic maid, cleaning houses for local families. They added to their meagre incomes at various times and seasons with basket making, which we did as a family. This not only supplied us with needed cash when times got tough, but also socialized among us the traditional knowledge of their parents and ancestors, along with stories of them.

Houlton is a small border town that had potato farming as its mainstay, to which all the schools contributed in helping get the crops in each fall. Mi'kmaw families from Maritime reserves came to Maine during this time and set up camps, bringing their children, most of whom would be out of school for up to a month, making it very difficult for many to graduate or catch up in the school year. The economic livelihood of Mi'kmaq having to take up seasonal work with their children—as well as the fact that their education, or lack thereof, was in the hands of the Canadian federal government (responsible for on-reserve education) and the dreaded Indian residential-school system—was what kept many Mi'kmaq from being able to achieve anything beyond elementary school. My own older sister Eleanor endured the Shubenacadie Indian Residential School for three years while my parents got settled in Maine, before bringing her to Houlton. Those years of that horrific experience on top of the racialized climate in Houlton, permanently affected Eleanor's life, and ours. At the age of sixteen, the legal age to leave school in Maine, she did. The rest of my siblings and I made it through high school, and my brother and I went on to college and university. Eventually I finished graduate degrees at two of the most coveted schools in the world, Harvard and Stanford, and my brother also graduated from Harvard.

Annie and children visiting Eleanor at residential school. N.d. Cape Breton's Magazine, 1993, vol. 64: 32. *Courtesy,* Cape Breton's Magazine.

In 1973, my parents finally went home to Potlotek First Nation, which then became my family home base. I had begun my graduate study at Stanford, focusing on the history of Mi'kmaw education and policies, trying to understand what had led to the devastating outcomes for Mi'kmaq in education and economic development under the Canadian Department of Indian Affairs (now INAC). Grand Captain Alex Denny had come to California to recruit me to begin a bilingual-bicultural education system for the Mi'kmaq and move toward regaining Mi'kmaw control of education. That would become my quest and a target that had many parts to it, including helping to develop a teacher-training program for Mi'kmaw teachers at the University of New Brunswick—as Nova Scotia universities refused to provide such a program then—and then creating, advocating and administering a program at Mi'kmawey School in Potlotek, with newly trained Mi'kmaw teachers. Denny also inspired me with his vision of the treaty imperative to regain Mi'kmaw control of education.

After receiving my doctorate in bilingual-bicultural education, Potlotek First Nation hired me as their education director and principal of their band-operated school on the reserve. From that experience, and from working in Eskasoni School as curriculum coordinator, I came to a deeper appreciation of what my parents had left behind, and why they returned. The large extended Mi'kmaw family grew into a collective that gave much to my emerging self immersed in Mi'kmaw life. My new job was my experiment in language and cultural education within the context of reserve life, with my newly minted skills from the Stanford University School of Education. It was an exciting and vibrant time of learning and experimentation with my newly minted teachers—from the Mi'kmaq Maliseet Education Program at the University of New Brunswick, and new teachers Murdena Marshall and Elizabeth Paul, along with several community educators, Beverly Johnson, Lillian Marshall and Charmony Johnson—an experiment I have discussed elsewhere (Battiste 1986, 1987). In the next section, I take you through some historical events that illustrate Mi'kmaw desire for education, the kind they wanted and what they were given.

Mi'kmaw Control of Education in the Mi'kmaw Treaties

While I was getting my doctorate, Grand Captain Alex Denny called me up and asked me to come home to help with a language-restoration project. He took me and my family under his large family to ensure that I had what I needed to begin. He made it clear that Mi'kmaq had to restore control of their education and that this control resided in Mi'kmaw families' right to have their own education under the treaties. None of the treaties, he stated, granted the Crown or government the right to interfere with the traditions of Mi'kmaw people to educate their own, nor justified attempts to destroy our traditional knowledge system and language—i.e., with residential and day schools. While he wanted Mi'kmaw children to know both Mi'kmaw and English (and/or French), and to appreciate both knowledge systems, which he saw as complementary, he rejected the existing assimilative education system. We spent many long hours over tea, talking, laughing and playing with the kids, as we discussed the past and present and the strategies needed to make the changes. As it turned out, Denny was right—on just about everything. From my historical study of the Mi'kmaq (Battiste 1984), the records show we never gave away control of education.

Mi'kmaw control of socializing children through education was a covenant learned from our Creation story and its teachings. The Mi'kmaw educational traditions were focused on enabling the potentiality and gifts of the Creator in each person and nourishing the learning spirit throughout the many cycles of life. Mi'kmaq deep love for their children, for learning and for sharing knowledge, including an on-going curiosity and capacity for the deep learning of diverse ecologies and societies, was part of Mi'kmaw socialization, hospitality and protocols of place—all shared with the newcomers as reported in the travel logs of explorers and missionaries and priests for centuries.

Initially, alliances with the Holy See and with French settlers in Mi'kma'ki made possible the tenets of reciprocal relations built on Mi'kmaq agreeing to allow French—and, later, British—families and settlers, to live as Catholic relatives of the Mi'kmaq. These alliances established particular protocols and reciprocal arrangements. The French and British colonists who married into the Mawio'mi were considered relatives (*no'kmaq*), those who did not marry into the Mi'kmaq were regarded as friends of a different nationality (*ntutem*). Some colonists established schools based on their knowledge systems and heritages, and sometimes they schooled together with Mi'kmaq. The Mi'kmaq sent a few of their people to the colonists' schools, but they did not give up their seasonal activities that assured their livelihood. Eventually, a lingua franca of a Basque-Mi'kmaw dialect (Upton 1979), suggests that there was, at least at one point in the colonial relationship, a very different one than that of today.

These relationships even created new blended families, as illustrated by how the Mi'kmaq protected the French merchant Charles La Tour after his 1625 marriage to Louise (Llul's) (La Tour 1631), a prominent Mi'kmaw woman. They were married in Mi'kmaw tradition, and he reported that his wife and her family had taught him to become proficient in Mi'kmaw, adding to his learning a variety of dialects through trade with the Mi'kmaq and the Wabanaki allies.

With his marriage into the Mi'kmaq, La Tour and his partners were able to expand their trade. According to La Tour, the years 1623 to 1627 "were our most prosperous years in terms of monetary gain" (La Tour 1631). His family lived in the Kespukwitk (lands end) district of Mi'kma'ki, at Fort Loméron at Cape Sable (Sandy Cape), which is now in the Barrington municipal district of Shelburne County, Nova Scotia (Fisher 2008: 438-39). In a letter home to France, La Tour (1631) referred to Mi'kmaq as "the people of this country" rather than the usual "savages."

In 1630, Récollet priests arriving in New France blessed Charles and Llul's' marriage. The priests also baptized their three young daughters, Jeanne, Antoinette and Marie. The marriage was a short one as Louise died in 1632. La Tour travelled back to France with delegates who the Mi'kmaq had selected, Quichetech (Tchichetech) and Nenougy, along with his three daughters with the idea of securing a good French education for them in a convent (MacDonald 1982: 44). The daughters had been raised in a bilingual tradition, sharing their time between their mother's village and their father's forts, where they learned the trading system. While his oldest daughter Jeanne refused a religious education, his younger daughters, Marie and Antoinette, did join a convent in France for their education, where Marie died. While little is known about Antoinette, it is noted that she became a renowned singer and later a nun, in 1649 (*Yarmouth Vanguard*: 50-51). The girls' Mi'kmaw relatives, however, were noted as being distraught over La Tour's decision to leave the younger daughters in convents in distant France, as they thought they should be raised according to their Mi'kmaw traditions.

In the summer of 1632, the king of France, Louis XIII, ordered Captain Isaac de Razilly to retake possession of La Cadie (Acadia) after three years of Scottish occupation. The king declared that de Razilly and La Tour would share the royal governorship over the restored territory. Under de Razilly's authority, fifteen French families and three Capuchin friars created a new coastal enclave at La Hève, which became the capital of Acadia (Fisher 2008). The Mi'kmaq took this opportunity to request a school for their children, so that they would not have to be sent away to convents for their education. The Capuchins missionaries created the first school in La Cadie, one that was for the use of both colonists and Mi'kmaq. This school provided Mi'kmaw children with French-language skills and French students with Mi'kmaw language. The bilingual school thus educated the children to be intermediaries in commercial trade.

In the Mi'kmaw treaties with English and British monarchs from 1629 to 1779, Mi'kmaq preserved their ancestral control over education. In preparation for the negotiation of the proposed peace and friendship treaty of 1725, colonial Nova Scotia representative Jean-Paul Mascarene promised the Mi'kmaq that they would not be molested "in the Exercise of their Religion provided the Missionaries residing amongst them have Leave from ye Govemour or Commander in Chief ... for So doing" (PRO CO 1725). In the understanding of chiefs and nation, education in the treaties was protected as part of spiritual and religious beliefs, and was the choice of the families. While they exercised their freedom of religion, and sought missionaries to assist them in education, Mi'kmaw families directed the education of the children to find their additional gifts. Subsequent attempts of government and its Church to take over education violated the treaty promises of the free exercise of their religion.

In the 1726 treaty, which ratified the proposed 1725 treaty, the British representative affirmed to the Mi'kmaw chiefs—and subsequently in other ratifications in 1749 and 1752 treaties—"that the Said Indians shall not be Molested in the Exercise of their Religion, Provided the Missionary's Residing amongst them have Leave from this Government for Soe Doing" (PRO CO 1726). In an attempt to implement the proposed treaty of 1725 (ratified by the Mi'kmaq in 1726 and 1728), Jonathan Belcher, governor of Massachusetts, met with the nations of the confederacy to "renew friendship" in July 1732, at Falmouth, MA (Mandel 2003: 384-91). Belcher declared that he planned to hire ministers at Fort Saint George and Fort Richmond. The ministers would have two functions: they would instruct Mi'kmaq in the "Principles of the Christian Religion" and to "teach your Children to Read and Write, which all be without any cost to you" (390). At this treaty conference, Governor Belcher, himself a graduate of Harvard College, promised free education at Harvard to the children of the nations of the Wabanaki Confederacy, a larger confederation of New England and Eastern Canadian tribes, which included Mi'kmaq, Maliseet, Passamaquoddy, Penobscots and Abenaki: "[i]f you are willing to send your Children to Boston, they shall be brought up to Learnings at the *College*, that so they may officiate as Fathers among you and teach you the true Religion, and their Education shall cost you nothing" (390). He committed these promises to paper, which the ambassadors acknowledged as additions to the treaties, which the Mi'kmaq ratified in 1726 at Annapolis Royal.

Governor Belcher vigilantly addressed the issue of education: "The Government is willing to instruct you on free Cost.... [W]e shall willingly send ... Schoolmasters to teach you to read and write; And if at any time, you will send your Children among us to be educated, they shall be treated with that Kindness, as if they were our own Children" (Mandel 2003: 390). The Wabanaki Ambassadors replied, "As to what was said of our Children, we are not qualified to answer as to the Proposal for their Education, we being but few here, and the other Tribes being concerned in it" (391). The Mawio'mi (Mi'kmaw Grand Council) accepted the proposed free education, although they did not send any children to attend Harvard College. However, the Mawio'mi rejected the Protestant minister in favour of Catholic priests.

The Mawio'mi also rejected colonial Nova Scotia's attempt to replace Mi'kmaw control of education, protected in the Crown treaties, with colonial educational systems and with teachers from Protestant religious groups (Battiste 1984). Similar to Belcher's promise, Nova Scotia provided for the instruction of Mi'kmaq free of charge at any publicly supported school. The chiefs had made promises to observe the treaties in the most solemn manner; this included the preservation of their ancestral knowledge, language and ways of life. In the mutual treaties of peace and friendship with the Crown, they did not delegate any authority over the education of Mi'kmaw children or their way of life. The chiefs retained and preserved this ancient power to the Mi'kmaw families.

In negotiations of the 1761 treaties, as affirmed in the 1779 treaty, Nova Scotia Lieutenant Governor Jonathan Belcher, son of Governor Belcher of Massachusetts, affirmed at the ceremony marking the treaty signing: "Your Religion will not be rooted out of this Field [of English liberty]. Your Patriarch will still feed and nourish you in this Soil as his Spiritual Children" (PRO CO 1761. The Mi'kmaw chiefs asserted an exception, "the one thing that bind me more strong and firmly to you that I can possibly express and that is in your indulging me in the free Exercise of the Religion in which I have been instructed from my Cradle" (PRO CO 1761). Under the Mi'kmaw treaties, Mi'kmaq Catholicism, founded on their own spirituality, ensured protection of Mi'kmaw educational practices and other chosen ways of life.

In 1814, the governor of colonial Nova Scotia created and financed a planting-out system that provided subsidies for farmers who took in Mi'kmaw children for a year to teach them the colonial ways of domestication and farming. British officer and social reformer Walter Bromley, who established the Royal Acadian School in Halifax for marginalized people, criticized this policy, asserting, "if Indian are to be civilized, it could only be done by general consent of the tribe" (Bromley 1814: 46). In 1829, the provincial assembly legislated another free-tuition scheme for the Mi'kmaq to obtain their consent to provincial schooling. Still, the Mi'kmaq retained control over education. The province appointed a commissioner of Indian affairs, Joseph Howe, armed with an 1842 *Act to Provide for the Indians and Permanent Settlement of the Indians*, to consult with the Mi'kmaq; that did not lessen the resilience of Mi'kmaq to retain control of education under the treaties. The *Act* provided for erecting a "school house" at permanent Indian settlements, and the commissioner was authorized by the *Act* to arrange for Mi'kmaw children to go to provincial school. Mi'kmaw parents were unwilling to give up their traditional education system, and with it, in effect, their knowledge system and language. Commissioner Howe reported to the assembly that "[w]ith few exceptions, I at first found nearly the whole tribe strongly prejudiced against learning to read or write any other language than their own" (Canada 1843: 7). Later he reported that, after a few experiments, the Mi'kmaq seemed "desirous of obtaining the knowledge of reading and writing, but they cannot afford to spend their whole time at it" (122). The assembly recommended that Protestant religious groups be given control of the money and the education of the Mi'kmaq (164).

In 1847, Howe faced the resistance of the Mawio'mi and the Mi'kmaw families. Mi'kmaw women expressed their disapproval "of any of their children being educated in the White Man's school—because, when so educated it would break off the natural ties of affection and association between them and their Tribe, and mutual dislike and contempt would be the result" (NSARM 1842: 146-51). Additionally, the Mi'kmaq resisted the discipline of the provincial school system and curriculum (NSARM 1843: 205-206). The Mi'kmaq asserted that day schools be established exclusively for Mi'kmaw children, with the recommendation that they be instructed in their own language. The tension between what languages and what knowledge systems were used was beginning to create a rift between the Mi'kmaq and the colonists. The commissioner thus recommended integrating Mi'kmaq with other children (Canada 1847: 122) with instruction probably in French. Moreover, he recommended to legislators that day schools should be phased out in favour of a return of the outing system by establishing distant boarding schools for Mi'kmaw children. After Confederation, when the British Crown's authority was transferred to the newly created Dominion of Canada, the latter recommendation generated the federal residential-school system, based on the forced assimilation and cultural genocide of Aboriginal peoples (TRC Executive Report 2015). In 1883, Canada's first prime minister and first minister of Indian affairs, Sir John A. Macdonald, declared to Parliament the goal of Canada in regard to Mi'kmaq and other Indians:

> When the school is on the reserve the child lives with its parents, who are savages; he is surrounded by savages, and though he may learn to read and write his habits, and training and mode of thought are Indian. He is simply a savage who can read and write. It has been strongly pressed on myself, as the head of the Department, that Indian children should be withdrawn as much as possible from the parental influence, and the only way to do that would be to put them in central training industrial schools where they will acquire the habits and modes of thought of white men (Canada, House of Commons Debate [9 May 1883]: 1107-1108)

This was a deep betrayal by the federal government, which violated treaties and destroyed much of the Mi'kmaw traditional knowledge and language at the generational level.

Treaty Implementation for Mi'kmaq Education

Probably one of the most misunderstood quandaries to Nova Scotians—the fact that Mi'kmaq receive an education provided by the federal government, implemented by the Mi'kmaw Kina'matnewey, and not by the provinces—the answer to Mi'kmaw control of education is under Crown treaties. To comprehend the importance of the Mi'kmaw treaties, educators should comprehend how, in regard to education, the Aboriginal and treaty rights of the Mi'kmaq has reoriented the constitutional framework of education in Canada. There is a mandatory force of treaty implementation through the various constitutional powers in the Constitution of Canada, as found by the Supreme Court of Canada, that was created to converge these different constitutional sources of power, creating a complex intersection of issues that should be addressed in transforming current and future educational outcomes.

The Supreme Court has termed the affirmation of Aboriginal and treaty rights "an underlying constitutional value" (Reference re Secession of Quebec: paras. 32, 82, 96) and "a national commitment" (*R. v. Marshall* (No. 2): para. 45). The Supreme Court, in *R. v. Cote* (1996), has stated that for every constitutional right of the Mi'kmaq, there is a corresponding constitutional duty to teach those rights.

The Mi'kmaq have proven in court that they have unique constitutional rights, including Aboriginal and treaty rights. These rights, based on Mi'kmaw traditional knowledge, are part of the constitutional right to lifelong learning and to generating an enriched livelihood of the Mi'kmaq. Constitutional supremacy has to be respected by all Canadian and provincial governments and institutions, and is especially relevant for education systems and educators.

The constitutional rights of the Mi'kmaq are a constitutional imperative attached to all educational institutions, and represent a dual (Aboriginal and treaty) inheritance of each Mi'kmaq. Every educational institution in Canada, especially in Atlantic Canada, is obligated to implement the constitutional rights of the Mi'kmaq. Respecting constitutional rights in education systems and institutions requires that the provinces and federal government, where they have schools, must take into consideration ways to advance Mi'kmaw education by reforming their vision, rules and regulations to implement and fulfill these constitutional rights.

The recognition and affirmation of these foundational and institutional imperatives is an essential prerequisite for respectful relationships, collaborative efforts and mutual benefit going forward. These imperatives are embodied in s. 35 of the *Constitution Act, 1982*; they are both implicitly and explicitly described in the Crown treaties, and are specifically described in the United Nations Declaration on the Rights of Indigenous Peoples (2007). Canadian courts have stated that constitutional and international law must be read together to comprehend and implement the Canadian constitutional framework.

The Supreme Court of Canada has declared that these constitutional rights have to be read together with the other constitutional provisions (see *Paul v. British Columbia* 2003: par. 24), and, as such, it has held that no part of the Constitution can abrogate another, as no power or right is absolute. Under this constitutional framework, the federal government, under s. 91(24) and s. 132 of the *Constitution Act, 1867*, and the provincial governments, under s. 92 and 93 of the same *Act*, must be read with Mi'kmaw rights in s. 35 of the *Constitution Act, 1982*, to allow each level of constitutional governance to fulfill the honour of the Crown within their receptive fields of competence and implement the treaty rights (Henderson 2007).

Canadian courts have recognized that the constitutional rights of Mi'kmaq affirmed in s. 35 were not created by Canadian legislation, but predate the formation of the Canadian state. The ancestral knowledge system and language of the Mi'kmaq, their Aboriginal rights, were preserved in Crown treaties. The Mi'kmaq did not delegate any control over education to the Crown. Because of their constitutional status, the Aboriginal and treaty rights protected by s. 35 and 52(1) of the 1982 *Act* impose positive and honourable obligations on government.

The recent clarification by the Supreme Court of Canada in *Grassy Narrows First Nation v. Ontario (Natural Resources)*, a 2014 decision, provides the constitutional framework for truly transformative change, away from the unacceptable status quo. The Supreme Court held that the provinces and the Government of Canada are each constitutionally responsible for the implementation of Aboriginal and treaty rights within their constitutional powers. No longer is the constitutional responsibility for implementing the constitutional rights of Mi'kmaq assigned to Ottawa alone.

This decision ends the regime of denial, uncertainty and conflict by assigning to the provinces of Atlantic Canada the role of implementing the constitutional rights of Mi'kmaq in education. (The division of powers in Canada's Constitution assigns the constitutional responsibility for education to the provinces.) As a result, the provinces are the primary source of education funding. Accordingly, the provinces of Atlantic Canada have the primary responsibility to implement the constitutional rights of the Mi'kmaq in education, in consultation with the Mi'kmaq and, in Nova Scotia, their educational agency, Mi'kmaw Kina'matnewey.

The Constitution of Canada creates a legal division of authority between "Indians" or First Nations, Inuit and now Métis, and for new Canadians who later become citizens and residents of a province. Identified in the *British North America Act*, the Queen in Parliament passed to Canada the implementation of treaties with the Mi'kmaq nation (s. 132), as well as jurisdiction over Indians and lands reserved for Indians (s. 91[24]). Later, in s. 35 of the *Constitution Act, 1982*, the Queen in Parliament subsequently affirmed and recognized the education rights of treaty Indians that were preserved in the Crown treaties. Aboriginal rights include, but are not exclusive to, language, culture, family values, socialization, communal relations and customs, spirituality and religion, governance structures, and lifelong learning, among others, all of which is considered as indigenous knowledge.

In the absence of a treaty with the Crown, pre-existing Aboriginal rights continue to empower education for Aboriginal peoples, which is based on indigenous knowledge and the choices of indigenous parents and how they want their own indigeneity or indigenousness taught in schools. The existence of educational rights in Aboriginal and treaty rights cannot negate the constitutional law-making powers under s. 91(24) of the *Constitution Act, 1867*, toward Indians. Conversely, federal legislation, like the *Indian Act*, cannot negate the constitutional rights of education to Aboriginal nations or peoples. In other words, all legislation and policy enacted pursuant to a valid constitutional power has to be consistent to be legitimate with all parts of the constitution. This recasts Nova Scotia's *Mi'kmaw Education Act* as part of treaty implementation consistent with the constitutional rights of the Mi'kmaq. It is a way for federal government and Mi'kmaq to fulfill the shared constitutional competency to take action to preserve and promote the distinct knowledge, traditions and distinctive education systems that underlay these rights. The Mi'kmaw Grand Council and chiefs view the *Mi'kmaw Education Act* as part of the implementation of the rights reserved to the Mi'kmaq under their treaties as required by s. 132 of the *Constitution Act, 1982*. Parliament, by its constitutional power in s. 91(24), implements the Mi'kmaw constitutional right to control education.

The need for treaty implementation of Mi'kmaw control of Mi'kmaw education in the *Mi'kmaw Education Act* is rooted in the failure of existing federal and provincial systems to recognize the needs of Mi'kmaq, both parents and children. The Auditor General of Canada (2000, 2004) has estimated that First Nations students will require more than twenty-four to twenty-seven years of accelerated and restorative education to catch up to the national average for high-school graduation. Yet Mi'kmaw Kina'matnewey has already achieved, under Mi'kmaw control, the needed acceleration of education in their high schools.

Despite the successes of that Mi'kmaw educational authority, other provincial schools are not doing as well with Mi'kmaw students. The national averages show that 40 per cent of Aboriginal students aged twenty to twenty-four graduating from secondary schools through the last three censuses (Richards 2008), compared to 58 per cent of the Canadian average. Only about 9 per cent of Aboriginal students have graduated from post-secondary schools. The negative legacy of education policies represents a significant educational challenge and a crucial test and resolve of many educators, policy-makers and Mi'kmaq; that they must be part of this dialogue and action to effect different outcomes from the past. Understanding and remedying this failure of education has been challenging for many agencies, federal and provincial.

Since education of Mi'kmaq is a core constitutional authority of the Mi'kmaq and of the federal government and the provinces, the latter must consult with Mi'kmaq on the best way to implement their shared constitutional responsibilities for fulfilling the treaties. Many Atlantic provinces have made education of Mi'kmaq a priority through the Aboriginal Affairs Working Group of the Council of the Federation, which is comprised of the provincial and territorial first ministers. The Council of Ministers on Education, Canada, is committed to support Mi'kmaw students interested in pursuing teaching as a career.

Court decisions and the institutional imperatives generate an occasion in education systems in Atlantic Canada for a new source of vision and leadership. It will require a revision of the support of an appropriate institutional framework and a commitment to set specific targets with timelines. This provides the Mi'kmaq, the federal and the provincial governments with an opportunity to remedy the past abuses and generate a robust and respectful agenda for supporting the knowledge system and languages of Mi'kmaq for its students. It can ensure coordinated support and equality in educational outcomes.

Under the doctrine of constitutional supremacy embodied in s. 52(1) of the *Constitution Act, 1982*, all federal and provincial legislation in regard to education has to be consistent with the existing Aboriginal and treaty rights of the Mi'kmaq as affirmed by the Constitution. The existing legislation must affirm the constitutional rights and not affect them negatively. This requires Canada and the Atlantic provinces to ensure that existing and future laws and funding are consistent with the constitutional rights of the Mi'kmaq.

Treaty implementation is an important critical educational response in patriated Canada. Only through recognition of the constitutional rights of the Mi'kmaq in Atlantic Canada can the provinces generate an economic, political and social future., and a responsive and non-discriminatory Canadian educational system. The Supreme Court of Canada has identified several constitutional purposes that include determining the historical rights of Mi'kmaq and giving Aboriginal and treaty rights constitutional force to protect them against legislative powers (*R. v. Sparrow* 1990: par. 65); sanctioning challenges to social and economic policy objectives embodied in legislation to the extent that Aboriginal and treaty rights are effected (par. 64); and a commitment to recognize, value, protect and enhance their distinctive cultures (*R. v. Powley* 2003: pars. 13, 18). To ensure the continuity of Aboriginal customs and traditions, the Supreme Court has determined that every substantive constitutional right will normally include the incidental constitutional right to teach such a practice, custom and tradition to a younger generation (*R. v. Coté* 1996). Current education systems have not implemented these constitutional reforms in the education of Mi'kmaq. The constitutional framework and court decisions generate an emerging reconciliation of indigenous knowledge and culture in learning and pedagogy that must be translated into policy and practice in all public forms of education. It creates the context for systemic educational reform to include indigenous science, humanities, visual arts and languages, as well as existing educational philosophy, pedagogy and teacher education.

To some degree, under the emerging indigenous renaissance, Aboriginal educators have begun the reconciliation, in their academic and social-justice activist agendas now growing (e.g., Idle No More, social media and the Indspire Foundation that is seeking to recognize and empower Mi'kmaq to realize their educational goals and enter various professions). This is not the responsibility of Mi'kmaq alone,

Grand Keptin Alex Denny of the Mi'kmaq Grand Council speaks in the Nova Scotia House of Assembly, under a portrait of James William Johnston, a premier of Nova Scotia in the 1800s, during Treaty Day ceremonies in Halifax on October 1, 1999. The annual event commemorates the signing of the Treaty of 1752 between the Mi'kmaq and the British Crown. Michael Baker, Nova Scotia Minister for Aboriginal Affairs and Justice Minister sits at right. (CP PHOTO/Andrew Vaughan. All rights reserved.).

however. The federal and provincial governments must reconcile these constitutional rights to education and implement the treaty rights of the Mi'kmaq. At present, they have not done so, as evidenced in the lack of negotiation of these constitutional rights with the Atlantic provinces. The task is great.

We must sensitize Atlantic Canadians and Canadian politicians, policy-makers and educators to be more responsive and proactive to reconcile the national and provincial curricula, and to displace the continuing education failures of Mi'kmaq and Aboriginal peoples in the diverse educational systems across Canada.

References

"Amidst the Rock and Fog of Cape Sable; The Rise of Charles de la Tour" np. http://www.oocities.org/weallcamefromsomewhere/rise_latour.html

Auditor General of Canada. 2000. Indian and Northern Affairs Canada: Elementary and secondary education. *Report to the House of Commons*, Ch. 4. Ottawa: Minister of Public Works and Government Services Canada. http://www.oagbvg.gc.ca/domino/reports.nsf/html/0004ce.html/$file/0004ce.pdf.

Barman, Jean, Yvonne Hébert and David McCaskill, ed. 1986. *Indian Education in Canada: The Legacy*. Vancouver: University of British Columbia Press.

Battiste, Marie. 1984. *An Historical Investigation of the Social and Cultural Consequences of Micmac Literacy*. PhD dissertation, Stanford University.

———. 1986. Micmac Literacy and Cognitive Assimilation. In *Indian Education in Canada: The Legacy*, ed. Jean Barman, Don McCaskill and Yvonne Hébert. Vancouver: University of British Columbia Press.

———. 1987. Developing Mi'kmaq Linguistic Integrity. In *Indian Education in Canada: The legacy*, ed. Jean Barman, Don McCaskill and Yvonne Hébert, 107-125. Vancouver: University of British Columbia Press.

———. 1993. Annie Battiste: A Mi'kmaq Family History. *Cape Breton's Magazine*, no. 64. Wreck Cove, NS:.

Bromley, Walter. 1814. Mr. Bromley's second address, on the deplorable state of the Indians delivered in the "Royal Acadian School," at Halifax, in Nova Scotia, March 8, 1814. Halifax: Recorder Office. https://archive.org/details/cihm_20998.

Canada, 1843-1873. Administration of Indian Affairs Annual Reports. Ottawa.

Canada, House of Commons Debate, 9 May 1883.

Ceremonials at Concluding a Peace with the several Districts of the general Mickmack Nation of Indians in His Majesty's Province of Nova Scotia, and a Copy of the Treaty," 22 June 1761, United Kingdom [UK] Public Record Office [PRO], Colonial Office [CO] Series 217/ 18 n.p.

Eskasoni Elders' Curriculum Advisory Committee. 1991. Mi'kmaw. Eskasoni, NS: Eskasoni Curriculum Development Unit, Eskasoni School Board.

Fischer, David Hackett. 2008. *Champlain's Dream*. New York: Simon and Schuster.

Henderson, James Youngblood. 1995. Indian Education and Treaties. In *First Nations education in Canada: The Circle Unfolds*, ed. Marie Battiste and Jean Barman. Vancouver: University of British Columbia Press.

———. 2007. *Treaty Rights in the Constitution of Canada*. Scarbrough, ON: Thompson Carswell.

Letter from Armstrong to the [Duke of Newcastle or the Lords of Trade], 5 September 1726, CO 217/38, Nos. 7, 7 (i, x-xvii).

MacDonald, Marjorie Anne. 1983. Fortune & La Tour: The Civil War in Acadia. Toronto: Methuen.

Mandel, Daniel R. ed, 2003 *New England Treaties, North and West, 1650-1776*, vol. 20. In *Early American Indian Documents, Treaties and Laws, 1607-1789*, ed. Alden T. Vaughan, general edWashington, DC: University Publication of America.

NSARM (Nova Scotia Archives and Records Management). 1842. Letter, James Dawson to Howe, 25 June 1842, reporting on a visit to Merigonish Island, Indian MSS, vol. 432, 146-151.

———. 1843. Letter, William Walsh to Howe, 9 February 1843, Indian MSS, vol. 432, 205-206.

Paul v. British Columbia (Forest Appeals Commission). 2003. 2 S.C.R. 585.

PRO CO (Public Records Office [UK]–Colonial Office). 1725. Promises by Major Paul Mascarene on behalf of the Lt. Governor of N.S. to tribes in Nova Scotia and New England, December 2 5/898.

———. 1726. English to Indians, Treaty, 1726 (U.K.), 12 Geo I., no. 3 enclosure Armstrong to Duke of Newcastle, September 5, 1725, 217/38, Nos. 7, 7 (i, x-xvii).

———. 1761. Ceremonials at Concluding a Peace with the Several Districts of the General Mickmack Nation of Indians, 25 June 1761, Nova Scotia Archives and Record Management [NSARM], MS. Documents, vol. 37, doc. 14; UK Public Records Office, Colonial Office (London, U.K.), 217/18, 277r-83r.

R. v. Côté. 1996. 3 S.C.R. 139.

R. v. Marshall. 1999. 3 S.C.R. 533

R. v. Powley. 2003. 2 S.C.R. 207.

R. v. Sparrow. 1990. 1 S.C.R. 1075.

Richards, John. 2008. *Closing the Aboriginal and Non-Aboriginal Achievement Gaps.* C. D. Howe Institute Backgrounder, No. 116. Toronto: C. D. Howe Institute.

Royal Commission on Aboriginal Peoples. 1996. *Report of the Royal Commission on Aboriginal Peoples.* 5 vols. Ottawa: Canada Communication Group.

Secession of Quebec, [1998] 2 S.C.R. 217.

Truth and Conciliation Commission of Canada. 2015. Honouring the Truth, Reconciling for the Future, Summary of the Final Report of the Truth and Reconciliation Commission of Canada.

Upton, Leslie. 1979. *Micmacs and the Colonists: Indian-White Relations in the Maritimes, 1713-1867.* Vancouver: University of British Columbia.

Yarmouth Vanguard [Yarmouth, NS]. 1989. First Nun in North America was Born at Our Doorstep. May 30.

Appendix 1

Mi'kmaw Declaration of Aboriginal Rights

From the Nova Scotia Micmac Aboriginal Rights Position Paper, (1976. Union of Nova Scotia Indians, Sydney.)

As from the Heavens flow water which creates oceans, seas, lakes, rivers and streams, it will be so that:

From Aboriginal Title Compensation, flow Aboriginal Rights, guaranteed by treaties, royal proclamation, and statute, in the areas of Social—Economic—Cultural—Educational and Political concerns, as felt and advanced by the Micmac of Nova Scotia and beyond.

The Micmac concept that the free use and occupancy of the land, air, water and its resources to maintain a Social—Economic—Cultural—Education and Political areas of Micmac life has anthropologically, historically and legally been accepted.

Acceptance that a way of life was destroyed by the denial of our treaties that guaranteed our free use and occupancy of land, air, water and its resources, which has also been proven anthropologically, historically, and legally.

Acceptance that compensation for that loss has not been fully compensated for thereby contributing to present Social—Economic—Cultural—Education and Political disadvantages facing present day Micmacs of Nova Scotia.

Full cultural, social, economic and political justice to Micmac Indians can only be served through the recognition of Aboriginal rights preserved by the treaties;

The Chiefs and Councils of the Indian Bands in Nova Scotia HEREBY RESOLVED that the Government of Canada must compensate for Micmac aboriginal title by guaranteeing, through states, Aboriginal right in the cultural, social, economic, and political fields. These Aboriginal rights must compensate for the loss of a way of life and must contribute positively to a lasting solution of cultural, social, economic and political concerns as felt and as advanced by the Micmacs of Nova Scotia.

The failure of Government to recognize and guarantee Aboriginal right will show a complete disregard for the fulfillment of its lawful and moral obligation, and will show itself as contemptuous toward the Micmacs of Nova Scotia.

The collection of archaeological, anthropological, historical and legal data contain herein will establish, by white means, what Micmacs have "felt" for centuries, social, economic and political injustices which must be compensated.

ALEX DENNY, President
Union of Nova Scotia Indians
Mi'kmaw Sagmaq (Chiefs) of federal *Indian Act* bands in Nova Scotia

—

From time in memory, our ancestors have lived in this land. This is our land. This is our home. Our history and our allegiance are to this land and to no other. Today we still live in this land that belonged to our ancestors that still belongs to us and that we will pass on to our children yet unborn. Our existence to this land predates the coming of European explorers and immigrant settlers. Our existence in this land predates the establishment of colonial settlements and governments from Europeans. Our existence in this land predates the Confederation of Canada.

Before the English and French came, we were here. We are a pre-Confederation nation of peoples.

Prior to the coming of the European immigrants, our ancestors exercised all the prerogatives of nationhood. We had our land and our own system of land holding. We made and enforced our own laws in our own ways. The various tribal nations dealt with one another according to accepted codes. We respected our distinctive languages. We practice our own spirituality and with it beliefs and customs. We developed our own set of cultural habits and practices according to our particular circumstances. We, in fact, had our own social, political, economic, educational, and property systems. We exercised the rights and prerogatives of a nation and the existence of a nation.

It was as a nation and treaties with the King that our ancestors dealt with the European immigrants. These treaties preserved and protected our Aboriginal rights. It is as nations we exist today. It is our desire and intent to continue to exist as a nation of Micmacs.

As nations of Indian people or Indian nation, our rights and entitlements to this land were inherited from our ancestors. Our right to the ownership of the land precede and supercede the claims upon our land by Europeans. We have prior right of ownership and entitlements to this land does not arise by virtue of any rights granted to us by foreign sovereigns of the Europeans or their succeeding government; rather, the European immigrants and their descendants live in this land by virtue of the rights we granted them. The rights granted them by treaties merely the rights to use and share the land with us.

Vast portions of this land still remain Indian land. Our continued ownership and rightful use of our land has not been terminated. Even though succeeding governments of our European immigrants attempt to dispossess us by seizing and claiming all our lands, we maintained the European peoples and their successive government have not, at any time or in any way, rightfully acquired these lands. We further maintain we are deserving of the recognition, restoration and compensation for the wrong seizure of our lands and resources thereon. We will continue to inhabit, occupy, and use these lands for our survival and subsistence according to the rights we have inherited from our ancestors.

We have paid a very grave and exorbitant price. We face the danger of being wrongfully dispossessed of much of our land; our spiritual beliefs and practices were outlawed. We were denied the use our language. Our music, dances and art were declared barbaric. We were prohibited to live and practice according to our own cultural customs. Our entire way of life, based on the land, was endangered and weaken by deliberate acts of destruction of the animals which sustained us and our movements were restricted so that our survival was made perilous and precarious.

Yet we have survived. We have not perished. We have not vanished. We are not also merely people of the past; we are of this land today; and we will be at this land in the time yet to come. Our survival in our land today is still perilous and precarious.

If we are to survive as a people in the future, to be strong and independent as we once were, we must develop and strengthen our existence with a special relationship with the European in this land today.

Therefore, let it always be known, as it has always been known and accepted by us, that we are nations of Indian people; and that we declare and proclaim a special relationship with the Canadian federation.

This is the understanding that exist in the minds and hearts of our people.

We, as a people, submit our aboriginal rights and statutory right claim as the only avenue through which the Micmacs of Nova Scotia can achieve social and economic justice. The negotiations of these claims are our future and our children's future.

Appendix 2

Archival Research, Treaties, and the Nova Scotia Mi'kmaq: Aboriginal Rights Position Paper and Acknowledgements

by Stuart Killen

Preface

The following speech by Stu Killen, former researcher to the Union of Nova Scotia Indians, was given to the chiefs and assembly during the annual meeting of the Executive and Membership of the Union of Nova Scotia Indians on September 30, 2009, at the Lord Nelson Hotel in Halifax. It is in reference to the Aboriginal Rights and Treaties position paper of the Union of Nova Scotia Indians paper that was presented to the Minister of Indian Affairs in Eskasoni in 1974. More than 41 years later, nothing has been done about it. Copies of the Aboriginal and Treaties claim has been deposited in the Nova Scotia Archives.

At the outset, I want to acknowledge the Mi'kmaq staff of the Union of Nova Scotia Indians, whose contributions resulted in the research that discovered the many treaties in the archives, formulated the 1976 Aboriginal Rights position paper, and provided the foundation for the litigation on Aboriginal and treaty Rights. This short essay reveals the scope and depth of their research effort that was accomplished and the deep appreciation that must be shared with many as the contributed the judicial victories of aboriginal and treaty rights of the Mi'kmaq

I also want to begin by acknowledging the lessons learned from the late Grand Chief Gabriel Sylliboy of Eskasoni, and the late Grand Chief Donald Marshall, as well as the late Chief Ben Christmas of Membertou. All were my guiding influences as Research Director for the Union of Nova Scotia Indians. Next, I would also want to acknowledge the influences of the UNSI Presidents, the late Chief Noel Doucette, the late Grand Keptin Alex Denny, the late Chief Stanley Johnson, and finally Chief Alex Christmas. All of these presidents help mapped out the research in the Mi'kmaq rights initiatives as well as the "Band Meeting Consultation" Process and Strategies that brought attention to the Treaty and Aboriginal rights. Special acknowledgement goes to Grand Keptin Alex Denny's, the heart and soul of the Mi'kmaw rights agenda for economic development, a great Mi'kmaw leader, a great husband and father.

My deepest gratitude is reserved to all Union of Nova Scotia Indian staff as well as band members at large, who were directly involved in the research and the position paper. Namely, Donald Julian my assistant; Joe B. Marshall, Tripartite Liaison; Peter Christmas, MicMac Cultural Studies; Bernie Francis, the first Union of Nova Scotia Indians court worker as well as MicMac Cultural Studies linguist; and the late Roy Gould, the editor of *Mic Mac News*, who published much of our research material, when no one in the non-First Nations news media would publish.

The Union of Nova Scotia Indians emerged out of the White Paper policy with the expressed purpose of "United We Stand: Divided We Fall." It was a direct response to the March 1969 White Paper, introduced by the then Minister of Indian Affairs Jean Chrétien and authored by the then, Prime Minister of Canada Pierre Trudeau. Simply put, in the White Paper policy, the government was trying to extinguished the King's treaties with the Indian Nations. This policy introduced the abandonment of the Federal Indian legal fiduciary responsibility under the Mi'kmaq treaties under the constitution of Canada, the *Royal Proclamation of 1763*, section 91(24) and 132 of the *British North American Act of 1867*, now the *Constitution Act, 1867*.

APPENDIX

In the *Royal Proclamation of 1763*, enacted after most of the Mi'kmaw treaties connected with the King of Great Britain, King George III commanded that provincial governments respect the Mi'kmaw territory that had not been ceded to or purchased by the King as part of the Mi'kmaw reserves under the existing treaties:

> And whereas it is just and reasonable, and essential to our Interest, and the Security of our Colonies, that the several Nations or Tribes of Indians with whom We are connected, and who live under our Protection, should not be molested or disturbed in the Possession of such Parts of Our Dominions and Territories as, not having been ceded to or purchased by Us, are reserved to them, or any of them, as their Hunting Grounds.

For the present, the King commanded the provincial authorities were forbidden to survey or make grants of these reserved Hunting Grounds. They were forbidden to allow people to make purchases or settlements on the reserved Hunting Grounds, without special leave and licence from the King. And the King commanded them to remove any person who inhabited the reserved Hunting Grounds:.

> And, we do further strictly enjoin and require all persons whatever who have either wilfully or inadvertently seated themselves upon any lands within the countries above described, or upon any other lands which, not having been ceded to or purchased by us, are still reserved to the said Indians as aforesaid, forthwith to remove themselves from such settlements.

Moreover in the future the King commanded with the advice of our privy council that provincial authorities

> strictly enjoin and require, that no private person do presume to make any purchase from the said Indians of any lands reserved to the said Indians, within those parts of our colonies where, we have thought proper to allow settlement;

After 1763, the King established the exclusive way to acquired the reserved Hunting Lands from the Indian nations:

> if at any time any of the said Indians should be inclined to dispose of the said lands, the same shall be purchased only for us, in our name, at some public meeting or assembly of the said Indians, to

be held for that purpose by the governor or commander in chief of our colony respectively within which they shall lie....

Section 91(24) of the *British North America Act, 1867* delegated to the newly created federal government authority on the subject matter of "Indians and lands reserved for the Indians" that was previous in the King and then the provinces, This included the reserved Hunting Grounds under the Mi'kmaw treaties. Moreover, section 132 of the *British North American Act, 1867* required for the implementation of the treaties:

> The Parliament and government of Canada shall have all powers necessary or proper for performing the obligations of Canada or of any province thereof, as part of the British empire, towards foreign countries, arising under treaties between the empire and such foreign countries.

A 1973 court case, known as *Calder*, affirmed that Aboriginal title existed until the King purchases their land according to imperial law not colonial law. This caused the government to withdraw the White Paper, and to create both the comprehensive claim process based on Aboriginal title as well as specific land claims under treaties and other lawful obligations.

From that decision and the federal government comprehensive claim process, the Union of Nova Scotia Indians requested funding for research into the areas of Comprehensive (Aboriginal Title and Aboriginal Rights preserved in the treaties and royal Proclamation of 1763) and Specific Land Claims.

During my time as Research Director all the above mentioned were involved in the research of Archaeological, Anthropological, Geographical, Historical and Legal documents from the Public Archives of Canada and Public Archives of Nova Scotia and New Brunswick, also Colonial Office Papers in London England, Journals of the House of Assembly of Nova Scotia and New Brunswick, and many published and unpublished manuscripts and theses. As well as the Public records office London England, Indian Affairs in Ottawa, the Amherst Regional Office and all the Indian Affairs offices at the reserve level, as well as every Registrar of Deeds in all of the counties of Nova Scotia, also, legal analyses of all the legal statutes, of pre- and post-Confederation governments.

The many legal articles including those published and unpublished as well as, all written records of the 18 Archaeological sites in Nova Scotia.

The Mi'kmaq research team, whose work and dedication was the backbone of the position paper and treaty research, consisted of the following: Executive and Research Assistants: Dr. Donald Julian, Joan Johnson, Barbara Sylliboy (MacDonald), Barb Gloade (Dorey), Lillian Marshall, Carol Moore (Paul) and Russell Marshall. Also, to the many Mi'kmaw summer students who were involved in archaeological digs sites, as well as those, who took part in gathering and recording Mi'kmaw Elders "Oral History." affidavits and statements.

Over a million and half hours of research was accomplished by this team.

The Mi'kmaw Aboriginal Rights position paper was a statement of the broader legal issue of Aboriginal Title of the Mi'kmaq relative to constitutional law of Canada under the Comprehensive Law Claim policy. International and constitutional law paves the way for Mi'kmaw peoples' compensation for the loss of use and occupancy of their reserved Hunting Grounds land and its resources that had never been purchased by the King of Great Britain under the treaties and the imperial constitutional law of United Kingdom.

It was this type of research that resulted in the UNSI being able to prove, what Mi'kmaq have known from time immemorial, that they have existed from time immemorial and have occupied and have an inherent right of use of the land and its resources to maintain a "Way Of Life." That use and occupancy by the Mi'kmaq of the land and resources meets the required definition of Aboriginal Title under United Kingdom and International Law. Aboriginal Title was the prior use and occupancy of the land and its resources before the European arrives, which resulted in a way of living. Ironically, we have proven Aboriginal title by the use of the "visitors' own documentation or laws"!

During reserve general band meetings, it was clear that the Mi'kmaq have always known that the treaties never ceded their Aboriginal title to the King and that the King never purchased the Aboriginal title. They would ask; "Why do we have to prove we were here first and we still own all of our traditional lands and waters. Can the King show a deed of sale for our land???? Don't they know it is never was for sale?

This brings me a very important acknowledgment: to all the Mi'kmaq who attended the many, many band meetings throughout all of the Mi'kmaw communities throughout Nova Scotia. These were Band meetings held on each reserve, and over the ten years, they numbered well over 400 Band meetings. Anyone who remembers these meetings knew you had to be prepared to deal with the many issues of the community. It was their input that resulted in the eleven points of the compensation package in the Aboriginal Rights Position Paper, for the loss of use and occupancy, comes directly from Band Meetings held in all of the Mi'kmaw communities.

The reason for compensation package was simple; a new way of life had, and still does need to be found in many areas for those who have lost a way of life. As it stood at that time, the Mi'kmaq have been dispossessed of their land reserved for them in the treaties, their Aboriginal Title, and Resources. Under international and British law, as early as the 1500s, it has always been understood, that people who have used and occupied land from time immemorial, have the inherent right to the title to the land and its resources to insure a living or way of life.

Also it is important to acknowledge of the federal *Indian Act* chiefs, who signed the Aboriginal Rights position paper on behalf of their Councillors and band members at the time, to Canada. Alphabetically, I wish to name the Chiefs for their courage, tenacity, and resilience in establishing the research initiatives in Mi'kmaw rights, for their support of the research, and for reviewing and approving of the Aboriginal Rights position paper: Chief John Basque, Chief Alex Christmas, Chief Raymond Francis, Chief Stephen Gloade, Chief Ryan C. Googoo, Chief Charles Labrador, Chief Reginald Maloney, Chief Peter Paul, Chief Peter Perro, Chief Leona Pictou, Chief Francis Pierro and Chief Gerald Toney.

Other Mi'kmaq need to be acknowledged for their efforts in the Aboriginal Rights position paper. Chief Rita Smith must be acknowledged, as she was very involved with the position paper, along with efforts to have her band recognized as the thirteenth First Nations Band, now known as the Gluscap First Nation. Acknowledgement must be given to Viola Robinson in her role, as President of the Nova Scotia Non–Status and Métis Association during that period of time, who provided me with thoughtful guidance. As well as acknowledgements need to be expressed to Sensi Jim "Jake" Maloney who has had a profound positive effect on my life and my best friend ever; to Eleanor Paul (Johnson) for her advice, to Carl Gould, Secretary Treasurer of the Union whose creativity with the research funds resulted in much more research being made possible. Also to the many Mi'kmaq at large who at a very early age gave me solicited and non-solicited sound advice, I thank you.

Equally important and deserving of honourable acknowledgement should be given to the Mi'kmaq who participated in ground level civil disobediences and non-violent activities that generated the Mi'kmaw rights initiative. Notably are the road blockades in First Nations of Afton and Millbrook to protest the division of their reserve lands by the Trans Canada highway without compensation. The Mi'kmaw warriors and youth took part in the siege of the Fortress of Louisbourg which brought the Mi'kmaw historical factor to the fort, and of course their many demonstrations need to be acknowledged for bringing the attention of the public to the issues along with the Pictou Landing Mi'kmaq who protested the pollution of Boat Harbor. There were many many more; however, I remember these because the police arrested me and others during these acts of defiance at blockades.

Today, because of the research by the Mi'kmaw people and others, there is no dispute that the Mi'kmaq have used and occupied the traditional territory of Nova Scotia from time immemorial, to maintain a way of life. It was the use and occupancy of the land and its resources that sustained the Mi'kmaq and their social, economic, educational, political and cultural systems and religious ways of life. Moreover, as of 1979 in the province of Nova Scotia, the Mi'kmaw research staff had identified and researched more than one hundred specific Land Claims, most still unresolved

From a Canadian settler and grass root level, let me be the first to apologize for my Irish ancestors, the "Killen clan's "savage and unforgiveable behaviour" in allowing the governments to dispossess the Mi'kmaq and violate their treaty rights. I am so, so sorry and I give my permission and encourage my government to acknowledge and compensate the Mi'kmaq for the wrongs done to them and to create a just society in Canada. The evils of the past must be acknowledged— to **ensure** it never happens again.

Nmultisup

Appendix 3

Communication to the United Nations Human Rights Committee About Treaty Violations

Ji'kepten Alex Denny
Eskasoni, NS
Before the Leaves turn colours, 1980

Me'taleyn:
The Jigap'ten of Santeoi Mawa'iomi of the Mi'kmaq Nationimuow has the honour to address you, as well as the sadness to communicate the substance of our grievances against the Dominion of Canada. The people of our tribal society are victims of violations of fundamental freedoms and human rights by the

Government of Canada: Canada has and continues to deny our right to self-determination; Canada has and continues to involuntarily confiscate our territory despite the terms of our treaties; Canada has and continues to deprive our people of its own means of subsistence; and Canada has and continues to enact and enforce laws and policies destructive to our family life and inimical to the proper education of our children.

We speak plainly, so that there is no misunderstanding. For three centuries, we have honoured and lived by our Treaty of protection and free association with the British Crown. We have remained at peace with British subjects everywhere, and our young men have given their lives, as we had promised, in defense of British lives in foreign wars. As the original government of the Mi'kmaq Nationimuow from time out of mind, and as signatories' and keepers of the great chain of union and association with Great Britain, we, the Mawa'iomi, have guided our people in spiritual and secular affairs in freedom and dignity in our own way, without compulsion or injustice.

Now, there is a great and terrible idea in this land. The government of Canada claims that, by virtue of its charter of self-government from Great Britain, the *British North America Act*, it has succeeded to the Crown in our Treaty. Furthermore, and in frank violation of the law of nations, the government of Canada claims power and right to ignore our Treaty at pleasure, and to seize our ancient lands, substitute, supervise, or abolish our government, remove our children to schools of its choosing rather than ours, prevent us from farming and fishing for our subsistence, and scattering our homes and families. They tell us we no longer are a protected State, but a minority group of "In-dé-ans," subject absolutely to their discretion and control, exercising the rights of property, self-determination, and family life only at their will. They offer our people political peonage and the destiny of dependence upon financial relief.

This, we cannot accept. Under the optional protocol to the International Covenant on Civil and Political Rights, acceded to by Canada on May 19, 1976, we submit this to the Committee on Human Rights.

For the Santeoi Mawa'iomi
Alexander Denny, Jigap'ten

NE'WT: ON STANDING

1. The Mi'kmaq Nationimuow is and always has been a distinct people, speaking its own language, free in the enjoyment of its own culture and religion, governed by its own officers and laws in its own territory, and recognized, until limited by its free association with Great Britain, as capable of engaging in Treaties with other States, both states native to this continent and states of Europe.

2. In accordance with our ancient laws and the law of nations, we recognize two Eurochristian allies or *racamanen* [Nikminen]: the Church of Rome and the British Crown. In 1621 our *jisagamow* Membertou, by his baptism and agreement, associated the Mi'kmaq Nationimuow with the Holy See, and ever since we have given the Church of Rome free access to our territory and people, the liberty to build and keep Churches, and the privilege of yearly renewing this association at our great meeting on Chapel Island. Agents of Great Britain sought us out as early as 1719 to treat for peace and political association, but, as we then were surrounded by settlements of France, we did not adhere to Britain's Treaties with our southern racamanen, the Penobscots, Passamaquoddies, and Maliseets. In 1726, as British arms displaced the French from our frontiers, we associated ourselves by Treaties with Great Britain, and by these Treaties have recognized that State, and they us, ever since.

3. The Mi'kmaq Nationimuow claims de jure, by 'ancient title and dominion, all that territory which it possessed, governed, used and defended at the time it entered into the protection of Great Britain. Sitqamuk, our national territory, includes the lands today known as Nova Scotia, Prince Edward Island, and parts of Newfoundland, New Brunswick, and the Gaspe peninsula of Quebec (Enclosure "B"), and extent of twenty thousand square miles, more or less. Although our Treaties of protection guaranteed us permanent enjoyment of this territory, save only for settlements of British subjects then existing (to the extent of one thousand square miles or less), we recently have been confined to small parcels of land in total less than fifty square miles. Title and right even to these parcels, denominated "Indian Reserves," is contested now by the government of Canada, yet we never have sold or ceded by deed or by Treaties a single acre of our original domain.

4. For evidence and proof of our territorial extent, we submit for your consideration that all physiographic features within these lands have ancient names in our language, which refer to our continuous use and possession of them, and identify the *wigamow* or settlements of our people that belonged to each of them. We offer to show these facts to you in our own country as you may see fit and convenient.

5. We have existed as an autochthonous people from the beginning of time. When the Mi'kmaq awoke naked in the world and ignorant of everything in it, they asked the creator, Nisqam, how they should live. Nisqam taught us how to cultivate the ground, and to respect the nations of the trees and their dependents; to hunt and fish, and to pray while we hunted and fished; to name the stars, the constellations, and the milky way, which is the path our spirits take to the other world. Most of all, Nisqam taught us to live together as one people, *ginuk*, in brotherhood with all other humans, animals and plants.

6. To lead the Mi'kmaq along the good path in their domestic relations, and to advocate their interests in foreign affairs; the Creator endows a few of each generation with special knowledge of the woodlands and the ocean, and concerns of the spirit. Long before our memory, these people of wisdom and responsibility joined together'" in a body, the Santeoi Mawa'iomi, or great league called the Grand Council by the Jesuitical emissaries of the Holy See who first described us to Eurochristians, and the Mi'kmaq Nationimuow by the diplomats of the British Crown with whom we made our Treaties of protection and association. As early as 1616, Eurochristian observers described the division of the Mi'kmaq state into seven great geographical districts under the direction of one Grand Council, and our affiliation with other peoples and autochthonous States in the relationship of confederation called by us racamanen.

7. From each wigamow or settlement of kinsmen and their dependents, the Santeoi Mawa'iomi recognize one or more gap' ten ("captains") to show the people there the good path, to help them with gifts of knowledge and goods, and to sit with the whole Santeoi Mawa'iomi as the government of all the Mi'kmaq Nationimuow. From among themselves the gap' ten recognize a jigap'ten ("grand captain") and jisagamow ("grand chief "), one to guide them and one to speak for them, and from others of good spirit they choose advisers and speakers, or putu's. The authority of our government is and always has been spiritual, persuasive and non-coercive. The cruelties of coercive laws and majoritarian oppression were unknown among us until the recent interventions of Canada. The continuity and authority of our state exists in our culture, in a common bond and vision that transcends temporary interest. This bond arises naturally from the fate of birth

into a family, community, territory and people—munijinik, wigamow, sitqamuk and ginuk.

8. Before the interventions of Canada, our gap' ten saw that each family had sufficient planting grounds for summer, fishing stations for spring and autumn, and hunting range for winter. Once assigned, these proper ties were inviolable, and disputes were arbitrated by our gap' ten individually or in council. We neither were settled nor migratory, as Eurochristians understand these things. The environment of our birth always has been suited best to seasonal use, so that, compatible with the rhythm of the earth, our families each owned a hunting home, fishing homes and a planting home, and travelled among them through the year in the beauty of our land. Today we keep these things as best we can, but our freedom to use our earth according to the annual cycle is much restricted, and the security of our cultivation, fishing and hunting rights much impaired by arbitrary laws and regulations of Canada.

9. We do not distinguish spiritual and secular affairs because we do not need to: we are one people entire. From time immemorial to this day, the Mi'kmaq Nationimuow have assembled each year in midsummer at Potloteg, the place Eurochristians know as Chapel Island, in Nova Scotia, to unite the people, ratify births and deaths, and share in prayer and thanksgiving. So, too, at this time, the Santeoi' Mawa'iomi have since before memory annually met to consider policy, and to send the jisagamow and jigap'ten to address the people, and to read the ulnapskog or records of our alliances. Whosoever doubt that we are one people with one government must observe this day and this place. The ground itself is worn into furrows by the passing of our feet, for thousands upon thousands of years.

10. As keepers of the chain of union between Great Britain and the Mi'kmaq Nationimuow, the Santeoi Mawa'iomi have direct and reliable knowledge of the condition of the Mi'kmaq people, the conduct of Canada in violation of Treaties and of international law; and of the destiny the Mi'kmaq people choose. We have witnessed the confiscation of ninety-nine per cent of our territory, and have struggled to save the spirit of our remaining ten thousand people from despair as their health and education decline. When our Treaties were made, we

had an abundance to eat and we lived and prospered in good health. Today we know hunger, malnutrition, disease, alcohol and drug abuse and suicide, all greatly in excess of what is known among our Eurochristian neighbours. These things alone would be sufficient basis for complaint that Canada had violated our rights, as individuals, to dignity, subsistence, health, education and life. However, the Santeoi Mawa'iomi also bear witness to a greater breach, Canada's violation of our Treaties of protection and association and it s guarantee of our freedom as a community. We speak for all the people: Canada seeks to destroy a state.

TA'PU: ON COVENANTS

11. When Eurochristians first appeared on our frontiers, we extended our brotherhood gladly. They came to us as refugees from overcrowded and hungry nations; many fled from injustices and intolerance. We fed them and showed them how to live on this continent. We listened to them speak of religion and, accepting Catholicism as consistent with our own faith and beliefs, in 1621 allied ourselves with the Holy See through the Church of France. Unfortunately, feuds among Eurochristian States over imaginary territorial lines forced us to assert our territoriality by force of arms. Although at first both British and French were welcome in our country, British efforts to expel French influence and religion from this hemisphere soon made coexistence impossible.

12. Sectarian Christian disputes and rum brought violence to our beloved forests and the smoke of European cannon mingled with the fog enshrouding Eurochristians' intentions. In their haste to destroy French settlements, British forces crossed and devastated our country and the lands of our Wabanaki racamanen: The Penobscots, Passamaquoddies and Maliseets. In response, we permitted the King of France to erect fortifications on our soil, and for fifteen years we seized and destroyed British shipping from north of Casco Bay to the Grand Banks. When French settlements on the mainland of Nova Scotia fell into British hands, King George II instructed his military governor to enter if possible into an association with the Mi'kmaq Nationimuow. No extensions of Eurochristian settlements were proposed, nor would

we have accepted them. Wherever our language was spoken was *sitqamuk*, and every part of this "territory," as sacred to us. Every tree, every shore, every mist in the dark woods, every clearing was holy in our memory and experience, recalling our lives and the lives of our ancestors since our world began. These things cannot be sold.

13. On 5 December 1725, representatives of many of our southern racamanen initialled Treaties with Great Britain at Boston, in which "they admitted to have breached their former Treaties of peace with that kingdom. Renewing these prior engagements," they promised to "hold and maintain a firm and Constant: Amity and Friendship with all the English, and never [to] confederate or combine with any other nation to their prejudice," to join British forces in the suppression of hostilities with other natives states, and to submit: future disputes with British subjects to "due course of Justice ... governed by His Majesty's Laws." The Treaties preserved the territorial status quo as it then existed, guaranteeing to Great Britain all of its "former Settlements" in New England and Nova Scotia, and reserving to our racamanen all the rest of their ancestral lands. Our southern allies, together with one of our own districts, the *gespogoitg*, ratified this Treaties at Casco Bay in what now is called Maine on 11 August 1726, the British "signatory, William Dummer, expressing his opinion that "this will be a better & more lasting Peace than ever was made yet, And that it will last to the End of the World."

14. Having made no former Treaties with Great Britain ourselves and wishing to remain non-aligned, the Mi'kmaq Nationimuow would not concede wrongdoing by adhering to the Treaty of 1725 as ratified in Annapolis Royal in 1726 and in Halifax in 1749, although that instrument purported to check further British expansion. For two decades British emissaries sought the assent of the various Mi'kmaq wigamow individually, but it was not until 1752, at the conclusion of another British war with the Nationimuow, that a Treaty was properly arranged with the Santeoi Mawa'iomi acting by its jisaya Jean Baptiste Cope. We agreed to abide generally by the terms of the Treaty of 1725 [Article l], thereby acknowledging British possession of existing settlements, and receiving Britain's acknowledgment of our title to the balance of our national territory. Our right to hunt and

fish, and to conduct trade, was guaranteed everywhere, even within British bounds [Article 4]. We consented, to litigate our disputes with British subjects in royal courts [Article 8], provided that we always be accorded "the same benefits, Advantages & Priviledges as any others of his Majesty's Subjects."

So eager were His Majesty's representatives for association with us, that we were paid reparations and aid [Article 5,6]. Our *jisaya* promised to bring all our wigamow into this racamanen [Article 3].

15. Treaties of association and protection were common among the autochthonous States of North America. Such Treaties "formed the covenant chains of the great Algonkin confederations, such as the Iroquois, and the Wabanaki. Britain's King George III took advantage of this shared understanding of the law of nations to neutralize the Algonkin States that bordered upon British settlements, placing them under permanent protection. Each remained a State, yet in perfect association with the British Crown. In its Treaties, the Mi'kmaq Nationimuow sold no land, and ceded no sovereignty over its domestic affairs. It became a protected State or dependency, as that term would come to be used and understood more generally a century later in the evolution of the British Empire into a Commonwealth of Nations.

16. We were conscious of the law of nations when we associated our districts with Great Britain, and we properly relied upon Great Britain's representations and on the practice of nations at that time. In 1761, shortly after the fall of French forces in Canada, Great Britain and the Mi'kmaq Nationimuow ceremonially renewed the Treaties at Halifax. Standing by a monument erected for that purpose, Nova Scotia Governor and Supreme Court judge Jonathan Belcher described our relationship, with the Crown in these words:

> Protection and allegiance are fastened together by links, if a link is broken the chain will be loose.
>
> You must preserve this chain entire on your part by fidelity and obedience to the great King George the Third, and then you will have the security of his Royal Arm to defend you.
>
> I meet you now as His Majesty's graciously honored Servant in Government and in his Royal name to receive at this Pillar, your

public vows of obedience—to build a covenant of Peace with you, as upon the immovable rock of Sincerity and Truth—to free you from the chains of Bondage—and to place you in the wide and fruitful Field of English Liberty.

The Laws will be like a great Hedge about your Rights and properties—if any break this Hedge to hurt and Injure you, the heavy weight of the

Laws will fall upon them and furnish their disobedience.

Assuring the Governor that our common religion would assure that the articles of agreement would be "kept inviolably on both Sides," Jisagamow Toma Denny replied, "Receive us into your Arms, into them we cast ourselves as into a safe and secure Asylum from whence we are resolved never to withdraw or depart," remaining the Crown's "friend and Ally."

17. British Nova Scotia was controlled entirely by prerogative instruments of the Crown such as Letters Patent, Instructions and Imperial Proclamations until 1867, and colonial officials had no power or authority beyond the terms of these instruments. The King in Council perfected the covenant chain with us by entrenching our protected status in the constitution of Nova Scotia. Letters Patent issued to Lord Cornwallis in 1749 to form a government for the British settlements directed that no grant of land be made or confirmed to British subjects, except out of territory freely ceded by the native proprietors. As earlier clarified by the Privy Council, this meant that land cessions be accepted only from the properly constituted governments of indigenous States, and not merely from their individual citizens, conformable to the law of nations.

18. The protection of territoriality always was central to our Treaty relationship with Great Britain. In 1761, the King in Council admonished the royal governors of Nova Scotia and other Crown colonies to keep " just and faithfull Observance of those Treaties and Compacts" which have been heretofore solemnly entered into" with indigenous States, and directed that action be taken to prevent unlawful settlements of British subjects on unceded lands. In 1762, Nova Scotia Governor Belcher implemented the Royal Instruction by proclama-

tion, ordering British subjects to remove themselves from any lands claimed by us, and to avoid molesting us in the exercise of our Treaty right to hunt and fish within the British settlements. In 1763, the King amplified Imperial policy by Royal Proclamation, strictly forbidding British occupation and settlement of lands "reserved under our sovereignty, protection, and dominion," on behalf of the several Nations or Tribes of Indians with whom we are connected, or who live under our protection. As an autochthonous State associated with Great Britain by Treaties, the Mi'kmaq Nationimuow indisputably was "connected" with, and "protected" by, the Crown. Thus after 1763 no subject or officer of Great Britain possessed authority to interfere with the territory we reserved in our Treaties, not only as a matter of the international law of Treaties, but as a matter of Imperial regulations limiting the constitutional power of the British colonies in North America.

19. A British royal commission in 1749 concluded that "[t]he Indians, though living amongst the king's subjects in these countrie are a separate and distinct people

> from them, they are treated with as such, they have a polity of their own, they make peace and war with any nations of Indians when they think fit, without control from the English,

Hence the law to be applied to relations between the Crown and indigenous States in North America was necessarily "a law, equal to both parties, which is the law of nature and of nations." The international status of protected States was well defined in the eighteenth century. Writing in 1760, Emerich Vattel explained in his treatise on the *Law of Nations*:

> We ought, therefore, to account as sovereign states those which unite themselves to another more powerful, by an unequal alliance, in which, as Artistotle says, to the more powerful, is given more honor, and to the weaker, more assistance. The conditions of those unequal alliances may be varied. Consequently a weak state, which in order to provide for it s safety, places itself under the protection of a more powerful one, and engages, in return, to perform several offices equivalent to that protection, without however divesting itself of the right of government and sovereignty—that state, I say, does not, on this account, cease to rank

among the sovereigns who acknowledge no other law than that of nations.

According to the American jurist, Henry Wheaton in *Elements of International Law*,

> Treaties of equal alliance, freely contracted between independent States, do not impair their sovereignty. Treaties of unequal alliance, guarantee, mediation, and protection, may have the effect of limiting and qualifying sovereignty according to the stipulations of the treaties.

To limit the capacity of a State, a Treaty must do so expressly; no State ceases to exist by implication only.

20. The protected status of North American indigenous states was further elaborated by the United States Supreme Court in the case of *Worcester v. Georgia* [1832], observing that the Crown's system of protection "involved practically no claim to their lands, no dominion over their persons. It merely bound the nation to the British Crown as a dependent ally, claiming the protection of a powerful friend and neighbor, and receiving the advantage of that protection, without involving a surrender of their national character. Following Vattel and Wheaton, the Supreme Court further concluded that

> a weak power does not surrender its independence—its right to self-government, by associating with a stronger and taking its protection. A weak state in order to provide for its safety, may place itself under the protection of one more powerful without stripping itself of the right of government and ceasing to be a State.

Similarly, British royal courts in India recognized the continuing validity of the *lex loci* of native protectorates, except where otherwise provided by treaty, and in 1823 Nova Scotia Judge T. C. Haliburton noted that, while the Mi'kmaq Nationimuow are considered British subjects in respect of their rights in royal courts, "yet they never litigate or in any way are impleaded. They have a code of traditional and customary laws among themselves." Under Crown precedents, a protectorate also often retains sufficient sovereignty to plead immunity from ordinary legal process.

21. In 1867, the British Imperial Parliament granted to Canada a charter of limited self-government, the *British North America Act*. The former Crown colony of Nova Scotia became a constituent "province' within a national confederation. The general government of Canada was not a State, however, until in 1931 the Statute of Westminster empowered it to conduct foreign relations independently of Great Britain. The *BNA Act* itself merely authorized Canada to "perfor[m] the Obligations of Canada or of any Province thereof, as part of the British Empire, towards Foreign Countries, arising under Treaties between the Empire and such Foreign Countries" [sec. 132] and regarding "Indians and Lands reserved for Indians" [sec. 91(24)]. It is possible that by this imperial *Act* Canada succeeded to the Crown's duties under our Treaties. Such may have been the intent of the Imperial Parliament, for while section 132 of the *Act* referred only to "Foreign Countries, "which ordinarily would exclude protected States, section 91(24) assigned to the general government of Canada, rather than the Provinces, responsibility for "Indians, and Lands reserved for the Indians." Assuming that we are "Indians" within the meaning of that provision, the Canadian Parliament may have authority and responsibility to implement our Treaties. However, delegation of legislative authority over protected native States was contrary to Imperial policy. Moreover, the *BNA Act* plainly was not a novation of our Treaties since we did not participate or consent in the imperial legislation of Parliament, and in international law "many treaty rights and obligations are clearly unassignable; e.g., ... in the case of rights or obligations under treaties of a purely political nature."

22. The issue of succession is not essential to our grievance: however, for either Canada or Great Britain must be obligated under our Treaties, and in either case Canada lacks lawful authority to interfere with our territory or self-government against our will. Great Britain never has denounced its Treaties with the Mi'kmaq Nationimuow; on the contrary, Her Majesty Queen Elizabeth II in 1981 declared that all Crown Treaties with indigenous peoples of North America would be respected. Implementing Imperial regulations such as the Royal Instructions of 1761 and Royal Proclamation of 1763 never were repealed. They were inalterably entrenched in the constitutions of North American Crown colonies, for "[no] colonial legislature could amend

its own constitution," and, unaffected by any express disclaimer or exemption in the *British North America Act,* carried over indelibly into the constitution of Canada. Indeed had it so desired, the Crown nevertheless could not have delegated to Canada in 1867 what it did not itself have. Since the Mi'kmaq Nationimuow granted the Crown no authority to dispose of its lands or to determine it s right of self-government, the Crown could pass no such authority to Nova Scotia or to Canada. Our status must be today as it was in 1752.

SI'ST: ON DUTIES

23. Great Britain or Canada, or both of them, are obligated to protect and secure for the benefit of the Mi'kmaq Nationimuow all Mi'kmaq national territory not settled by Eurochristians prior to our Treaties. They also are obligated to protect the right of the Mi'kmaq Nationimuow to political, economic, and cultural self-determination, and to make and enforce no laws limiting the authority of the Santeoi Mawa'iomi to govern the territorial affair s of the Nationimuow. All laws and acts of Great Britain and Canada tending to deprive the Mi'kmaq Nationimuow of territory or self-determination are void and of no effect as repugnant to (i) the obligation of Treaties in the law of nations, (ii) Imperial legislation regulating and forming the constitution of Canada, (iii) customary international law governing the territorial rights of autochthonous peoples and States, (iv) *jus cogens* as expressed in covenants, declarations and other binding instruments of the United Nations, to which Canada is a party, and (v) unilateral declaration s and under takings of Canada to abide by principles of international law and the law of the United Nations.

24. It is an ancient principle of international law that all Treaties are obligatory on the parties: *pacta sunt servanda*. The Vienna Convention on the Law of Treaties, acceded to by Canada on 14 October 1970 and accepted as generally declarative of nations historical practice, reiterates the, "universally recognised" rule that "[e]very treaty in force is binding upon the parties to it and must be performed by them in good faith." Treaties remain in force unless modified by agreement or suspended by a material breach, impossibility of performance, or a supervening peremptory norm of international law. Neither Canada

nor Great Britain have grounds to suspend or terminate our Treaties, for we have fulfilled every obligation on our part, and both Great Britain and Canada always have had power to fulfill their duties to us. It is no excuse that Canada and its Provinces have, since 1726, enacted municipal laws in derogation of our Treaty rights, for a State never could relieve itself from a Treaty by invoking provisions of its own domestic laws.

NE'W: ON VIOLATIONS

34. This we believe: No state can be made a non-State by the municipal laws of another State. No people's right to self-determination and the free, choice of its political, social and economic future can be lost because their capacity, as a State, to have entered into binding Treaties is later denied on the basis of their supposed race. No state can be deemed "conquered" and denied fundamental human rights, when in fact it has remained at peace with all nations for two hundred years. No State or people can be deprived of its territory and subsistence on the theory that its endowments exceed its needs. If we are wrong to believe these things, then your response will be our answer. If we are correct, Canada has violated our rights as a state, as a people and as individuals by depriving us of our territory, our destiny and our families under colour of colonial laws (prior to 1867), provincial legislation, and federal legislation such as the *Indian Act*. Great Britain has violated our rights by failing to defend us from the unlawful actions of Canada, as provided by our Treaties.

35. The first violation of Canada was and continues to be involuntary confiscation of our territory and resources, and involuntary supervision of our use of remaining, unconfiscated territory and resources. As described earlier in this communication, our Treaties, the terms of renewal in 1761 and confirming treaties, and the King's Instructions and Royal Proclamation of 1761 and 1763, respectively, secured to the Mi'kmaq Nationimuow all of its ancient territory, save that already actually occupied by British subjects at the time of the treaties.

40. Our Treaties reserved forever, in addition to lands, the right of the Mi'kmaq Nationimuow to hunt and fish "as usual" both in ceded and

unceded territory. Freshwater and coastal fishing always contributed a large portion of our subsistence and, as lawless encroachments on our farms and destruction of our fields increased, fisheries became increasingly necessary to our survival. [...] A century ago, in 1896, the Minister of Justice of Canada reported to the Governor General of Canada that Canada's policy was "that the utmost care must be taken ... to see that none of the treaty rights of the Indians 'to hunt or fish' are infringed without their concurrence."

42. The Mi'kmaq Nationimuow advised Canada that it considered itself to retain de jure ownership of all lands reserved by the Treaties. The government of Canada has responded by disclaiming any liability for occupation and settlement of our territory since 1726, arguing (i) that our rights to any lands outside of the "Indian Reserves" surveyed for us by colonial Nova Scotia have been "superseded by law," and (ii) that our Treaties was not a binding "Empire Treaties" but "only "a non-binding declaration of friendship. The government of Canada has not been able to identify any specific law that "superseded" our Treaties, and we maintain that any such laws, if they had been made, would be unconstitutional and in violation of the law of nations and imperial law.

43. Canada's position that our Treaties is non-binding reflects two antequated Eurochristian theories, both repugnant to international law. The first theory is, that treaties made with uncivilized nations have no binding moral force as against civilized and Christian nations. This theory is inapplicable to the Mi'kmaq Nationimouw in fact, because we were a Christian State in alliance with the Holy See for more than a century before we negotiated our Treaties with Great Britain. Furthermore, this theory is racist and violative of peremptory norms of international law, in that it conditions the rights of peoples, even under solemn international agreements, on their race, culture and religion. If this theory is admitted in the forum of nations, all future resolution of international affairs by treaty and peaceable engagements necessarily will be jeopardized.

44. Canada's position also reflects the theory that the territory of the Mi'kmaq Nationimuow was *terra nullius*, belonged to no state,

and therefore was entirely subject to the disposition of Eurochristian "discoverers." The International Court of Justice has twice rejected this theory as unacceptable in the law of nations, and its continued application to us must be regarded as unjust and racist. Terra nullius is, in fact, a *post hoc* rationalization of unlawful and unconstitutional failures of Great Britain, its North American colonies, and the government of Canada to perform their Treaty obligations to us since, as we have shown elsewhere in this communication, Great Britain's own municipal law until recently strictly respected our status as a protectorate and limited territorial sovereign. The principle of intertemporal law should apply to the interpretation of our Treaties: our capacity as a State was recognized then, and so must it be recognized now.

45. The second violation of Canada was and continues to be interference with our ancient institutions of self-government and self-determination. [...] The Mi'kmaq Nationimuow never consented to be governed by a Canadian bureaucracy of the *Indian Act*, or by the Provincial Assemblies, or by native institutions not of our own choosing designed and supervised by Canada. Our own traditional institutions are mild, confidential and theocentric; the imposition upon our communities of coercive, majoritarian agencies and foreign laws bearing no relation to our culture has bred little but conflict, bitterness, and despair.

47. The third violation of Canada was and continues to be the enactment and enforcement of laws and policies destructive of our family life and inimical to the proper education of our children. The erosion of our Mi'kmaq family life has, resulted chiefly from (i) laws limiting citizenship in the Mi'kmaq Nationimuow, and (ii) laws entrusting to the Minister of Indian and Northern Affairs absolute, control and discretion in the education of our children.

50. Most precious of all things to us are our children: they will discover our destiny, and the secrets Nisgam has entrusted to us to share with all peoples. Beginning in the early decades of this century and continuing for nearly forty years, the government of Canada removed our children against our will to "residential schools" managed by public or private organizations. At the Shubenacadie residential school, Mi'kmaq children were imprisoned like convicts, beaten for speaking

in our language, and often forbidden to communicate with their families. An entire generation of our people were embittered, and all of our families were separated by this program. Over the past twenty years, the government of Canada gradually has transferred responsibility for the education of our children to public Provincial schools, over which we enjoy no greater control. The Mi'kmaw language no longer is proscribed, but neither is it spoken in instruction. Public curricula are entirely irrelevant to our circumstances, resources and aspirations as a people, and teach disrespect and shame for our history and traditions. The consequences are plain. No significantly greater proportion of our children complete school today than did formerly during the residential school era, and, as shown by a 1978 survey conducted by the Union of Nova Scotia Indians, there is no correlation among our adults between years of school completed and either employment or income.

51. Through all these tragedies, Canada's thoughts and action were in violation of our Treaties, imperial law, the law of nations, and, now, the declarations and covenants of human rights. In the past, it could have been a problem of clarity and apprehension of our legal rights. Since the accession to the United Nations declarations and covenants by the United Kingdom and Canada, these excuses have been impounded by hesitations, objections, reservations and even vehement racism and sexism when faced with these violations against the Nationimouw's rights. There has been no truly constructive or effective contribution to human liberation since accession of the United Nations declarations and covenants; no change in policy, no acknowledge of error, no request for forgiveness—only more oppression in Canada. The United Kingdom Parliament has remained aloof in the controversy and failed to take corrective measures. The threat of force of arms continues to be the basic elements of Canadian policy, rather than human rights.

64. *Na nige' gespiatogsieg ag wi'gatiegen gagayag.* (Now our voices die away and our communication ends.)

About the Authors

Patrick Augustine is Mi'kmaq from Elsipuktuk Reserve. He has a master's degree from University of Prince Edward Island and is currently completing a doctorate degree at Carleton University in history.

Stephen Augustine is hereditary chief and keptin from Elsipuktuk in the district of represent Sikniktok "district" on the Mi'kmaw Grand Council. Holding a master's degree from Carleton University, he is the Dean of Unama'ki College at Cape Breton University.

Russel Barsh, an international advisor to the Mi'kmaw Grand Council, studied human ecology and graduated from the Harvard Law School, and has taught at the University of Washington (1974-1984), University of Lethbridge (1993-1999), and New York University (2000-2002). He has advised on Indigenous peoples and environmental issues at the United Nations (1984-2000) and currently doing research and living in Washington State.

Jaime Battiste, a Mi'kmaq from Potlotek First Nations, residing in Eskasoni in Unama'ki, is a graduate of Mi'kmaq Studies at the Cape Breton University and law school of the Dalhousie University. He is former assistant professor of Mi'kmaq Studies at CBU. Currently he is working on a treaty education project in collaboration with the Mi'kmaw chiefs of Nova Scotia, Mi'kmaw Kina'matnewey and the province of Nova Scotia. He is a published writer and researcher on Mi'kmaw history, culture, and law.

Marie Battiste is a Mi'kmaw educator from Potlotek First Nations, Nova Scotia, and full professor in the Department of Educational Foundations at the University of Saskatchewan. With degrees from Harvard and Stanford Universities, she is widely published in initiating institutional change in the decolonization of education and activating social justice and postcolonial educational approaches that recognize and affirm the political and cultural diversity of Canada.

Eleanor Bernard, a member of Eskasoni First Nation, is a BEd graduate of University of New Brunswick, holds an MEd from St. Francis Xavier University, and is currently working on a PhD in education, also from St. FX. She is executive director of Mi'kmaw Kina'matnewey and wife of Barry Bernard; mother of Candace, Barrie, Keenan, Hunter and Ted; and grandmother of seven.

Victor Carter-Julian is the son of Bridget Julian and Tavis Carter. Born in Boston, Massachusetts, he is a member of Pictou Landing First Nation. He received a joint bachelor of arts in economics and sociology from St. Francis Xavier University and a juris doctorate from Dalhousie University. Victor completed articling in Saskatoon and was called to the Saskatchewan Bar in 2015. He aims to use what he has learned to assist in nation-building. He enjoys time spent conversing with friends and family about ideas large and small and can be found often travelling between Boston and Nova Scotia.

Douglas E. Brown, a graduate of Mi'kmaq Studies at the Cape Breton University and Dalhousie University Law School, is a Mi'kmaw lawyer, published writer and researcher on Mi'kmaw history and law.

J. Youngblood (Sa'ke'j) Henderson, JD, IPC, FRSC, is a member of Chickasaw Nation. He is the former research advisor to Union of Nova Scotia Indians, advisor to the Mi'kmaw Grand Council and professor and lecturer at University of Cape Breton. Currently is the Research Director for the Native Law Centre of Canada, College of Law, University of Saskatchewan.

Stuart Killen is a former research director for the Union of Nova Scotia Indians. He was also a former Indian Affairs agent assigned to Nova Scotia in the early 1960s. His story reveals attitudes of the Indian Affairs and their treatment of Mi'kmaq, in the 1960s, that led to his eventually working with the UNSI and their research on Mi'kmaw treaties.

Fred Metallic is a Mi'gmaq from Listuguj in Gespe'gewa'gi District. Fred holds a PhD in Environmental Studies from York University. Fred was the first doctoral student at York to defend his dissertation in the Mi'gmaw language and in the community of Listuguj, Quebec. Fred is a member of the Mi'kmaw Grand Council and sits on the Mi'kmaw Ethics Watch. Fred works for the Listuguj Mi'gmaw Government as the Director of Natural Resources, and teaches in the Community Studies program of a satellite campus of Cape Breton University in Listuguj.

Naiomi Metallic, daughter of the late Emanuel Metallic of Listigutj, is a Mi'kmaw lawyer in Halifax at Burchells Law Associates. She is well known for her work advancing indigenous and Mi'kmaw languages.

Pamela Palmater is a citizen of the Mi'kmaq nation and member of Eel River Bar First Nation in New Brunswick. She has been a practising lawyer for sixteen years specializing in indigenous law and governance. She is currently an Associate Professor and Chair in Indigenous Governance at Ryerson University and has several publications on Mi'kmaw treaties and identity.

Daniel N. Paul, CM, ONS, is a Mi'kmaw Elder and passionate advocate for social justice and the eradication of racial discrimination. Danny is an outspoken champion of First Nations communities across Nova Scotia, which has garnered him many awards, including the Grand Chief Donald Marshall Sr. Elder Award, Order of Canada, Order of Nova Scotia, Honorary doctorate degree from University of Sainte-Anne, Honorary Doctor of Law Degree from Dalhousie University, Multicultural Education Council of Nova Scotia award, City of Dartmouth Book and Writing Award, and he is listed in Canada's Who's Who.

Kerry Prosper is a Mi'kmaq from Paq'tnkek First Nation, and a graduate of St. Francis Xavier University with an honours degree in anthropology. He is a published writer and researcher on Mi'kmaw knowledge, culture, fisheries and law.

Natasha Simon is a Mi'kmaq from Elsipogtog and a mother to two young children. She is a former PhD candidate in history at the University of Victoria and holds a master's degree from Carleton University. She currently strives to make post-secondary education more attainable to her community members by facilitating an Elsipogtog-Saint Thomas University partnership program, and is developing a university-accredited Mi'kmaw immersion program in Elsipogtog.

Index

Note that page numbers refer to the print version of the book.

Abenaki 19, 57, 266
Aboriginal Affairs Working Group 273
Aboriginal Language Initiatives Program 247
Aboriginal Languages Recognition Act 249
Act to Provide for the Indians and Permanent Settlement of the Indians 268
Adirondack Deer Law 201
African National Congress 124
Afton FN 14, 93, 222-25, 229-30, 233, 289, 309
Afton Day School 223
Ainu 126, 130
Alberta Indian Association 109
Alex, Andrew 3, 22, 153
Algonquian, Algonquin 19, 244
American Indian Movement (AIM) 131
American Indian Student Association 197
Amherst, NS 83-85, 185, 286
Amkotpigtu 53
Anishinaabe 238
ankukamewe 143
Annapolis Royal 16, 144-46, 267, 296
Apamuek 68
Apistane'wj 53
Arguimaut 55
Assembly of First Nations (AFN) 245, 247, 257, 259
Assembly of Manitoba Chiefs 89
Assembly of Nova Scotia Mi'kmaq Chiefs 161, 210
Atikamekw Nehiywaw 57

atwigen 114
Audette, Justice 77
Auditor General of Canada 272
Augustine, Agnes (Thomas) 16
Augustine, Chuck 234
Augustine, Egian 44
Augustine, Michael 16-17, 173
Augustine, Thomas 16
Augustine, Thomas Theophile (Basil Tom) 16

Barney's River 230
Basque, Chief John 288
Basque, David 242
Basque language 264
Basque, Mary 75
Basque, Will 68
Bastarache, Justice Michel 244
Battiste, Annie 3, 12, 68
Battiste, John 260
Bayfield, NS 225-26, 228
Belcher, Governor Jonathan 13, 22-23, 59, 166, 169-70, 172-73, 176-77, 194, 266-67, 297-98
Bernard, Allison Jr. 198, 204
Bernard, Joshua (*R. v. Bernard*) 111
Bill S-237 245
Binnie, Justice 59
Blackfoot 117
Boone and Crockett Club 200
Boston Friendship Centre 93
Botero, Ana 135
Bras d'Or Lake 75-76, 154
British Columbia Wildlife Act 211
British North American Act (BNA) 58, 284, 286, 301
Bromley, Walter 301
buoin (shaman) 54-55
Burnt Church FN 11, 49, 237

Calder et al. v. Attorney-General of British Columbia 99-100, 286
Canada Act 109
Canadian Human Rights Tribunal 247
Canadian Multiculturalism Act 247
Canton, MA 196
Cape Breton Highlands 211, 216-17
Cape Sable (Kespukwitk) Mi'kmaq 145
Cape Sable (Sandy Cape) 265
Capuchin 265
Caugnawaga (Kahnawake) 57
Chapel Island FN (Potlotek) 3, 22-23, 68-69, 96, 107, 153, 185, 292, 294
Charles, Francis 211, 219
Charles, King of England 59, 143
Charter of Rights and Freedoms, Canadian 157, 249
Charter of the French Language (QC) 249
Cheyenne 96
Chickasaw Nation 96
Chippewas of Rama First Nation 238
Chronicle Herald 22, 187, 220
Clarke, James 213
Coady Institute, the 141
Cobiere, Allen 238-39
colonial office 74
concordat 72, 135
Confederacy of Mainland Mi'kmaq 161, 186, 195
Conn, Hugh 87
Constitution Act, 1867 60, 271-72, 284
Constitution Act, 1982 58, 61, 81, 109, 157, 193, 196, 198, 207, 219, 245, 249-50, 270, 271-72, 274
Cope decision 109
Cope, Grand Chief John Baptiste 147, 158, 296

Cornwallis, Edward 24, 33, 145-47, 188, 191, 298
Council of the Federation 273
covenant chain of treaties 67, 71-73, 143
covenant chain wampum of 1764 239
Cross Lake 88, 90

Daes, Erica-Irene 134
Dalhousie Law School 11, 70, 141, 158, 197-98, 244, 307-309
d'Amours, Charlotte 22
d'Amours, Louis (Sieur de Chauffours) 22
Davies Rocks 226
Declaration on the Rights of Indigenous Peoples (U.N.) 13, 109, 129, 137, 246, 250, 270
Deer, Ken 128
Delgamuukw v. British Columbia 45
Denning, Lord 109
Dennis, Clara 3, 22
Denny, Anlte 67
Denny, Dianne 76
Denny, Grand Chief John 22
Denny, Janette 68
Denny, Michael L. (Mikelo) 79
Department of Fisheries and Oceans (DFO) 34, 160, 237
Department of the Secretary of State 60
de Razilly, Isaac 265
de Saint-Castin, Baron 21
Dickson, Justice 81
Doucette, Noel 72, 91-93, 121, 132, 142, 185-86, 198, 227, 242
Doyle-Bedwell, Patricia 244
Duncan, Justice Patrick 218-20

Economic and Social Council (U.N.) 129
Education Act (BC) 248, (Mi'kmaw) 249, (NT) 248, (NU) 248, (YK) 247

INDEX

elikewake 4, 144-45
Elsipogtog 16, 35, 53, 310
Epekwitk aq Piktuk 56
Esgenoopetitj 49-50
Eskasoni FN 11-12, 66-69, 79, 83-87, 91-93, 96, 98, 138, 151, 154-55, 182, 196, 198, 204, 211, 256-57, 263, 277, 283-84, 290, 307-308
Eskasoni Indian Agency 83-84
Eskasoni School Board 68
Eskikewa'kik 56

First Nations Education Act (BC) 248
First Peoples Heritage Language and Culture Act (BC) 248
Fort Benning, GA 197
Fort Loméron 265
Fort Richmond 266
Fort Saint George 147, 266
Four Directions Council 124, 127-28
Francis and Paul *See R. v. Paul* 199, 211-220
French River 230

Gakpesawtek 225, 228
Gaspé 9, 26, 71, 117, 251
George, King of Great Britain 2, 80, 146-49, 285, 295, 297
Gespe'gewa'gi 43, 47, 241-42, 246, 309
Glusgap *See* Kluskap
Gogan, Justice Robin 218
Gould, Carl 289
Gould, Roy 91, 142, 284
Governor-in-Council 148
Grand Council of the Crees of Québec 133
Great Council of Fire (Putuswakn) 57
Great Peace of Montréal 57

Halifax Herald See *Chronicle Herald*
Harvard College, Law School, etc. 12-13, 68, 155, 262, 266-67, 307-308
Haudenosaunee 57, 71, 123, 136
Heatherton 225, 230, 233
Herbert, Henry William 200
Hildebrand, Martín von 135
Hobson, Peregrine Thomas 147
Hokkaido 126
Holy Family Island, *See* also Potlotek 57, 76, 153
Howe, Joseph 189, 268

Idle No More 238, 274
Ilsipugtug also 44
Indian Affairs, Dept. of 12, 14, 26, 31, 60, 61, 80, 83-84, 86-88, 90, 92-93, 97, 102, 106-109, 182, 185-86, 195, 255, 256, 262, 283-84, 286, 308-309
Indian and Northern Affairs Canada 140, 253
Indian Branch 60
Indian Brook *See* Shubenacadie FN
Indigenous Affairs and Northern Development Canada (INAC) 97, 140-42, 152, 154, 161, 253, 262
Indigenous Bar Association 238
Indspire Foundation 274
Innu 19, 126-28
International Commission on Human Rights 197
International Labour Organization (ILO) 132, 135-36
International Monetary Fund 130
Inuit Language Protection Act (NU) 248
Inuktitut 244, 248
Inverness County 84
Iroquois League 57
Isaac, Stephen *See* also *R. v. Isaac* 107-108, 156, 158

Jay Treaty 183, 261
Jeddore, Noel 78
Jerome, Alma 44
Jerome, Louis 26
Johnson, Beverly 263
Johnson, Charmony 263
Johnson, Francis 224
Johnson, Greg 92-93, 142
Johnson, Joan 93, 287
Johnson, Margaret (Granny) 85
Johnson, Noel 284
Johnson, Patrick 68
Johnson, Stanley 92-93, 142
Joyal, Serge 245
Julien, Donald 93, 154, 186

Kainai 117
Kanesatake also Oka 128-29
Kejimukujik 71
keptin(s) definition and duties 56, 67, 72, 76
Kespe'k 25, 56
Kespukwitk 56, 145, 265
King's Road Reserve *See* Membertou FN
Kisulk (Creator) 11, 42, 46, 53, 71, 164, 264, 293
Kluskap also Glusgap 19, 42, 46, 51 53-54, 170, 176,
Knockwood, John 142

La Cadie (Acadia) 265
La Have, also La Hève 145, 265
Laidlaw Foundation 92
Lakes Confederacy of Ojibwa 57
Lakota 123-24
Lapatko'tikimk 153
La Redemption, QC 242
La Tour, Charles 264,-65
Laurent, Chief Paul 173
League of Nations 128
LeBel, Justice Louis 113
LeClercq, Fr. 54
Lennox Island Indian Agency 85
Lescarbot, Marc 72

Listuguj 34, 43, 49-51, 242-43, 246
'lnapsku 153
l'nu 251, 254
L'nuk 53
L'nu Sipu Kina'matnuo'ko'm (LSK) 254
Louisbourg 93, 171, 289
Louis, King of France 265

MacDonald, Associate Chief Justice Michael 209-10, 219
Macdonald, Sir John A. 269
MacEachern, Allan J. 92
MacPherson, Darcy 212
MacPherson, Joe 87
Madakwando, Chief 21
Maillard, Abbé 55, 146, 148
Malagawatch 76
Malagawatj 76
Malecite, 57
Malecite, Maliseet 57
Maliseet 19, 48, 112, 144-45, 263, 266
Maloney, Chief Reginald 142, 288
Managua 125
Manitoba 12, 86, 88-89, 248-49
Manitou Community College 242
Maori 136
Marshall, Albert 154
Marshall decision *See* Marshall inquiry, etc.
Marshall, Donald Jr. 34, 159, 194, 198
Marshall, Grand Chief Donald 138, 155
Marshall inquiry, decision *See* also *R. v. Marshall, Marshall 2,* 34, 59, 160-61, 219-20, 237
Marshall, Joe B. 135
Marshall, Lillian 263, 287
Marshall, Murdena 69, 76
Marshall, Russell 154, 287
Marten (Apistane'wj) 53, 55
Mascarene, Jean-Paul 147, 188, 266
Mawiomis (districts) 17

INDEX

Maybe, Don 90
M'Chigeeng FN 238
Membertou FN 77, 140, 237
Membertou, Grand Chief 72, 144, 292
Menchú, Rigoberta 134
Metallic, Emmanuel Nagugwes 241-43
Metis and Non-Status Indian Association of Nova Scotia 196
Michif 244
Micmac News 19, 35, 81, 91, 103, 131, 155, 157, 159, 198
Migmawei Mawiomi Secretariat 246
Mi'gmewey 50
Mi'kma'ki, also Mi'gma'gi 9-10, 16-18, 24-26, 31, 43, 48, 53, 71, 73, 76, 96, 99, 143, 145, 149-50, 153, 255, 264-65
Mi'kmaq College Institute (Cape Breton University) 141
Mi'kmaq Maliseet Education Program 263
Mi'kmaw Education Act 272
Mi'kmawey School 68-69, 262
Mi'kmaw Fish and Wildlife Commission 206
Mi'kmaw Grand Council, also Sante' Mawio'mi 3-4, 10, 13, 17, 19-20, 22, 60-61, 66-68, 70-76, 79-80, 95, 100, 105-106, 115, 120, 123, 137, 142, 147, 150-51, 153, 156, 158, 196, 267, 272, 293, 307-309
Mi'kmaw Kina'matnewey (MK) 162, 253-54, 257, 260, 269, 271, 273, 307-308
Mi'kmaw Treaty Day 7, 69, 82, 142, 156
miniku 153
Ministerial Task Force on Aboriginal Languages and Cultures 245
Mohawk 11, 48, 50, 57, 128-29

Mombourquette, John 206
Montréal 148, 171
Moore, Carol (Paul) 287
Moses, Ted 133-34
m'set nogemaq (all my relations) 62
Mulroney, Prime Minister Brian 134
Myran v. R. 207

NADACA (Native Alcohol and Drug Abuse Counselling Association) 204
National Indian Brotherhood 259
Native Council of Nova Scotia 53, 196
Nektowek 230, 233
neskwat 20
Netawansum 42, 46
netukuli'mk 11, 71, 55, 164
New Brunswick Court of Appeal 212-14
niganawitgen 114
Niskawtimk 153-54
Nnu 243
no'kmaq (relatives) 264
North Atlantic Treaty Organization (NATO) 126-27
Norway House FN, Indian Agency, etc. 86, 88-91, 94
Nova Scotia Court of Appeal 158, 207, 210-13, 215
Nova Scotia Department of Justice 197
Nova Scotia Federation of Anglers and Hunters 200
Nova Scotia Wildlife Act 199-200, 202-203, 208-12, 215
Nugumi and Nukumi 42, 46, 53
Nunn, Bruce 206

Official Languages Act 247-48
Osborne, Helen Betty 88

Palais des Nations 128
Palestine Liberaton Organization 125
Palmater, Francis (Frank) Xavier 26
Pannawamskewiak (Penobscot) 57
Papua New Guinea 129
Paq'tnkek FN *See* Afton FN
Passamaquoddy 48, 57, 144-45, 266
Patterson, Judge George 78-79, 82, 107, 190-91, 193-94
Patterson, Stephen 170, 172, 215, 218
Paul, Aaron *See R. v. Paul*
Paul, Elizabeth 69
Peace and friendship treaties 1, 8, 10, 16-17, 22, 32, 44-45, 147, 188, 190, 194, 197, 250, 266-67, 292
Peminawit, Kjisakamow 74
Penobscot 21, 22, 48, 57, 144-45
Peskada mokantiak *See* Passamaquody 57
petroglyphs 53, 137
pictoglyphs 53
Pictou Landing FN 14, 93, 235, 289, 308
Pomquet River etc. 225, 230
Port Royale 144
Port Toulouse (St. Peter's, NS) 22, 146
Potlotek FN, Chapel Island 11, 15, 20, 57, 67-69, 72, 76, 96, 107, 154-55, 259-60, 262-63, 307-308
putu's (wampum keeper) definition, duties, etc. 3, 22, 48, 67, 76, 153, 293

Québec 9-10, 19, 26, 43, 71, 128, 130, 133, 143, 171, 242, 246, 249, 251, 270, 292, 309

Rama FN 238
Ramos-Horta, José 134
Remissions of Penalty Act 217

Restigouche, River, etc. 43, 242
Richibucto 145, 173
Roma 126
Ross, Alan 89-90
Ross, Judge A. Peter 205-208, 210, 213
Royal Acadian School 268
Royal Commission on Aboriginal Peoples (RCAP) 245
Royal Proclamation of 1763 2, 25, 58-60, 100, 107, 149, 284-85, 299, 301, 303
R. v. Bernard 36, 111, 204-205, 208-210
R. v. Denny, Paul and Sylliboy 206-207, 215
R. v. Gray 36, 70, 112
R. v. Horseman 208
R. v. Isaac 107-108, 156, 158
R. v. Marshall 36, 59
R. v. Marshall, Marshall 2 See also Marshall inquiry, decision etc. 36, 59, 70, 110-11, 270
R. v. Morris 211, 213, 218
R. v. Paul 211, 217-19, 234, 211
R. v. Polches 212-14, 216
R. v. Prince 9, 26, 71, 85, 142-43, 152, 207-208, 249, 292, 307
R. v. Sappier 36, 70, 112
R. v. Secretary of State for Foreign and Commonwealth Affairs, ex parte Indian Association of Alberta 109
R. v. Simon 13, 36, 45, 69, 70, 81, 109-10, 156-59, 166, 190, 193-94, 226, 232, 310
R. v. Sylliboy [sic] 66, 70, 75, 78-79, 81, 107, 110, 190, 193
R. v. Van der Peet 215, 218
R. v. Wesley 208
Ryan, Judge David 204-205, 213, 216-18, 220, 288

sagamaw 47, 50
samgoneese 48

INDEX

Sami 126, 130
Sandinista(s) 125
Sante' Mawio'mi *See* Mi'kmaw Grand Council
Sark, John Joe 121, 133, 135
Shubenacadie FN 45, 79, 140, 145, 151, 178-79, 182, 185, 190, 254
Shubenacadie Indian Residential School 305
Shubenacadie Residential School 140, 180, 262
Sieur de Chauffours 22
Sikipnékatik *See* Shubenacadie 56
Sipekne'katik *See* Shubenacadie 147, 254
Skinner, Ernie 84, 91
Souriquois 19
St. Anne 54
St. Anne's Mission *See* also Holy Family Island 22, 57, 68, 72, 76-77, 80, 96, 153
St. Francis Xavier University 88, 91-92, 141
St. Georges Bay 225
St. Peter's *See* Port Toulouse
Students for Educational Access 197
Sylliboy, Grand Chief Gabriel *See* also *R. v. Syliboy* 4, 11-12, 22, 44-45, 66-68, 70, 75-80, 82, 86-88, 93, 105-106, 152-54, 156, 232-34, 284
Sylliboy, Tom 231, 233-34

tabagies 19
Task Force on Aboriginal Languages and Cultures 245
Têtes de Bule 57
The Pas Indian Agency, 88
Trail of Tears 236
Treaty of 1725 16, 23, 32, 144, 148, 189, 266, 296
Treaty of Utrecht 145
Truth and Reconciliation Commission (TRC) 8

Ugpi'Ganjig (Eel River Bar First Nation) 26
ulnapskok 121, 135
Unama'ki (Cape Breton) 44, 76, 307
UNESCO 67
United Nations Commission on Human Rights 123
United Nations General Assembly 130

Vatican 122, 135-36
Viti Levu, Fiji 119
von Gernet, Alexander 215

Wabanaki Confederacy, Federation, etc. 19-20, 48, 52, 57-58, 62, 110, 144-45, 147, 264, 266-67, 295, 297
Warzazi, Halima 129
We'koqma'q FN, also Whycocomagh 75, 76
Whitehead, Ruth Holmes 3, 53-55, 56, 232
white paper (1969 white paper on Indian policy) 92-93, 99, 151, 152, 244
Whycocomagh *See* We'koqma'q FN
Wicken, William 70-75, 78, 215-16
Wildsmith, Bruce 107, 158, 198, 205
Willemsen-Díaz, Augusto 134
Working Group on Indigenous Populations (U.N.) 125
World Council of Indigenous Peoples 126
Wulastegwiak 57